NIALL O'DOWD

AN IRISH VOICE

THE O'BRIEN PRESS
DUBLIN

First published 2010 by The O'Brien Press Ltd,
12 Terenure Road East, Rathgar, Dublin 6, Ireland.
Tel: +353 1 4923333; Fax: +353 1 4922777
E-mail: books@obrien.ie
Website: www.obrien.ie

ISBN: 978-1-84717-194-8

A catalogue record for this title is available from the British Library

1 2 3 4 5 6 7 8 9 10
10 11 12 13 14 15 16

Front cover photograph by Kit DeFever
Picture section photographs and back cover photograph supplied by the author.

Printed and bound in the UK by J F Print Ltd, Sparkford, Somerset.

Dedication

To Donal and Kathleen

Acknowledgements

Thank you to the many people who made this book possible: my colleagues at *Irish Voice* newspaper, *Irish America* magazine and IrishCentral.com; Michael O'Brien of The O'Brien Press for believing in the project, Mary Webb, for her patience and talent as my editor; and my wife Debbie and daughter Alana for their support always.

Contents

Chapter 1

INSIDE OBAMA'S WHITE HOUSE

When you step into the White House it is an extraordinary experience. The immensity of the seat of power in the most powerful of all countries hits you with full force.

On the walls are arrayed the predecessors of Barack Obama, the man we have come to honour this night of 17 March, St Patrick's Day 2009. The fine china and cutlery from Jackie Kennedy's state dinner service lies within touch, mounted on the wall. The silver goblets that Andrew Jackson used at his state events in the 1830s are all present and accounted for. For a country that is so ambivalent about the general topic of history the American White House reeks of it.

And tonight we are witnessing a slice of history that John F Kennedy and Andrew Jackson, the old Indian hater, could only have dreamed of – though in Jackson's case it might have been a nightmare!

The first ever black president of the United States, Barack Obama, is holding court for the Irish in the house that kept Irish and blacks out for so long. The 'No Irish Need Apply' signs only came down in the lifetime of many present here tonight. And the idea of a black man as president was the stuff of pure fiction and bad jokes only a few years ago.

Yet here we are: one group who came as slaves, and so many of the other in coffin ships. This is our night, to celebrate with this young African American man who has capsized the stars.

On the way to the East Wing the crowds are moving slowly, taking in the significance of the occasion. Marines in their crisp dress uniforms stand by, ready at a second's notice to spring into action to help the guests.

Even the coat check is intriguing, once the site of the White House private cinema where Jack and Jackie watched movies, where George W. Bush invited Ted Kennedy soon after his inauguration to watch a film about the Cuban missile crisis. Little did he know that Kennedy hated to watch footage about his beloved brothers.

But that is the past and Kennedy is not here tonight, laid low by dreadful illness, a brain tumour that has brought the lion of the senate to his knees, and will cause his untimely death five months' later, on 25 August, 2009. It is a shame, because he helped create tonight with his extraordinary support for Obama at a critical time in the primaries. That booming voice will not be heard tonight, and the event is a little poorer for its absence.

The guests stare at each other furtively. Who got on the list and who didn't is the great parlour game that has been resonating throughout the Irish American community for the past few weeks. But the Obama folk have focused heavily on their Chicago political friends, not necessarily Irish. That left many in the Irish American community out and very sore at the prospect.

Those of us who are there feel the rub of the green, the sigh of relief that we are still on the list. For others, including one Irish leader who stood outside, hoping that someone would shoo him in from the cold, it was a night to forget.

After we mount the stairs we are standing in the sweeping corridor walkway which connects the two parts of the East Wing. In the distance Hillary Clinton comes into view, alone, somehow vulnerable in the place she once called home and had hoped to do so again. She is Secretary of State, a powerful figure, but tonight she enters alone. We talk, as we always do. She asks about my family, I about hers. She remembers everyone's names, knows the issues, but you can tell also that she knows this is not her night. Before her conqueror arrives she slips away.

The band plays on as the guests gather, and soon President Obama and Michelle come striding down the corridor, accompanied by Taoiseach Brian Cowen and his wife Mary. It is, in the best sense of the phrase, 'a sight to behold'.

President Obama in person is remarkably slight, thin as a spindle. They say he will only play basketball in a track suit in order to hide his skinny legs. It is the smile that captivates, however, the broad flashing megawatt grin that he uses so effectively when greeting everybody. His body language this night is very relaxed, very open. He is clearly among friends. The Chicago bosses gather round him like bees at a honeycomb. He is the biggest star in the universe and they know it.

Michelle is striking, much more so than he. She has the duskier complexion, reflecting her broader African roots. She is also the warmer of the two, grabbing people and hugging. He stands back and waits for people to come to him.

The President and Taoiseach speak twice, once in the East Room and once in the West Room in order to satisfy the 300 or so present. Obama is utterly at ease. He knows this crowd. He grew up with Irish pols in Chicago and many were his mentors. Somewhere in the audience, Chicago Mayor Richard Daley is smiling quietly. His father made JFK and now he has helped make Barack Obama.

And what a politician this president is. When Brian Cowen accidentally begins reading from Obama's speech on the autocue, he pretends to read from Cowen's speech when it is his turn, smoothing over the moment and utterly putting his guests at ease.

One of his close advisors told me that Obama wanted to move into the White House as soon as he could, so he could still remember what it was like to put the garbage out and have a normal household for his kids, before all the various staff took over the everyday duties of daily life. As an example of how distanced one can become in that sort of situation, Nancy Soderberg, who was Deputy National Security Advisor for President Clinton, told me she found it shocking when she had to hail her own cab instead of having a limousine fetch her from home the day after she left the White House.

Unlike previous occupants, Obama had never entered that bubble of being a governor where normal life fades and is replaced by a battery of worker bees ready to carry out your every whim, and he had not been a senator for very long.

This night he was happy. As he surveyed the room, that golden smile flashed again and again; he had made it and no one could take it away from him. We Irish certainly had no desire to. We loved seeing history being made and having an underdog rewrite it.

As for me, I reflected how, just a few months ago, I had been working very hard to defeat him. Not anymore, he was my president now too. But, honestly, I never thought it would happen.

Chapter 2

A SOLDIER IN HILLARY'S
LOSING BATTLE

'Niall, have you met Barack?' asked Senator Hillary Clinton, taking me by the arm. We were in the ballroom of the Mayflower Hotel in Washington. It was July 2008 and the presidential election had entered its decisive stage.

Against all the odds, the first-time Senator from Illinois had defeated the heavy favourite, Hillary Clinton, who I had avidly supported for the Democratic nomination. Now we were all playing the good guy game, her key supporters meeting for the first time with the young man who had overturned our world, all in the name of Democratic unity.

Though the flesh was willing, the spirit was weak. Everyone seemed ill at ease. Even Obama himself lacked the radiant presence we had come to expect. When Hillary addressed us, he stood with arms folded, eyes fixed in the middle distance, betraying all in his body language. For Hillary, this moment was an especially tough blow. Yet she had soldiered on through so many crises in her life that she bore this one bravely too. She certainly looked better than when I was backstage with her after the final primaries a few weeks before.

<hr>

The venue back then was telling, a cavernous basement in a public building in lower Manhattan. The lack of light and grim glares from campaign staff added to the sense of foreboding doom. The numbers would not lie and Hillary was crashing to defeat despite winning most of the delegates in the late states. She looked pale and tired, sniffling from a cold and strangely vulnerable. Her rhetoric was still upbeat, her husband was still plunging into the crowds with reckless abandon and shaking hands, but the Fat Lady was busy warbling off stage.

Now, in Washington's Mayflower, she was looking more composed, but I recalled sitting in this very hotel about a year earlier and hearing such an upbeat assessment of her chances that defeat was out of the question. In July 2007, about thirty of her closest supporters gathered at the Mayflower for an all-day seminar on the campaign. We were convinced that it was all over bar the shouting. Barack Obama was a new face who was highly unlikely to run, and if he did was sure to be crushed. The woman who hoped to be the future leader of America had gathered her brains trust here to work out the plan of campaign that would land her in the White House – or so we all believed. We were wrong.

We heard from all the heavyweights: Harold Ickes, Bill Clinton's old enforcer, pollster Mark Penn who assured us that the trends were completely in our favour. I remember one brief moment of doubt on looking around the room and figuring that everyone there was over fifty. But that was a fleeting thought. These were the pros who had delivered an unknown Arkansas governor to the White House on two occasions. They were hardly likely to fail with a far better known candidate, albeit his wife. On the campaign trail Hillary's victory had seemed assured until the voters actually cast their ballots.

The most upbeat assessment was by Terry McAuliffe, Hillary's chief fundraiser, who stated flatly that defeat looked out of the question. I would remember those words in the months to come as the impossible took shape.

A few months later I heard the same McAuliffe mantra. It was November 2007 and we were in Winterset, Iowa, in a little country hall deep in the heart of the Irish belt in a state where over 18 per cent of people were of Irish extraction. Nearby were the bridges of Madison County, made famous by the bestselling book by Robert James Waller and the Clint Eastwood film of the same name. Not far away was the farm field where, in October 1979, 300,000 Catholic Iowans had gathered to hear Pope John Paul speak to Middle America.

I had spoken ahead of McAuliffe to the fifty or so Iowans present and told them what an extraordinary job Hillary and Bill Clinton had done in helping bring peace to their ancestral land. They seemed charmed by the Clintons and glad to hear of their good deeds in Ireland. All the signs pointed positive. Outside the snow was falling but the promise of spring and political renewal seemed in the air. Mc Auliffe told them, as he had told so many before, that Hillary was so far ahead everywhere that it was only a matter of counting the votes.

Somehow, somewhere it went tragically wrong. I think I know where. The night after the Winterset meeting, Saturday, 11 November, we were in Des Moines at the Jefferson Jackson dinner. Hosted by the Democratic Party, it allows the candidates to speak at length to over 10,000 Democrats crammed into the local state fair hall. It is also the first major media event of the primary season. It is a beauty contest, a night when the candidates put on their rouge and try to make the maximum impression. I was seated at one of Hillary's tables with famed record producer Quincy Jones. The expectation was that she would hold her own with the mesmerizing young talent from Illinois who was threatening to pull off the huge upset.

When she spoke, Hillary was adequate. She was never the best speaker; is much better in intimate surroundings, talking quietly about the issues she cares most about, such as health care. That night her campaign had saddled her with a ludicrous refrain which had something to do with being able to stay in the kitchen to withstand the heat. She referred back to it again and again but it came across as phony and hokey.

Obama could not have been more different. He bounced onto the stage and commenced a thirty-minute oration on how the country was being steered in the wrong direction, a speech that had his exuberant supporters cheering and clapping. His cadence and rhythm was that of the old-time preacher. His rhetoric was from the gut, reflecting the disgust and despair in America at large with the Bush years. In spite of my Hillary sympathies, I found myself gripped by him as was everybody else.

Beside me there was a sudden commotion. The Hillary people had come for Quincy Jones, escorting him to the side of the stage for an urgent photo op with Hillary. It was a clear attempt at a diversion – to showcase a prominent black supporter at a key moment for her main opponent. It didn't work, however – nothing would have – we were witnessing the birth of one of the most incredible political stories in American history.

The following day, David Gepsen of the local *Des Moines Register* called the Obama speech a defining moment. Coming from him it was like a pronouncement from the local Oracle. It felt like that too. Hillary never quite grabbed back the mantle of leadership after it.

Iowa proved to be a shocker of a magnitude that no one had predicted. Her gurus had expected about 150,000 people to vote in the Democratic caucus in Iowa and believed they had a winning majority at that level. In the event, 227,000 showed up, and as the busloads of Obama supports rolled in, the faces of the Clinton people got glummer and glummer. The final insult was when John Edwards shaded her for second place.

We felt like the Polish mounted cavalry that faced German tanks in September 1939 soon after the outbreak of the Second World War. We were that outdated and overpowered.

I spent days in New Hampshire as the campaign counted down and Hillary looked to be on the ropes from her shocking setback in Iowa. The Clinton canvassers were clearly being outgunned by the Obama machine. At every stoplight, at every town centre, the Obama message blared out and canvassers gathered to hoot and holler for their man.

Inside the Hillary headquarters, a shabby office in an anonymous office building, the mood was grim. The Iowa defeat had stunned the mandarins, setting off a cascade of finger pointing that would last to the very end of the campaign. Only the candidate herself seemed unperturbed, still resilient and confident despite what had happened.

Then Hillary pulled off a stunning upset in New Hampshire, and for a time it seemed that yet another chapter in the comeback saga of the Clinton family was about to unfold, but it was not to be.

Obama simply outorganized us. Whenever Hillary won a big state – and she won plenty – Obama would have locked up a caucus in a small state somewhere else where the Clinton Poo-bahs had neglected to organize, always keeping a critical margin ahead. It became like snakes and ladders, where we'd climb and tumble and climb again, always frustrated that he was just a few squares ahead of us.

I attended many Clinton campaign meetings and fundraisers during those fraught months. I was reminded vividly of the scene in the movie *Butch Cassidy and the Sundance Kid* when Robert Redford and Paul Newman keep wondering who is following and outsmarting them as they try to escape. Like Butch and Sundance we'd mutter, 'Who are those guys?' and promise to do better in the next stage.

The week of the Texas primary, I was at a fundraiser at the Dakota Building in Manhattan, famous as the location where, in December 1980, Beatle John Lennon was gunned down by Mark Chapman. It felt like a shooting this day too. Super Tuesday had just passed, Hillary had done well but not well enough, and now, for the first time, I could feel it in the air that her hard core supporters had lost heart. Even Hillary herself looked pale and wan and on her uppers. She knows she's lost it, I thought.

She fussed around as usual, spent time with my daughter, Alana, signing a campaign poster for her and asking her about third grade. She's a pro, I thought, one of the best ever. My heart went out to her. There was no stopping her and she was as fiery in her remarks as ever, drawing strength, as her husband always did, from the support around her and the love many there felt for her.

But the calculations had changed. There was nothing, short of an utter meltdown by Obama, that would give her victory. The game was up after Super Tuesday.

Now, a few months later, we were gathered in the ballroom of the Mayflower to pay homage to the new nominee of our party. In person, like many famous people close up, Barack looked impossibly young, hardly the face of a man ready to run the western world.

We spoke briefly. I asked him if he intended to go to Ireland. He flashed that wide grin. 'Of course. I have relatives from there,' he answered, referring to the Moneygall, County Offaly roots of his great great-grandfather, Falmuth Kearney. How soon would that be? 'I need to get elected first, but I'll definitely get over there,' he stated, flashing that high wattage mile. He turned to meet with someone else, but then turned back. 'I will definitely make it there as president,' he said. I could almost feel Hillary wince.

On Tuesday, 4 November 2008, I stood on 125th street in Harlem, surrounded by African Americans and giant screens as one of the most extraordinary days in American history unfolded. I interviewed Shirley Waller, a seventy-year-old woman from South Carolina who had moved to Harlem from the Deep South years before. She was the great grand-daughter of a slave and had never thought this day would come. 'I thank God I lived to see it.'

But there was still fear until the Pennsylvania result was announced – fear that somehow, some way the election would be stolen from them. The cheer that went up when the Keystone State went in the Obama column was an electric moment, as it signified certain victory. A black man was going to be president of the United States. Harlem rejoiced and it was a rare moment to share with them.

America had done it. Putting aside all the fear and negativity of the Bush years, the voters had reinvented their country and indeed the world. From Africa to Asia never again would the world look the same, with a man of colour leading the most powerful country in it.

On 20 January 2009 I stood with about a million and a half others in Washington DC as Obama was inaugurated. It was Mardi Gras and Super Bowl days all mixed up together. When Obama accepted the oath of office, a noise like rolling thunder spilled out across the stage and down through an audience that stretched as far as the eye could see. It was the sound of sheer exultation.

A few moments before, a helicopter had roared overhead, bearing the former president George Bush away to exile in Texas. The crowd began singing spontaneously, 'Na Na Na Na, Hey Hey Hey, Goodbye'. Thus in such absurd moments are political dynasties ended.

A few weeks earlier, Obama had shown his political smarts by appointing Hillary as Secretary of State. Declan Kelly, a Tipperary-born New York businessman, hosted a small brunch in her honour. He would later be named her economic envoy to Northern Ireland – an inspired choice, I thought, as he cared deeply about his home island and the issues it confronted in getting the peace process completed.

Over eggs and bacon in his Tribeca loft, Hillary held forth on the world as she saw it. She made clear that what she had experienced in Ireland would help shape her vision of the world. She spoke about the importance of special envoys such as George Mitchell to help mediate conflicts when heads of governments cannot do so. She spoke of her Irish experience of talking to previously untouchables on both sides. 'We make peace with our enemies, not our friends,' she remarked when I asked what the overwhelming lesson of the Irish peace process was for her.

That sounded right. I felt glad I had been able to help her and Bill to discover that. It had been a long journey for me.

Chapter 3

THE WISDOM OF BILL

The Clinton residence in Chappaqua, New York, a town of about 10,000 residents some thirty miles north of Manhattan, is in a cul de sac named Old House Lane. The neighbours are far closer than you might expect for the residence of a former President and First Lady of the United States. They moved in on 6 January 2000, just before Bill left the White House and Hillary took over as US senator for New York from Daniel Patrick Moynihan.

It is a beautiful old white clapboard house situated on a few acres, ironically not far from the world headquarters of the now bankrupt *Readers Digest* empire, one of the most influential right wing publications in its heyday.

On this cool autumn evening in September 2002 it was finally action time for the 2008 Hillary for President campaign. Of course it wasn't billed as such, just as a party for close friends. We were all part of a group cloyingly known as 'Hill's Angels', essentially the core group tasked originally with winning her US senate seat and eventually the White House. No one would have described it as such that night, and her presidential run was many years away, but, equally, no one was under any illusions. 'Will Hillary run for president? Does a bear shit in the woods?' as one close Clinton aide said to me pungently.

A number of us had gathered at the sprawling residence where a marquee had been set up to accommodate the attendance. Hillary greeted everyone personally, remembering spouses and kids' names in that effortless way that she and Bill have mastered. She was dressed in a summer outfit and looked more relaxed than I had seen her in years. She was clearly enjoying her term in the senate and had proven herself a dedicated and talented legislator. Now came the next step.

I knew some were urging her to run in 2004, not a strategy I favoured. The events of 9/11 had made Bush into a two-term president in my opinion, and Hillary, with only two years in the senate, would face withering criticism that she was a carpetbagger who took the seat only to run for the White House.

As the evening progressed, my wife Debbie and I took a stroll through the residence. It was clear that there was a definite geographic division of labour between the couple. Bill's study, office and gym were all on the east side of the house, while Hillary's rooms were on the opposite side. His library was packed roof to ceiling with books and, incongruously, some gym equipment. I spied three Irish titles on his shelf: a book of poems by Seamus Heaney, Conor O'Clery's book, *Daring Diplomacy,* about the Clinton work on the Irish peace process, and George Mitchell's book, *Making Peace,* on the same subject.

Outside we found Bill Clinton sitting back in an easy chair, holding court with a few friends on the state of American politics. As night began to fall, we joined the inner circle and listened to perhaps the greatest pure politician of his generation. He was discussing his favourite topic – how to win the White House – and spoke of the need to listen closely for the cadence of the times. Was it a time to run on a platform of change or to run on continuity and a steady compass? If someone was running for president, they had to know the mood music – what the American people were focused on that year – and be pitch perfect, he said.

As night drew in, the circle around Clinton grew and we hung on his words. He is always worth listening to. He is the son of a father he never knew [his father died in an accident before he was born], the stepson of an abusive alcoholic, the spurned candidate who only won the Democratic nomination in 1992 because all the insiders thought that Mario Cuomo, the popular governor of New York, was a shoo in and they decided not to run. When Cuomo pulled out, Clinton spreadeagled the field.

Now he was saying that if a politician was deaf to that mood music he or she could never succeed. Amazingly, he and Hillary made that mistake, by not running on a change agenda in 2008 six years later. No one except a complete outsider, an African American senator from Illinois, would pitch that note.

It is almost forgotten now, but Hillary's support of the Iraq war was what doomed her at the start of the 2008 campaign. The necessity to stay onside on that issue with broad American public opinion was a fundamental mistake that many other politicians also made. Perhaps Hillary's coterie can be blamed for looking past the primaries to the general election and being overconfident that she would win the nomination.

But that was all in the future back in October 2002. That night, I left Chappaqua with the clear belief that Hillary would run, not in 2004, but wait until 2008, having made a calculated decision that Bush was unbeatable in 2004, an election year bound to be overshadowed by the events of 9/11.

I was looking forward to her running for the White House in 2008. I had been there from the start of her political journey and before that for Bill's first run for the White House.

Chapter 4

HOW HILLARY EARNED HER SPURS

T he call from Hillary Clinton in the autumn of 2000 could not have been more urgent. The soft money ban, in place in her senate race against Congressman Rick Lazio in New York, which had set maximum contributions at $2,500 for individuals, meant that she was almost out of funding with the crucial last few weeks in the race yet to come. Could I organise a major fundraiser, one that the president himself would attend if we could swing at least $150,000 in hard cash, she asked. I thought it over for a few seconds before responding that yes, I could do that. After putting down the phone I wondered if my enthusiasm had not overwhelmed my judgment. Getting 150 people separately to write a cheque for $1,000 was an uphill battle, particularly in a community where many held very mixed views on the Clinton White House.

Over the next few days I ransacked every filofax entry I had, and with enormous help from Steven Travers, one of my work associates, began calling around non-stop. I got some blunt refusals; others promised help but never delivered. The majority, however, hard-working Irish businessmen and women, were only too happy to oblige. Because of the Clintons' extraordinary role in the Irish peace process there was a reservoir of goodwill and commitment there that had never been truly tapped. Many of the contributors were staunch Republican party members who appreciated above all else what the Clintons had done in Ireland. I discovered that the best way to fund-raise was to get a few heavy hitters who could then bring in five or ten others, who could bring in a few more, in a sort of daisy chain reaction that ensured that we reached out the length and breadth of the Irish community in New York. Thus several leaders in the Irish community signed on as co-chairs. Soon the total began mounting, until I fully used up the favour bank I had built up over many years in New York. We passed the $100,000 mark and headed confidently for the magic $150,000. The Clinton staffers were obviously astonished. At the end of a long drawn out political campaign – the most expensive senate race in history – they thought they had tapped every conceivable donor and ethnic group, but here were the Irish, delivering.

On the night itself, some 200 or so of us packed the lobby and bar area of Fitzpatrick's Hotel in midtown Manhattan. It was a crush, as it always is at Clinton functions, with everyone determined to get close enough to get a photograph with the world's most famous couple. As MC and chief organiser I was run off my feet trying to cater to every big contributor. Worse, of course, the Clintons were late, as they always are, and Hillary arrived before Bill, throwing our programme into chaos. As always, Hillary was cool and calm despite the crush of bodies. One of the secrets often missed about the Clintons is how much they actually enjoy the flesh pressing part of the political game. Whereas most people would recoil from another sweaty room and hordes of excited devotees trying to grasp their hand, I have seen both Clintons thrive on it on many occasions.

When she began her senate race, Hillary was more standoffish, but by the end she was almost a match for her husband, one of the most electric personalities ever to light up a room. As First Lady, Hillary had often seemed aloof, and many of her supporters questioned whether the rough and tumble of political life as a candidate would suit her. They need not have worried. Hillary was also very comfortable with the press, something not generally realised because of all the scrutiny she has undergone. Once, when hosting her at a St Patrick's Day event in 2000, there were throngs of media waiting to interrogate her upstairs in O'Neill's restaurant. A small group of us huddled together downstairs to prepare her for possible questions. Midway through my briefing on Irish issues I realised she was actually looking forward to the grilling, to giving as good as she got and walking the tightrope of unscripted media appearances, which fewer and fewer politicians do. She strode upstairs almost eagerly, the light of battle in her eye, ready to face the klieg lights and the assembled horde.

On this night in October 2000, when I introduced Hillary I talked humorously, I hope, about the 'Irish' senate seat she was running for, one held by Daniel Patrick Moynihan, Kevin Keating, William Buckley and many other Irish Americans, going back decades. Even though she wasn't directly Irish, I said, we were going to accept her as one of our own, and no Italian like Lazio was going to take the 'Irish' seat. She enjoyed that and she launched into a spirited outline of all she and her husband had done for the Irish peace process. She was interrupted several times by tumultuous applause. After her remarks, Hillary went upstairs to a holding room to await her husband who had been delayed. I sat out in the front bar area where he was going to make his entrance, with some secret service people and John Fitzpatrick, a close personal friend and owner of the hotel and a man who had devoted enormous time and energy to the Clinton cause over the years.

Hillary joined us and we stood chatting for over ten minutes while waiting for the president to arrive. When he did, it was his usual bear-hugging, backslapping entrance, striding into the cordoned-off room and immediately becoming the centre of gravity. He posed for pictures with the bartender, with John Fitzpatrick and me. Then he and Hillary huddled together for a few moments, within earshot. Seeing them together for any extended period of time you cannot but be struck by the easy body language. Numerous books have been written, and

indeed an entire industry has grown up, speculating on their relationship. Having seen them close up and so easy with each other on innu-
merable occasions, the answer seems obvious to me. Despite all the
difficulties and trials of the past decade, they remain in love and
indeed infatuated with each other.

She visibly relaxes in his company. He often plays the jokester,
anxious to put her at her ease. He talks, she listens. He leans in,
forming almost a protective barrier around her. She can be remote,
tightlipped and distant in certain situations, but never around him.
There have obviously been tradeoffs, as there are in most
relationships, but they have stayed together for over thirty-five years,
far longer than the relationships of many of their chief critics who
espouse 'family values'. On this evening he was advising her about an
aspect of her campaign for senator. He has a computer-like facility to
remember even the most arcane aspects of any political race and he
was telling her the percentage of the vote he thought she needed to get
in several upstate counties. 'Governor Pataki got 71 per cent there in
his last election' he told her, referring to some remote New York state
region, 'I think you can get over 50 per cent'.

When he was in Dublin in 1995, in Cassidy's bar, he regaled
Congressman Tom Manton and me with the figures from almost every
precinct in Queens from the 1992 presidential election. When he had
finished and moved on, Manton, the Queens' Democratic leader and
an old-style boss, turned to me and said, 'He knows more about votes
in Queens than I do'.

When we entered the main lobby from our private meeting in the
bar, you had the immediate sense of a room listing to one side, as the
crush to meet the president became an unruly scene. Perfectly poised
businessmen and women who were calmly sipping cocktails and
munching on hors d'oeuvres, suddenly dropped all pretence of
sophistication and rushed to meet and greet Clinton. With great

difficulty we established a receiving line and I stood beside the Clintons to ensure that everyone they met was properly introduced. It is always astonishing to watch people's behaviour in Bill Clinton's presence. 'Clutchers' is the secret service name for those who just won't let go, and there were quite a few in our crowd. One woman in particular did everything but strip in front of him, rubbing her breasts against him and clutching on to his hand until I gently disengaged it. I saw Hillary signalling to me when another woman engaged her and her husband in a discussion about her dreams, which included the nugget that she dreamt about Bill every night. These people apart, the Clintons seemed to genuinely enjoy the warmth of the welcome. Bill, as one aide said, is addicted to 'junk love' – the extraordinary reaction he gets from crowds. This evening he was a trifle weary by the end of the handshaking, however, and asked me in a humorous aside if I was going out into the street to bring people in to meet him.

After his brief speech I escorted him back through the curtain into the bar area where we stopped for a few moments and chatted about the North. As usual, he listened intently. His ability to soak up knowledge on a myriad of complex issues is perhaps his greatest political talent. I knew this was the last time I would see him as president and I thanked him for all he had done to bring peace to my country, the first president who ever cared enough about it. As we walked to the door he suddenly put his arm on my shoulders, looked me in the eye and said, 'We did some great work together, didn't we?' I couldn't think of a better tribute than that to my time in America. I had come a long way too.

Chapter 5

MY FATHER'S DREAM

We walked along the road to the beach. He gripped my hand in that urgent way reserved for fathers walking with their sons, not as comfortable or steady as my mother's. He was at home here. It was his place: West Kerry with its soaring mountains and mutinous sea crashing endlessly against the rugged shoreline. His family had been here for several generations and his nephew still farmed the lumpy land just a few miles from the beach. He knew every field, every yard of the old homestead. He even knew the ghosts. He told me he thought they walked beside him, those solemn spectres of family past. I know he talked to them in Irish, the native language still spoken in this remote part of Ireland. He missed them all, he told me, and more than ever now that he was bringing their grandchildren down to this most westerly part of Ireland.

Years later I would go back and find out who he was communing with.

❦

When the 1911 Irish census first came on line it covered only four counties: Antrim, Dublin, Down and Kerry. Luckily, the O'Dowd old homestead in the townland of Kilcooley, about seven miles from Dingle, was included. My brother Fergus called me excitedly from Ireland and referred me to the Kilcooley parish records from 1911 – and there, at last, was my father's family.

It was an extraordinary moment to reach out and touch the souls

29

who came before me and made me what I am today. Some names I knew, others I never would. They were there under the heading: 'Residents of House No. 8, Kilcooley, Kerry'. My great-grandfather, Edward Dowd (they didn't use the 'O' back then) was the family patriarch in 1911. He was seventy-two years old and married with four children.

He signed his census form with an X, which meant he was not literate, a fact the census taker duly noted. He had been born just a few years before the famine in 1839 and had gone through it. Edward was a farmer, and he and wife Mary, 69, had married in 1861 and raised four kids there in their two-room house and small farm. Now, in 1911, they shared the two-room house with thirteen others – an incredible number of people, but a fair indication of the awful economic times.

There was Michael, my grandfather, and his wife, Catherine Kennedy, from a nearby townland. They were aged 45 and 38 respectively when the census was taken on the night of 2 April 1911. I remember my grandmother dimly, my grandfather not at all. They had nine children at that point and the census taker noted that ten had been born but one did not survive – something none of my family today ever knew. There was Mary who went to Detroit, Jack who followed her there, Michael, who would eventually inherit the farm, Ellen, who became a nun in Savannah, Georgia, then Patrick, who became a priest in the black hills of South Dakota; there too was Donal, my father, five years old on 2 April 1911, who later became a schoolteacher.

Underneath his name were those of Edward, who went to London, and Thomas who became a Christian Brother. Not yet born were Dennis, who also became a Christian Brother, Brid who came to New York, and Matt who became a Christian Brother and died tragically young. Also living in the house at the time were two of my grandfather's brothers.

Everyone was listed as farmer or scholar, except for my grandfather's brother, who was listed as a fisherman. Everyone except Edward was literate, but only in the Irish language. It seemed from the census that there were more people living in my great- grandfather's house than in any other home in the parish. A family called the O'Connors had a six-room house, which must have made them the envy of the Dowds and everyone else locally.

What amazed me too was the fact that, almost a hundred years later, the same families still occupy the village. Next door, as they were in 1911, are the Hurleys and the Sheas. The old homestead is now farmed by my cousin Padraig. We know from Griffiths' Valuations, an 1852 survey of land prices in West Kerry, that Michael and Mary Dowd were living in Kilcooley back then, though there is no further information on them. There is a wonderful timelessness to all this, the sense that the rhythms of life in an isolated part of rural Ireland pass down from generation to generation. I felt that a chapter on a previous life of my father's family had suddenly been opened up and the history suddenly come to life.

That was all in the future, of course. On this day when I was young, my father and I reached the beach and walked to the end of the pier. We gazed out at the vast expanse of water and the headland in the distance. The clouds were settling in over Mount Eagle, a harbinger of rain to come. A distant roll of thunder echoed across the bay. A storm was coming. Other children were there with their parents, shouting and laughing. A little boy ran past, pursued by his father as they raced to their car to beat the storm. I realised for the first time that mine was older than most of the fathers and that he would find it hard to run so fast. It didn't bother me. He didn't seem to mind the rain as it fell and the sky darkened. His eyes were fixed on the wide horizon, staring far out to sea, past the crashing waves. 'What is out there, Dad?' I asked him. He looked at me, smiling. 'America,' he said. 'That's the next parish.' It was the first time I had ever heard of the place.

Chapter 6

CALIFORNIA HERE I COME

There's a stretch of wilderness, like a no-man's-land, between Wyoming and Salt Lake City, where what seems like thousands of miles of hard sand and rock undulate on either side of the highway. On a clear summer's night in 1978, with a full moon reflecting eerily on the lunar-like landscape, it was like nothing I had ever seen. Inside the Greyhound bus speeding me across this vista I was conscious of a great stirring.

I was twenty-five years old and truly on my own for the first time. Behind me lay the East Coast and the city of Chicago, where I had spent the past six months. Ahead lay the Western shores, first Nevada and beyond that California – my final destination. There is a moment, as Solzhenitsyn has remarked, that your life leads up to and everything after leads away from forever. This was mine. Perhaps it had been the lights of Cheyenne reflecting in the rear view mirror of the bus and that lonely, indescribable feeling as I faced into the night and the unknown. Maybe it was the sheer enormity of the land we now travelled through that brought about the dawning realisation that nothing again would ever be the same. Nor would it be.

Back in Chicago, just two hours after I had left, a telegram arrived informing me of my father's heart attack back home in Ireland. If I had stayed, or even been delayed by a day, I would have immediately rushed home to be with him. The attack was not fatal, but a later one soon after would kill him. If I had returned from Chicago I would have been there when he died from the second attack. I would have settled down in Ireland and become the schoolteacher he so desperately wanted me to be. I would have figured, fatalistically, that my life had taken that turn for a reason and would have just allowed myself to be carried along in the familiar flow of family, a decent job and lots of friends. It was not to be, because of a two-hour time lag.

Strangely, my father had said goodbye to me on the phone just the week before, calling me up out of the blue to chat about America, a land he had never seen but which lived vividly in his imagination. He had given me my love of it, filling my childish head full of tales of westerns and Zane Grey novels where the heroes always looked cool and clean. Cowboy films were one of his few relaxations away from his seven children, and he replayed many of the scenes to me from memory. I loved the old movies too; titles like *The Man from Laramie* and *Shane* were part of my boyhood mythology. Finally I was living the dream I had had since I was a kid, of travelling to the American West. Indeed, since I was a child all of America had taken a grip on my imagination. I loved *Superman* comics and the visits home by my uncle, a priest in South Dakota. I was enchanted when he talked about the endless plains and the vast prairies where one could drive for a full day and never meet anyone, and the crashing thunderstorms and bolt lightning that lit up the night sky like day.

The life I lived in Ireland, solidly middle class, one of seven children of my father, a schoolteacher from Kerry, and my mother, a housewife from Clare, seemed sadly unoriginal by comparison. Because he was quite deaf at that stage, communication was difficult with my father during our final phone call, but I told him what I could about how well I was doing, the thing each parent wants to hear, despite the reality of my circumstances. I would always be glad of that last awkward goodbye.

Now I would never see him again and the telegram would pursue me across the United States, arriving ten days later when I was settled in California. As he lay ill and on his final journey I was on the Greyhound bus contemplating a rebirth, a new life in a land where I knew no one, having cut all the ties to Chicago and home. I had never felt happier in my life. I knew nothing of his illness, intent on my American odyssey.

Years later, my mother told me that when he heard I planned to move to San Francisco from Chicago, he had studied maps of America from his hospital bed and plotted my course from Chicago to San Francisco with the excitement of a wagon train scout planning a new route. Perhaps he was with me on this trip, a ghostly presence out beyond the flatlands. Indeed, during a fitful sleep on the Greyhound bus I dreamt vividly of him that night. I even jotted down a note about it when I awoke. In the dream I pictured him as I saw him on one of the last occasions in the Franciscan Church in Drogheda, my home town, half way up the aisle, a short, stocky man with his black cap for once in his pocket. He was kneeling, as he always did, yet in his own world, too deaf to hear the prayers, too proud to admit it to anyone but his family. In the dream he was reading from his old Irish language missal, the one with the ornate symbols and exotic Irish phrases. He caressed it often, as though it was one of his children. The litany of the saints always sounded much more intriguing in the Irish language, the fine strong words tripping off his tongue; he had a beautiful lilt when he spoke the language. I would remember that dream forever. Ever after, on hearing the booming opening lines of his favourite prayer in English: 'Hail Holy Queen, Mother of Mercy, Hail our life, our sweetness and our hope', it would take me back to that moment.

Sometimes he would meet his friend, Stephen Ryan, like him an Irish speaker, and they would drive in Ryan's old Fiat to the seaside, usually to Mornington, a sleepy little village just four miles from town. There the Irish Sea washed in, far calmer than the bold Atlantic on the other side of the country, and the hungry seagulls perched on top of the ruins of an old abbey. Cars carrying courting couples parked near the water and waited for the onset of nightfall. From across the fields you could often hear the tolling of the Mornington church bell, its rich peal echoing over the strand. On clear days my father and Ryan could look across the bay and see Ireland's Eye, the little island perched off the Irish coast, and further on the shimmering lights of North Dublin, the gateway to the big city. Sometimes they drove in that direction, but they never actually reached it. They were two country men, not really at home in the big cities. Ryan was a travelling salesman and had spent a lifetime traversing the highways and byways of Ireland and he knew every twist and turn. My father had travelled little, never learning to drive.

Once I was lucky enough to accompany them to Mornington. We drove out on a harsh night with rain spitting against the windows of the tiny car. I sat in the back, wedged behind the front seats. I was eleven or twelve at the time, fast coming into maturity. They spent the entire time talking about how scandalised they were at the appearance in Dublin of American film star and sex symbol Jayne Mansfield. A sex symbol in Ireland! I couldn't wait to read about her and dreamt about seeing her in the flesh.

The sins of the flesh, of course, were non-existent in Ireland at the time, or so we were led to believe. A generation later it would all come spilling out about paedophile priests, the horrific abuse in some orphanages and the dreadful acts committed on some single mothers who were forced to give up their children and live in total servitude. Back in the Ireland of the 1960s, grim, brooding and bitter, you didn't try and stand up or stand out, you just conformed, even as a kid. You knew better than to question your elders and betters. A fundamentalist mindset reigned. 'Who made the world?' 'God made the world.' No room for doubt there.

That all seemed far behind me now. Now I was in Jayne Mansfield's country: rich, voluptuous, different. The bus sped on. From time to time we pulled off the highway into some unnamed or unremembered town, stopped briefly to discharge or take on a passenger. The night sky was star spangled all the way to the horizon, the moon was full and the only sound apart from the hum of the bus was a soughing wind when you opened the windows to breathe in the perfect air. From the back of the bus wafted the acrid smell of a marijuana joint, and later some muffled giggling. Two black guys I had befriended at the Cheyenne stop were doing the smoking. When I invited them into the bar near the bus stop they politely declined. Once inside I knew why. Everyone there was white and they would hardly have been welcome.

Inside the bar I got into conversation with two cowboys seated at the counter. One told me he thought Ireland was somewhere off Africa. The other inquired, for some reason, about exporting cars to Ireland. I found it all exotic and exciting. Back on the bus after hours of crossing the flat terrain, Salt Lake City finally loomed in the distance, home of the Mormons, and not much else that I knew about it. As we traversed the downtown streets it seemed like a ghost town, with no one except occasional cops and a bum or two in sight. The Greyhound bus terminal was in a seedy part of town, as they invariably are, and the brightly lit waiting room was the only oasis in what seemed a dark and unfriendly neighbourhood. This was my terminus too, the place where I would pick up another bus to California. Within an hour I would have to choose between a bus to San Francisco or Los Angeles, a decision that would alter the course of my life forever.

In retrospect, my decision was obvious, but at the time it hardly seemed so clear cut. I was expecting this to be the definitive journey of my life, not merely another passage to some unknown place. San Francisco had been part of my imagination since the Scott McKenzie song of that name strummed its way into my head several years before. As a student in Dublin, damp and dreary nights in cold apartments were often whiled away dreaming of California. Since I was a child it had fired my imagination, why I will never know, yet it had been a constant urge to go there. Now I was finally on the way.

Los Angeles was also an option because a friend of a friend in Chicago had invited me to go there and work with him. It was not a city that had ever inspired me, however, but the prospect of a definite job and a place to stay after this exhausting trek across country was inviting. My ticket terminated in Salt Lake and as I waited in line to buy passage to my next destination I felt an eerie calm about the decision I was about to make.

San Francisco seemed an antidote to life in narrow, constricted Ireland, a place where they wore flowers in their hair and nobody cared where you were from or where you were going and where there seemed a sense of youthful idealism and a real meaning to life. There was also a name I had of someone in San Francisco, one Martin Mulkerrins, a brother of a good friend of mine in Chicago. I didn't know his address or phone number, merely the name of the tavern called 'The Abbey' that he hung out in. It was better than nothing, and besides, it was an improvement over Los Angeles for which I felt no tug at my soul. San Francisco it would be. After a two-hour wait, the bus finally pulled out of the station as dawn was breaking. I settled back in my old seat, conscious that the two young black men had disembarked and that I knew not a living soul from here to California. I suddenly loved that feeling. Soon we drove through the Salt Lake itself, resplendent in the dawn light, how I imagined the Dead Sea would look in a scene from biblical times. It was easy to see why a man would put down camp and establish his church here under what one writer later called the 'Banner of Heaven'.

As we went further west the terrain had begun to change. The flat monotony of Iowa, Idaho, Nebraska and the plains states were behind us, and first the foothills and then the sheer stark ridges of the Sierra Nevada loomed in front of us. What a bountiful land, I thought, looking at the lakes, streams, rivers, mountains and forests that had begun to dot the landscape in the morning light. I could picture the old pioneers, so many of them Irish, coming across this land after the exhausting trek across the plains and imagining they had reached Nirvana. A hundred years or so later, that's how it looked to me as well. In Ireland, from the tip of one end to the extreme at the other, the island is no more than 350 miles long. I would travel that distance in a single day now and still make no dent on the never-ending landscape which stretched out in front of me.

The notion of following the horizon without falling into the ocean I found a very powerful one. Sometimes I felt miscast in this century, much preferring to have tackled these same hills and mountains as part of a pioneering expedition. In a strange way, as I watched the landscape slip by, I felt I was back to where I had never actually been. If there was such a thing as a previous life I believed I must have spent part of it here in the American West. Our first stop on the bus was Reno, an isolated bluff of a town lying at Nevada's northern edge. The opening lines of the old song 'Don't Go Down to Reno'... 'In Reno town for a few dollars down' played in my head as I made my way to the casino near the bus station. It was early morning and I was weary. There was just enough time to lose some money on the gaming machine before the last leg of the journey to San Francisco commenced.

Somewhere between Reno and San Francisco, a group of motorcyclists began buzzing the bus, first three in front and three behind, then all six riding perilously close together just a few bumpers' space from the bus itself. Though the driver tooted his horn and hollered, they were obviously having great fun. Finally the leader of the pack, a heavyset, bearded guy, stood up straight in his saddle while his female pillion passenger pulled his jeans down to reveal his butt cheeks to the startled bus passengers. Some of us laughed, others looked away in disgust. As a cheeky welcome to California, it took some beating.

It was late evening when we reached the San Francisco Greyhound bus station. By now I was sufficiently exhausted to have slept the last hour of the journey or so but I woke up disoriented, having dreamt that I was back in Ireland playing football. Instead, here I was, inside a station in a seedy part of the Mission district with a backpack and about $200 dollars in cash. The effect was like a cold shower, the grand dreams and designations of the bus trip giving way to a scary reality. The old saying that it is sometimes better to travel than to arrive crossed my mind. Now it would be a matter of taking care of basics such as food, work and accommodation.

A good-looking young couple accosted me as I walked towards the station entrance. They were members of a commune, they explained, and I was welcome to join them if I so wished. The woman was blonde and California looking, with glasses perched on her forehead, the man clean and well dressed and very polite. 'Do you need a place to stay or some food?' they asked. It was a California cliché come alive for me. Years later I figured they were probably Moonies. Luckily, after briefly entertaining their offer, I declined.

Once outside, I asked directions to the Abbey Tavern on 5th and Geary, and was directed to a nearby bus stop. Having eventually figured out how to pay the fare, I found myself on a bus travelling up Geary Boulevard with Ocean Beach as its final destination, a route that would soon become very familiar to me. San Francisco was beautiful. The moonlight played off the Victorian mansions, their colours a pale kaleidoscope of blues, yellows and pinks, all the different colours giving off a warm glow. The hills were majestic and magnificent as the bus clambered up each one en route to the Richmond District. The bus seemed to pause as if to catch its breath before the top of each hill and the next traffic light. In the distance I could see the twinkling lights of San Francisco Bay and the looming mansions of Nob Hill that the very rich called home. This was like nowhere I had ever been before, a city yes, but a magical place too, where the very air seemed full of possibilities and a young man's imagination would find room to breathe. I was well pleased with myself.

The Abbey was a hive of activity when I stepped inside. A large pool table in a side room was a central gathering point, while the bar itself was circular in shape and extended fully around the room. On the wall were faded photos and mementos of Ireland. In one of them a donkey ambled happily down a country road, in another an old Guinness ad: a man balancing a horse and cart over his head after getting the energy from drinking a pint of the black stuff. The place had a somewhat run-down feel, which added somehow to its attraction. I learnt later that during the day it was man's bar, a hard-drinking oasis in a city where alcohol was becoming decidedly uncool. Late at night, however, the big old bar would fill up with wives and girlfriends and single girls intent on meeting a lonely Irishman. Then the atmosphere changed.

I pulled up a stool to the bar and eyed the clientele. Who to ask here about Martin Mulkerrins? I immediately saw my target; amid the blond and bleached California looks was a man with a map of Ireland face, dressed for all the world like he was ready for a night out in a West of Ireland ballroom around 1955. I strolled over and tapped him on the shoulder.

'Hello, I'm just off the bus from back east and I'm looking for Martin Mulkerrins,' I announced.

'Martin?' he said, hardly skipping a beat. 'He was here about a half hour ago but he left. You'll probably find him at the Blarney Stone – it's on twenty-second and Geary.' He paused for a moment, no doubt taking in my long hair, straggly beard and generally unkempt appearance. 'Where are you from yourself?' 'Tipperary,' I answered, the place where I was born before our family moved to Drogheda in County Louth when I was ten, knowing it was a safe enough answer and glad I didn't have to say 'Dublin'. If I had, there would have been an immediate mistrust. 'Jackeens' were generally considered too clever by half by other emigrants.

'Oh, right so. Well, I'm from Mayo. Will you have a drink?' he offered. We sat and drank a beer and then he ordered two shots, which I had, of course, to reciprocate. Already I could feel the $200 beginning to seep away, not to mention a warm buzz filling my head. 'This is a good town,' he told me, having introduced himself as Pat Curran. 'Plenty of work for them that want it. Good weather all year round. Constructions indoors, outdoors, no winter season like Chicago and back east. If you can play Gaelic football you'll get along fine.' The last point was one I knew already. For generations, young Irishmen like myself had made their way to America to play Gaelic games. If you had no relatives in the country it was about the best way to get your start. The teams, if you were very good, paid your fare out and got you work. If you were even a little above average they could ensure that you got the all important 'start' or first job in construction. 'Any chance of the start?' was a common refrain. Playing football was also a wonderful way to make friends, to bed down with your own kind. Years later, I often heard people remark scathingly that the young Irish wanted to stick with their own, making it some kind of criticism of them. What else would you do straight off the plane and in a strange land? There would be lots of time to find out about the great American culture later on. Thus, skill at Ireland's national game, played fervently by exiles all over America, was the equivalent of a ticket to travel and to work. I wasn't the greatest player around, but had the advantage of being relatively new from Ireland at a time when not many were coming over. In San Francisco that was even more the case. If five or six journeymen with football skills arrived every summer that would be it. I was part of this year's crop. I knew that Martin Mulkerrins was tied in with one of the San Francisco teams, so that could be my ticket to a job and putting a roof over my head. I had made the mistake back in Chicago of aligning myself with one of the poorest teams who could provide very little in the way of job opportunities or accommodation. I was not about to make that same mistake here. After another round of drinks I said goodbye to my new-found friend and stepped outside the Abbey bar. I gazed up for a long time at the California sky and thought of all the times in my dreams I had come to this place and time. Now I had actually arrived. It was time to get started on my new life.

Chapter 7

SAN FRANCISCO DREAMING

T he Irish neighbourhoods in San Francisco – the Sunset and the Richmond – were adjacent to each other, separated at their furthest points by Golden Gate Park. Each was bordered by the ocean, spectacularly so. Ocean Beach is one of the most beautiful urban stretches of strand in the world, with the Pacific breakers reaching shore within a taxi ride of downtown San Francisco. Each neighbourhood was home to a polyglot of constantly changing cultures, but a strong Irish presence remained despite the shifting cultural sands around them.

Here it was that generations of Irish emigrants made their living, by my time mostly by constructing what came to be mockingly called 'Micktorians' – basic two-family apartments about as far removed from the glorious Victorian mansions as Los Angeles is from San Francisco. The Irish would make no apologies for that. Most of the emigrants in the 1970s and before had left hopeless lives on small farms on the western seaboard. Not for them the endless grind of their fathers' lives, making enough on the Fair Day to keep going for another few months. They got out, and the luckiest of them came to California. Building dreary apartments in California wasn't a bad option, given the alternatives, and the weather was surely a lot better.

Many had stopped off in Alaska first, lured by the work on the giant oil pipeline there. References to places like Prudhoe Bay and Fairbanks were as common as talking about Dublin or Cork in many Irish circles. 'When it's Springtime in Alaska', a country and western song, was on as many jukeboxes in Irish bars as any Irish song. Those who went to Alaska were inevitably marked by the experience. The money was great, of course, and many arrived in San Francisco with a life's fortune. But the conditions were cruel, sometimes nineteen-hour days, and the long and interminable stretches of boredom and loneliness in the far north affected some men for the rest of their lives. Some could not cope with what San Francisco offered after they left the wilderness, and drank, drugged and whored themselves into a kind of permanent stupor. Occasionally you would see one of these stumblebums falling around the place as the bars closed. Other times they would show up at the Gaelic games, standing away on their own, lonely figures shunned by many, or, sadly, made fun of by others.

The majority, however, used their cash wisely and started construction businesses. Many were the same age as me, twenty-five when I arrived in California, but were already well on their way to millions in their mid-twenties. I had no such background, of course, and was barely passable as a construction worker, something I had learned to my cost in Chicago. Having two left hands was part of the problem, but a pronounced fear of heights when balancing on a scaffold or a forty-foot ladder didn't help either. Later I would learn that there was something about California that crept into the soul of Irish men there, made them more congenial, less eager to judge or hurl the bitter word like so many of their countrymen back east. But when I arrived I was intent only on finding work and a place to live. That was proving difficult to do that first night.

I arrived at the Blarney Stone to discover that Martin Mulkerrins had just left, and I felt suddenly like I was chasing a ghost. A few more beers gave me the courage to talk to some other Irish men at the bar. They felt certain that Martin would be at the dance that night in the nearby church hall, hosted by the Sean MacDermott's football team. I could surely find him there. I walked out into the night air which had now turned decidedly chilly and damp. Unknown to me, I was experiencing the famed San Francisco fog for the first time. I had my bag and about $150 in cash. I had to make a connection at the dance. Finding the church hall was no easy matter. The church itself, an old Spanish style adobe building, was easily located, but the hall was tucked away at the back. I could hear the sound of the Irish music, but could not find an entrance. Finally, in desperation, I clambered over a wire fence and crossed what seemed like a school playground, in the direction of where the music was coming from. Eventually I arrived at a church door and a sign which read 'Parish Hall'. Once inside, I discovered I could have been back in any parish hall in Ireland.

The band, as the posters advertised, was from Boston: John Connors and the Lightning Express – a rare treat for the San Francisco Irish. They belonged in a ballroom in Mayo, not here in this city by the bay, 6,000 miles from there. They were blasting out the old country numbers to a packed hall and it took me some time to negotiate the heaving and swaying mass to get to the bar. A giant of a man, who looked to be in his early thirties, with thick curly hair, stood at the bar nursing a Budweiser. Over the din of the music I shouted that I was looking for Martin Mulkerrins. He took a long look at me and said in Irish, '*Tá tú ag caint leis.*' (You're talking to him.) I breathed a sigh of relief. At long last, a stroke of luck. I mentioned his brother in Chicago and said that he had told me to look him up.

'I know. I was looking for you too. Have a beer. You're staying with me tonight.' No sweeter words had ever been uttered to me. Bushed after the long journey and feeling the light-headed effects of too much beer, I was only too anxious to find a bed to lie down. Martin, however, was going to enjoy the dance for a while more. We stayed at the bar sipping our beer and I learnt quickly that he was a man of few words and one of the most relaxed human beings you could ever be around. Nothing bothered him. He fitted right into San Francisco, where laid back was a way of life.

The women were beautiful, and tired as I was, I could not but admire that golden California look that so many sported. Many of the dancers seemed to know the Irish dances and soon the floor was a whirling dervish of couples turning and dancing in different direction. It was a captivating moment. Here it seemed every person in the room was out for the 'Siege of Ennis' or the 'Walls of Limerick', swirling around the floor with great abandon. A pretty young girl grasped my hand to part-ner her in one of the waltzes. I couldn't believe my luck that a woman had asked me to dance. As we stumbled around the floor she told me she was a schoolteacher and a native San Franciscan whose father was from Ireland. She seemed to know more about 'the old country' than I did and reeled off a list of places she had stayed on vacations over there. I hardly got a word in edgeways. We danced a few more sets and she gave me her phone number; such a display of forwardness would have been unheard of for an Irish woman back home. I liked her but was simply too tired to even think about following up.

At around two o'clock that morning, Martin had enough and we went outside where he slung my canvas bag into the back seat of his car and we set off for his home, a modest two-bedroom apartment in the Richmond district, just a stone's throw from the ocean. The address was 1418 La Playa, an anonymous apartment building, but I would not have been happier to see the Waldorf Astoria.

I met his roommate, a fellow Connemara man, Tom MacDonagh, who, amazingly, I knew from Chicago where he had been a roommate of a friend of mine. The omens were good. I had just enough energy to shake hands and exchange pleasantries before falling dead asleep on a mattress on the floor. I had made it to California and had a roof over my head. Things hadn't started off too badly, unlike when I had first moved from Ireland to Chicago.

Chapter 8

THE CITY OF BROAD SHOULDERS

'In the city of Chicago
As the evening shadows fall
There are people dreaming
Of the Hills of Donegal'

W hen I landed in Chicago in the summer of 1978 I had struggled mightily to put a basic life together. It started when I joined the wrong Irish football team – St Mel's – the weakest of the Chicago area sides. That meant no easy job in construction or an apartment share. But St Mel's had paid my flight out so I was beholden to them. At the time I knew no difference between the teams, so I was very happy to get the subsidised trip. That morning I had bid goodbye to Ireland and to my parents, my father, as it turned out, for the last time. At my version of an American wake the night before I had got thoroughly drunk with my best friend Eddie Holt and confided in him my desire to leave for America for good. 'I'm making the break,' I told Eddie as we sipped our beers. 'I'm like a fish out of water over here, I need something else.'

'Be careful what you wish for,' he responded. 'If America doesn't work out, you might be forced to come back here with your tail between your legs. Now that might prove very awkward.' He was right of course, yet I didn't care. That night we took our usual late night walk around town, out to the furthest streetlight on the road towards the town of Navan. It was raining, a dull drumbeat that splattered off the slatternly roofs of the small cottages we passed on our way. I wouldn't miss this, I thought, not at all. Well after midnight we went back to his house to drink a few beers while his parents slept upstairs. I felt oddly exhilarated as if the witching hour had come for me and a journey long contemplated was about to begin.

I had little choice but to leave. School teaching, I had discovered, was not for me. I lacked both the patience and the temperament for a job that I had always aspired to. A year in an inner city Dublin school, barely holding an unruly class in check, had convinced me of my mistake in my first career choice. Some of the other teachers I knew held their classes together by sheer fear and meted out corporal punishment at will. I was unable to do that, having suffered from it too much in my own schooldays. I had the idea that I would be a different kind of teacher and that the pupils would become my friends, but I learnt all too quickly that this was a mere pipe dream which shattered on contact with reality.

It was tough to teach kids some of whom undoubtedly did not have enough to eat that morning. At the parent/teacher meetings, I quickly learnt that it was always the parents you wanted most to see about their errant kids who never showed up. All in all, a dispiriting experience and one that convinced me that I needed to look elsewhere. It had finally come to a head when I came unmercifully close to hitting one kid who had been bothering me for some time. As a Christian Brothers' boy, I had been well used to getting physically knocked around by some of the bullying brothers and lay teachers, but I didn't ever want to be part of that mindset myself. The psychology involved in teaching had changed, I realised. Whereas in my father's time it was a prestigious job with the emphasis on learning, now it was more a matter of just keeping order for successive forty-five-minute spells.

The only time I had felt good about myself in the role was teaching night classes in the Dublin suburb of Finglas, which had ferocious social problems. The area had originally been set up by relocating families from the tenements in the centre of Dublin. It was a disastrous move. Whereas they had at least a sense of community in the city centre, in Finglas they lived on soulless, sprawling estates where the only patch of green was some miserable vegetable gardens some residents tried to grow. However, because the night class pupils were adult and obviously highly motivated, I communicated much better, learnt a lot and enjoyed the experience thoroughly.

So I knew I had to move on. But to where? In Ireland at the time there were very few other options: unemployment was a booming business and the emigrant trains and planes were starting to fill up after years of relative prosperity. I had a visa allowing me to work for four months in the US. It seemed the only way out.

Chapter 9

THE LEAVETAKING

The next morning, still suffering from the effects of the booze, I staggered downstairs at 9 o'clock. Outside the skies were a gun metal grey and rain sweeping in from the west was forecast. Some things never changed. A deep sepulchral gloom hung over the household. My mother cooked her usual gargantuan breakfast – her greatest fear was always that one of her brood would go hungry. Her heart wasn't in it this morning, however. Only since becoming a parent myself do I realise how difficult it is to part from a child. I didn't really know then, but I know now that it must have broken her heart each time a member of her family took off for foreign climes.

My father was not a demonstrative man but he threw his arms around me in a rare display of emotion. Then he waited out in our back garden as I climbed the embankment to the nearby railway bridge in Drogheda, a fast short cut to the station. He watched as I walked across the railway lines spanning the river Boyne to the train station proper. Did he suspect that this was the last time he would see his son? I would never know the answer to that but my mother said he seemed more upset than was usual when one of his brood of seven went away, as was a frequent occurrence. I think of him now, as I became a smaller and smaller speck on the horizon, walking further away from him at every step. I don't know if he was thinking those dread thoughts of his own mortality, so close to his own death, but there was no question that he must have felt a deep sense of loss.

Later, my mother told me that my father plotted every yard of my journey, picking each of the cities I flew over en route to Chicago, living the trip he had never taken but had always wanted to. He had almost moved to America himself in the early 1930s. A letter survives from a friend who had gone to Boston, inviting him out. Huge numbers from his own area had left for that city when the bleak depression began hitting home in Ireland. The friend wrote that you were as likely to meet someone from home in Boston on a Sunday morning on the way to mass as back in West Kerry. Another letter survives in which the friend makes it clear that times were now just as bad in Boston as they were in Ireland. My father had been due to take the train to Cork and the emigrant boat just a few weeks later. He never made it.

My mother had never contemplated crossing to the 'Fresh Land' or to 'Bright City' as New York was called. She had had a tragic early life in Ennis, County Clare, losing her father and three brothers before her 21st birthday. One brother was killed playing rugby, another died from meningitis, and a third was killed in the RAF at the end of the Second World War. Her father had died of a haemorrhage. She had briefly considered following her remaining sibling, her sister May, to England and becoming a nurse during the Second World War, but her mother's illness meant she had to stay close. Against all the odds, my father had become a schoolteacher, the first in his family, and indeed his village, to get a teacher training college education. He spent his early years traversing several counties, usually on a bicycle, teaching the Irish language which was undergoing a huge revival after Irish independence. His heart was alive to that challenge and he was full of daring during those years as he felt he was playing an important role in creating the new country. He met my mother in Tipperary when she came to his class and they married in January 1946. There is a photograph of them on their honeymoon in Dublin. He is confident, square-jawed, looking the camera flush in the eye as he strides along O'Connell Street, the main thoroughfare. She is more reticent, looking a little to the side, shy perhaps, but very beautiful in a dress that hugs her figure.

❧

On the train to Dublin I met a priest from the diocese, a family friend who was going to Dublin for the day.

'You must be halfway to heaven by now,' he said. 'Your poor father hardly stops between the prayers and the holy water worrying about you and the journey west.'

I laughed, but his words struck home. It was a lonesome journey. The beautiful countryside I was passing through did not inspire an exile's heart for the flight ahead. The blaze of the sun cast its warm rays across the fields. I could see the cows scatter at the train's approach, heavy, beautiful animals, their great clumsy strides eating up the rolling fields as they sought sanctuary from the approaching noise. There are few Irish sights as beautiful. At the airport, sad scenes of emigration, similar to those stretching back generations, were all too evident. Loved ones embraced at the gate. Tearstained parents bid their offspring goodbye. Hard times had come to Ireland again and the planes were filling up. I thought then of those generations who had left by boat, knowing that they would never return, and how tragic that must have been. Parents who never saw sons or daughters again, children who never saw their parents grow old or bounce one of their grandchildren on their knee. In a country where family ties are everything, such partings must have been pure heartbreak.

Many of the emigrants on this day, however, once having bid goodbye to their parents, had a spring in their step as they made their way to the departure gate. It wasn't all about sadness, but about opportunity for a lot of them. I felt much the same way. Jennie was there, as I expected. She was my love, the Donegal woman I had shared my life in Dublin with for about three years. We had met at college and she stood by me during a particularly tough time in my life. We lived together in a little flat in Leeson Street where we played house, like all young couples do. We, two penniless students, had dreams of buying it and settling in Dublin where we would both get teaching jobs and live happily ever after. The dreams melted away because of the heat of my ambition and my disappointment with teaching. I was going to get out.

Jennie was not coming with me. Her heart was in Dublin; the same intimacy and closeness that repelled me attracted her. She loved the craic, the gossip and the eternal backbiting, the friends she had gathered to her and me, because she was far more outgoing. Taking her out of that would have been like tossing a starfish on a rocky shore. She was meant for Dublin. We embraced.

'I love you,' I said.

'I love you too,' she replied, but I knew she had a sense that we would find it tough to overcome this separation. We talked about how she would come over when I had some money put together and she put on a brave smile, but her eyes were sorrow-filled when I kissed her. At last we let go of each other and she strode off without glancing back. She was wearing the same Afghan coat she always did then and I watched as it disappeared into the distance. I was severing my single biggest tie to Dublin.

At the gate I linked up with several friends who were on the same flight. The early morning blues and the farewell to Jennie had now given way to a rising excitement, and, with the arrogance of youth, I quickly forgot those left behind. Like giggling schoolkids, we were all looking forward to this trip into the wild blue yonder. Most were stopping off in New York, some going to points further west or to Boston. We were some of the lucky ones, the first generation, really, that would never be more than a plane flight away from home. For centuries exile had been a death sentence, with few ever coming back. Now it was different. On the plane we drank and talked about how great America would be, perhaps to cover our nervousness. None of the others, as far as I knew, was set on emigration as against a summer fling. Just before take-off a group of schoolchildren from Dublin got on for the trip to Shannon, probably an educational tour. They were wet-nosed and red-eyed from their early morning start and I could imagine the excitement in their homes as they rose and prepared for this trip. I looked at their sleepy little faces and the first pang of homesickness struck me.

At Shannon, the bar and the duty-free store beckoned. I chose the bar and whiled away the waiting period building up my bravado with Dutch courage for the trip ahead. It was a scene I would repeat many times over the next few decades. But I was taken with a sudden fit of melancholy as the furthest islands off the western Irish coast dropped away beneath the plane's wings and I realised that this might be the last time for a long while that I saw the land of my birth or my family. I tried unsuccessfully to sleep, but I was never a great flyer and each dip and yaw of the plane startled and woke me. Far from calming me, the drinking seemed to have the opposite impact as my heart pounded every time we dipped, and I gripped the seat tightly. Finally, over Newfoundland, I got up and strolled to a window at the back of the plane. There I looked out and saw the snowcapped tips of mountains, huge gorges, mighty rivers and as still a landscape as in an oil painting. It was my first view of the American continent.

A fellow traveller, a young priest, was gazing out the window with me. Like me, it was his first trip to the US. He told me that he was on his way to a parish in Florida. He was an only son from Leitrim, an isolated county, and it was soon clear from what he told me that he was his mother's pride and joy. They were small farmers and now his aging father would be left alone to manage the few cattle, the poor soil and the lumpy hills. He had one sister, but she had already left to be a nurse in England. He told me how his mother had dumped an entire bottle of holy water over him at the airport as he left on his first foreign assignment. His father had not come, preferring to stay on the lonely farm. The night before, they had got drunk together, and in the small hours of the morning, the worse for drink, his father had broken down and cried and cursed that he had ever become a priest. 'There will be no one left at home,' he told him. 'I wanted you to have the farm, to raise your children here.' Now that would never happen.

The priest's eyes welled with tears as he told me the story. He was moving to Boca Raton, leaving Leitrim, his parents and the seminary in Dublin far behind. 'It's a lonesome feeling,' he told me. 'Going to live among strangers. I've been told I won't be home for two years. It's enough to make a grown man cry.' I wasn't feeling the most robust myself: too much booze, the late night before, and my mouth as dry as sandpaper from dehydration. My bravado about the prospects for my new life had dimmed somewhat.

Chapter 10

NOT SO WELCOME TO AMERICA

After six and a half hours, the city of New York hove up on our right. I rushed to the window on the other side of the plane, as did many others, to catch a first glimpse. As far as the eye could see there were vast urban landscapes interspersed with patches of green. As we swooped in over Long Island, we could see the long stretch of pristine sand and the Atlantic waves lapping up against the shoreline. Now the airport lay dead ahead, beyond the broad expanse of water. The runway seemed to stretch on forever. A strong crosswind produced a final bump as we approached, and then, mercifully, the wheels touched down so softly that I hardly knew we had landed. Some of the passengers applauded. Six hours and forty-five minutes after leaving Ireland I was in the New World. The sailing ships had taken weeks, the steamers five days or so. I was there in less than a good night's sleep.

The Aer Lingus plane disgorged us amid some heartfelt goodbyes and pleas to stay in touch. If there were personal doubts or misgivings we hid them well from each other.

Once on the ground we were directed to the immigration control area. It was hard not to feel intimidated by the sight of the burly agents, hunched over their machines, closely examining every arrival. A few years later, returning to the US illegally, I panicked when I realised I had a business card from my American company still in my wallet. I had only one option as the line snaked towards the counter. I slipped it in my mouth and chewed it, swallowing it with a great effort just as my turn at the counter arrived. I was lucky on that occasion; they asked me to remove the contents of my wallet and I would certainly have been caught. I had heard many tales of people stopped because they had American labels on clothes or a receipt from an American store. There were apocryphal stories too, about carpenters showing up with their work tools in their bag and construction workers with their California driver's license. I knew of one case where a slightly inebriated friend tried to chat up a cute immigration inspector and he ended up back on the next flight home. On this occasion, armed with my valid temporary work visa, the inspector was perfectly courteous. As were the custom officials.

I strolled outside for my first view of the city. The hot breath of a New York summer enveloped me immediately. The temperature was somewhere in the 90s, but the humidity made it feel even hotter. In moments I could feel the sweat gather on my body. Cold winters and lukewarm summers in Ireland had not prepared me for this. In all my life I had never experienced such heat. Despite that, Kennedy Airport seemed somehow familiar to me. With America it is always difficult to separate the reality from the endless movie reel in our heads, but I sensed a familiar yet not known landscape. My attention was immediately grabbed by the sight of the holstered gun on the policeman on traffic duty. Up to that point I don't believe I had ever seen a real gun in my life. Then there were the people, charging off in every direction, a cacophony of noise and excitement and different languages, all combining to produce a frenetic effect. It was exciting and awful at the same time. Why were such people in a hurry, where could they possibly be going? Little did I know that in a few years I would become one of them.

After an hour or so of sightseeing around the airport, I went to the TWA terminal to catch a flight to Chicago. I was now on the last leg of my journey and surrounded by strangers. The by now familiar pangs of homesickness struck and I found myself wondering what my family and my girlfriend were doing at that particular moment while I was heading away from all of them at over 500 miles per hour. The flight was full of people going back to their homes and spouses. My seat-mate was a banker, returning from a business trip to New York.

'You only have to watch one thing in Chicago,' he told me, when I explained that it was my first time there.

'What's that?' I said, my interest piqued.

'The niggers. Be careful where you go and don't ever go into their neighbourhoods. A friend of mine got stuck on the Dan Ryan express-way in a rainstorm and got knifed to death.'

This was surprising talk to me. It was my first introduction to the kind of casual racism that some Americans practise, seemingly without a thought. To my shame I didn't even demur, preferring to study the in-flight magazine and while away the time staring out the window. We were crossing over the Midwest plains. Every so often, city lights spar-kled off the starboard wing and the pilot would tell us where we were. The plane pitched and yawed as it hit a turbulent patch. I gripped the seat tightly and hung on for dear life. Two hours or so later we descended into the Windy City, passing over the city itself on our descent. For what seemed like an eternity we taxied on the longest runway I had ever seen. O'Hare Airport was the size of an average Irish city, I reckoned, looking at the gleaming lights that headed off to the horizon. Eventually we came to a stand at the gate and disembarked. As I said goodbye to my banker friend, he pressed his card into my palm and said, 'If you ever need help getting work just call me.' It was the kind of instinctive kindness you will often find from complete strangers in Amer-ica, even one who swore about the 'niggers' taking over his city.

Once off the plane, I looked for the person from the football club designated to pick me up. Vainly I searched the sea of faces at the exit gate until I saw a large, heavy man with an unmistakable Irish gait come panting up the arrival lounge. It was indeed my contact, a kind soul called Joe Gleeson from Kerry, the Chairman of St Mel's, the club I was to join. 'Welcome to Chicago,' he said, out of breath and looking at me a little askance.

I didn't blame him. I was dressed in my usual outfit: an ill-fitting pair of jeans and a scruffy sweater and shirt, with a straggly beard and long hair. I wasn't big on appearances, in fact quite the opposite. It was a source of pride to me that neatness in dress or appearance didn't matter. I knew he was thinking that this surely wasn't the big hired gun he had paid to come over from Ireland. 'You're welcome to Chicago' he said, again, his voice containing not an inflection of the twenty years or so he had spent in America. It was just as though he had stepped out of his Kerry village on the same flight as I came on. 'Thanks,' I said. 'It's great to be here. We went outside into the warm Chicago night and I could immediately feel the clammy air stick to my skin. 'Don't worry, you will get used to it,' Joe advised as we walked towards the parking lot. 'Even I can stand it now.'

Joe lived in a modest townhouse on Chicago's West Side, a typical suburban residence where Joe could dream of Ireland all night long, as he told me he did, yet live his own modest version of the American dream by day in the construction and furniture business. I was introduced to his wife, Sally, and their two children, Kevin and Sean, who were on their best behaviour for this total stranger suddenly landed in their midst. Exhausted by the long trip, I asked for a beer and made small talk for an hour or so before Joe decided I needed to call it a day. I was completely bushed and couldn't wait to tumble into bed – any bed.

That first night, in a gesture of hospitality that only a fellow Irishman could understand, and despite my loud protests, Joe had his wife sleep on the couch while I slept in their best bed. It was an uncomfortable feeling to begin with, but it became a lot worse when Joe himself climbed into the bed beside me. He lay down and talked to me of 'the old country' as if it were the most normal circumstances in the world. To outsiders it might have seemed like a scenario for a homosexual tryst: two grown men lying side by side in a bed in a darkened room in suburban Chicago. But it was no more than an act of exaggerated hospitality on the part of my hosts. Nevertheless, I spent my first night in America wide awake, listening to the loud snores of a 300-pound Kerryman. I thought of Jennie back in Ireland, alone in our little flat. No doubt she had the transistor radio on to the pop station, Radio Luxembourg, to help her fall asleep. She always smoked a cigarette and we often lay in bed together watching the arc of the cigarette and humming along to the hits. Just now, that seemed like heaven. I wondered if she was thinking of me.

At some point towards early morning Joe awoke and lit a cigarette, its red glow casting an eerie light across the room.

'Are you awake?'

'I am.'

'It's a great country, America. You'll do well here.'

'I hope so.'

'I just have one piece of advice for you: stick to your own – it's the best way to get along.'

Years later I would read the same advice as it was proffered to Frank McCourt of *Angela's Ashes* fame when he came to the US. Perhaps it was built into the DNA of Irish emigrants everywhere and from every generation.

'I will,' I lied.

'Good man,' he said, extinguishing his cigarette. 'You'll do fine so.' There was silence for a moment and then he said, 'I miss it, the old country I mean.'

The expression was to become very familiar to me in my years in America, but this was the first time I heard 'the old country' used in relation to Ireland.

'I think I know what you mean,' I said, because I was missing it too, after just one night, particularly my warm bed back in Drogheda that I never had to share with a large Kerryman.

'Not a day goes by that I don't think about it,' he told me. 'I still wonder what field they're planting this year on the old farm and what the neighbours are up to.'

'I understand,' I said, although I didn't. Reared in an urban environment, I had no feeling for nostalgia about farm life.

'I wish I was back there.'

'I know.'

'It'll never happen, I suppose.'

'I suppose.'

'Do you know the old Tom Jones song, "The Green Green Grass of Home"?'

'Yes, I do.'

'We'll sing it together,' he said. And so we sang, two men in a bed, our voices softly echoing across the Chicago night:

The old home town looks the same, as I step down from the train,
And there to meet me is my mama and papa,'

Joe was near tears now, something he was easily moved to.

'... Down the road I look and there runs Mary...'

'Shut up in there!'

It was Sally, trying to sleep on the couch. Obviously this wasn't the first time her husband had decided to belt out a song at four in the morning. We stopped singing. In the silence he lit another cigarette and the glow arced across the room.

'Stay away from the American women now.'

'Why?' I asked.

'They are too smart for the likes of us.'

'Okay,' I said, neglecting to point out that he himself was married to one, and a wonderful person at that. He probably wanted me to continue our conversation but I was too exhausted and soon fell asleep.

I was quickly to learn that each generation of emigrants holds their version of the truth close. Paul O'Dwyer, the happy warrior of Irish America, told me once that when he came out in the 1920s, the emigrants from the 1890s didn't think much of him and his fellow new arrivals. The oldtimers didn't believe the newcomers worked as hard as they had to and that they got it much easier. So it has been for every successive emigrant stream since.

In the last century, emigration from Ireland has seemed to follow a thirty-year pattern. In the 1920s, those who left were the men and women, like O'Dwyer, who were on the wrong side in the Irish civil war, many of them embittered, glad never to return to the partitioned country they left behind. The next tidal wave of emigration occurred in the 1950s: the sons and daughters of small farmers from the western seaboard of Ireland, fleeing harsh economic times. Conservative by nature, many never had the opportunity to further their education. In the main they stayed close to neighbourhood and religion and greatly resented any erosion of either. Then there were the 1980s group, who, like the men and women of the 1950s, were fleeing harsh times. This was a much more dispersed wave, with almost every county in Ireland contributing. These emigrants should have prospered in the new land, but by a cruel twist found themselves victim of the new immigration laws. They were the best educated, but in many ways the most deprived generation, as they could not use their skills in the US until they managed to finagle a green card. Nowadays Ireland's economic woes are sparking an exodus once again, much of it to Australia.

As for myself, once my four-month J-l student visa expired, I would be on my own, illegal in the United States. When you are young such matters don't seem as bothersome, but if I were to face such an uncertain future now, as many still do, it would be nearly impossible to cope.

Joe woke me up by turning on the morning television shows. He gave me a running commentary to demonstrate how much he knew. 'Now we'll hear from the weatherman,' he told me at one point. 'Now they will go back to the news.' And so on. All I could see was a gaggle of fast-talking, slick-haired men and women discussing what seemed to me the most inane topics. Soon Joe was struggling into his construction gear and on his way to work. When he had gone, I continued my introduction to the great American way as portrayed by television. The advertising seemed to come on every five seconds or so and after a while I grew irritated and turned it off. I went out to the living room where Sally had cooked me an enormous breakfast, the first of many, and she had thoughtfully put the air conditioning on full blast. She knew from Joe's relatives arriving from Ireland that the Chicago heat could utterly defeat many emigrant sons.

In the afternoon Joe returned early from work and took me on the grand Chicago tour. Situated where the endless Midwestern prairies and farmlands finally wash up on the shores of Lake Michigan, it remains the most quintessentially American of cities. We went on the Dan Ryan expressway and I remembered the man on the plane telling me about the person who had been stabbed there. I told Joe about it, and he put his foot to the accelerator until we were back close to home. 'We never had much to begin with,' he said as we neared his house, telling me the tale of rural poverty that he grew up around. I told him how my father had gone to school without shoes most of his young life and that there were fourteen of them in a small cottage.

Paul O'Dwyer once told me about the time his father had seen a local farmer come up the road from the Fair Day, lurching from side to side. 'Look, he's drunk, Daddy,' Paul said to his father. 'No, he's not,' his father replied. 'He wasn't able to sell his cow so he's just pretending to be for appearances sake.'

Chapter 11

TRYING TO FIT IN

Every time I have returned to Chicago since that first time I think of Joe and have the same sense of awe at the city's glistening and seemingly endless skyline from Lake Shore Drive. I have never stopped feeling that there will always be a part of me that calls it home, for it was during my brief six-month stint there that I learnt so much about my new country. That first night it gleamed like a jewel through the heat and humidity and I felt the by now familiar throb of excitement as I contemplated my future there. By the second or third day I was feeling a little bit cocky in my new environment, chancing taking a downtown bus which landed me on Michigan Street in the heart of the city. Sally had given me detailed instructions on how to take the bus and where to go in Chicago but I soon ended up hopelessly lost in the downtown area. I approached a stranger, a woman with shopping bags and a kind face.

'Can you tell me how to get to Lake Street?' I asked her.

She looked at me. 'Is that a brogue I hear?'

'It is,' I said.

'Well, my grandparents were O'Briens from Tipperary. Do you know the family?'

'No,' I said, thinking how there must be ten thousand O'Briens in that part of the country.

'I was over there in 1970,' she continued. 'We had a wonderful time.'

She didn't fit the stereotype, this elegantly dressed woman. From seeing many Americans who came to Ireland, we had the notion that most Irish Americans looked like they just stepped out of a laundromat in Cleveland, with ill-fitting, baggy pants, shamrocks on their caps and probably also on their underwear, and, worst of all, fake brogues. She sent me on my way with detailed directions. I got lost twice subsequently, but the kindness of strangers – putting me on the right road, even offering to take me to the bus station – was a revelation, having heard so much about how Americans were stand-offish and unhelpful. My experience was quite the opposite.

On the second night, Joe took me to meet my new Irish football colleagues, and we were indeed a motley lot assembled in a playing field on Chicago's west side. I soon turned out to be perhaps the best footballer there, not for any brilliance on my part, but because the others had hardly kicked a ball in anger since the previous season, twelve months ago. Many had been out of Ireland for a considerable time, some were Americans with only a basic acquaintance with the rules, some were past their playing best when the Summer of Love commenced in 1967 in San Francisco. Paradoxically, the ease with which I was scoring made me aware that this could not be a very good team, given that I knew that the standard overall in Chicago was quite high. It was no surprise to me then, when we adjourned to a nearby tavern after practice, to find out that drinking was a much more favoured pursuit for many of them, and that no one had work or accommodation available to me. I would be staying with Joe for the foreseeable future.

This was a blow because I had heard from so many of my mates at college in Dublin that they had been fixed up with apartments and jobs on their first nights in America. I had somehow expected the same but now felt foolish about it. There were no big construction owners attached to the St Mel's team, just a bunch of workaday folks. Indeed, I soon found out that getting my fare together had probably been a major stretch for them. So I was stuck with Joe and no work. As the weeks went by I got to know Joe as a big loveable mutt, a man moved to tears, alarm or humour easily. His wife, Sally, was a gem of a woman, patient and kind, who never uttered a cross word about the unwelcome intrusion into her home life. Their welcome however, was wearing thin, for them and me. No job meant I was spending hours just walking around the neighborhood or playing with their two children while I was waiting for something to turn up. My teammates were looking increasingly unlikely as a source of help in that regard. Granted, I had not helped my cause with them after the first game of the season.

The night before we had attended an Irish dance, during which copious amounts of beer were consumed. I was still unused to American beer, but after a bellyful of it I was proclaiming myself well able to handle it – which I undoubtedly did until the next morning. The dance itself seemed a blur. I was a popular man because I was just over from Ireland. Two women asked me to dance, an unheard of occurrence, and I got a little drunker on the strength of it. One of them took pity on me and took me outside, where we sat on a wall. She smoked and I asked her about her life. She was a schoolteacher living in the suburb of Evanston. Her father took her to Irish events nearly every weekend. She loved the 'craic', the Irish word for fun. She wanted to meet an Irish guy and marry him because it would definitely please her father no end. It was all said in a matter-of-fact way, so straightforward that it astonished me. Here was a modern, pretty American woman, and all she wanted was to find an Irishman just like her dad.

My image of American girls had been of 'mall rats' – girls consumed by what they wore, their boyfriends and who was hot right now. A million American movies had convinced me that the last thing they wanted to do was find someone like me.

'Maybe we could go out,' she said between puffs on her cigarette.

'Maybe,' I said as our lips touched and my hand slipped around her waist. She kissed me hard and then I never saw her again. The last sight was of her driving out of the car park in a large Oldsmobile. I immediately loved her.

Greatly fortified by my romantic experience, I stepped back inside and made my way directly to the bar. By the end of the night, as the band played 'The Siege of Ennis', I could barely stand up on the floor. Several women avoided my come-on look as the dizzy dancers stretched back and forth across the floor. I was making a fool of myself and I dimly realised it. I woke up with the worst hangover of my life, accentuated no doubt by jet lag. My mouth was as dry as a desert, there was a fire in my head and when I spoke to Joe on the way to the game I could hear my voice inside of myself. To make matters worse, it was one of those mercilessly hot Chicago summer afternoons, with humidity close to 100 per cent. I stepped out on the field already drenched in sweat and afraid of my life at the thought of the first physical contact, which I felt would probably cause me to pass out.

American Irish football is far rougher than the version played in Ireland and referees are not known for their strictness in applying the rules. In other words, it is every man for himself. I got my 'welcome to Chicago' about five minutes into the game from an American lad, playing the sport of his father but with only a hazy knowledge of the rules. As I came down the field with the football, he delivered a tackle that felt like I'd just hit a shithouse wall. I collapsed in a heap, but foolishly, after a few minutes decided to play on. By now, the ringing in my ears from the tackle had joined with the hammer in my head to provide a symphony all of their own. After twenty minutes I made my way over to the sidelines and beckoned to the coach.

'I can't go on. I'm completely out of it,' I mumbled.

'Listen, son, that is not why we brought you from Ireland. Besides, I have no substitutes,' he replied evenly.

'Oh fuck,' I said.

'Get the fuck back in there and don't be letting down the boys,' he suggested kindly.

And so I went back on, ending up in the corner forward line by half-time, the worst position on the field. I tried to come off again early in the second half but this time the coach was even more blunt.

'I'll have your ass on a plane back to Ireland if you don't stay on,' he threatened.

'I can't,' I said desperately, heading for the bench. I didn't even make it before I began retching, great deep hiccups that caused much disgust to many in the vicinity. 'Get away,' I heard one father bark to his two children, and I had an image of all scattering before me. But I was past caring. All that was important was that I was able to lie down. I lay full length on the ground for the remainder of the game. Figures stepped over me from time to time and there was more than one sarcastic comment. 'Look what they are sending out from Ireland these days,' was one of the nicer ones. What my new teammates felt about this great talent they had flown in from Ireland I will never know, but at least I was spared their commentary in the tavern afterwards by going directly home. There I collapsed into Joe's bed, and a choir of angels, or even Joe climbing in beside me, would not have wakened me.

Chapter 12

BUILDING SITE BLUES

Four weeks into my stay I finally landed work. It was a measure of my desperation that I took it with a construction company notorious for their exploitation of 'Paddys' like myself, just off the plane. I had no choice, my meagre funds had dwindled away and I was living off hand-outs. In the Abbey bar on the North side a player from one of the other football teams took pity on me and called a friend who landed me the job with Redmond the bricklayer.

'He pays well but is a bastard to work for,' he advised me.

He proved to be exactly right. I started work on a typical Chicago summer day on the city's south side. The heat penetrated everything and sweat formed with the slightest physical exertion. Redmond, my new boss, put me in charge of the mixer, feeding the brickies as they laid the foundations for another batch of 'Micktorian' houses among the decaying structures already there. I knew I was in trouble straight away when he put me in charge of mixing the mortar. Every twenty minutes or so I heard the urgent shout of 'More mortar, More mortar' belching down the wind to the place where I was working. The cry soon began to resonate in my head.

I shovelled each load onto the wheelbarrow. Then I ran with the barrow, a dead run past the serried ranks of bricks, over a narrow defile and onto the gangplank where a slip was fatal. Tip the wheelbarrow there and you were automatically fired. Up to the first brickie, throw down the mortar, then on to the next man, and so on down the line until I had 'fed' four of them. Back then to mixing the mortar and awaiting the next baying call. By ten o'clock I was exhausted and the heat was only starting to rise. Somehow I made it through to the break at 11 o'clock and grasped at the fifteen minutes in the shade. Then it was back to work with a vengeance. 'Shovel or bust' as the construction men say.

Redmond had it in for me from day one, because I was educated, I guess. Fear was a large part of it: anyone who was anyway different, who stood out, was to be feared and belittled. These immigrant men like Redmond had never got anything easy, were used to living by the sweat of their brow and suspicious of those who got the education they never had. I had come across many similar in London where I had worked for summers during my college years. It was a legitimate sense of frustration in some ways, seeing young men coming out with bright futures while all they faced was the eternal mixer, but men like Redmond went far beyond that. Humiliation was his stock in trade.

He came over to me at the mixer, watched me for a few moments and said, 'You shovel like a sissy.'

I ignored it, merely grunting in reply. I had been warned.

'Did you hear me, lad? You're shovelling like a sissy with those soft little hands.'

I felt the anger rise in me, the blisters on my fingers reinforced what he was saying.

'I'm doing my best.'

'My arse you are! You college boys are all the same. Even the narrowbacks can do better.'

That was the ultimate insult, being compared to the Irish American kids, nicknamed narrowbacks because, unlike their fathers, they never had to work too hard. I just had to grin and bear it. For the next four weeks I put up with a daily dose of his sarcasm. At night I dreamt of mortar trays and when I woke up in a sweat I thought I had slept hours when it was only minutes. It was the hardest physical work I ever had to do and the days seemed to be endless. The only respite was a bar called The Blue Fox at lunch time, a seedy place with a pool table and a resident hooker who often disappeared into the ladies room with one of the men. It was heaven, however, for the air conditioning alone, cooling bodies that were raw from the morning sun. Some of the men congregated there after work as well to drink the hours away. It was a sad way to spend your life, one I had also witnessed in London, but it was all they knew.

Strangely, if one of them had been fired, a regular occurrence with Redmond, the other men would not drink with him, almost as if he could spread the contagion to them. It was an example of the fear that Redmond had instilled into them – you could not associate with someone who had angered the boss. Redmond had his spies in the group and could hear everything back the next day. I had seen that type of cowering behaviour in London, too. Many of the construction workers there lived in rooming houses owned by other Irish immigrants who exploited their work and their poverty by cashing their cheques for them, taking a percentage off the top and then charging them inflated rents. Many men worked for the same man who owned their accommodation and who therefore ripped them off on the double.

Years later I read that Irish immigrants in Britain 'on the lump', i.e., paying no taxes all their life, were the saddest of all the retirees, unable to work anymore, broke and often thrown on the mercy of the welfare system. It was not Godless Britain so much as other Irishmen who visited such indignities on them. There are lots of similar stories in America.

Redmond fired me for the mortal sin of showing up in shorts one day. My only workpants had been stuck to me the previous day, a combination of sweat and mortar. I had fallen asleep right after coming home. When I woke up, the mortar had hardened and the pants were

71

as stiff as a board. They could have walked to work themselves. There was nothing for it but the football shorts. As soon as I stepped on the site I knew it was a mistake. The bevy of catcalls that greeted my appearance was led by Redmond who obviously considered such a sartorial breach the equivalent of showing up naked. Why someone could not wear shorts on a building site, especially in killer heat, was never explained to me. It was a rule and when you asked about it you were told to shut up because that was the way it was. Maybe it was against the 'rules', but it was actually the convenient excuse that Redmond had been looking for. He came down to where I was working and jerked his thumb in the direction of the gate.

'You're out,' was all he said. I felt a rush of blood to my head.

'You fucking muck savage,' I said. 'You wouldn't treat a dog the way you treat people.'

He looked at me in complete surprise for a long moment. 'Get out of here, sonny,' he said, raising his fists, 'or it will be very bad for you.'

I threw the shovel at his legs. It missed and he came forward, a grim smile on his face, fists up.

'Now, sonny, let's see how soft you are.'

The scene is still vivid in my mind: the backdrop of the construction site, the Chicago sun high in the sky, sweat pouring down my brow, mortar everywhere. I knew he could easily kill me. He had a mad look in his eyes. I directed a kick at him, aiming for his balls, but he swatted it away like he would a fly. He circled me and I stood still, watching him. I kept trying to kick him, to ward him off. Finally, he grabbed my foot on the upswing and pushed hard. I fell on my back on the mortar tray, the cement clinging to me like a wet blanket. I could feel it running down my back. I pulled myself to my feet. Then I turned and ran. I heard him laugh. Soon all his mates joined in and I could hear the distant echo of their laughter as I hoofed it off the site. My cheeks were red with embarrassment.

For nights afterwards I dreamt that I had stood up to him and delivered a good hiding. In my dream he was on the ground and I was kicking him. He pleaded for me to stop but I was merciless. I now discovered I had made a major mistake. I should not have fought him until I had been paid my last cheque. Back then, three hundred and fifty dollars was a fortune, and of course I never got it. It was a tough lesson to learn.

My next construction experience lasted all too briefly. Soon after being fired I landed work with a company called World Plumbing that was laying huge pipes in a major construction site in downtown Chicago. To an immigrant, the pay was phenomenal – one hundred dollars a day. It was a fortune and I was determined to hold on to the job. An Irishman called Jim Purcell from Tipperary made sure I had the best shot possible. Patiently he explained the work to me, how to dig the space for the pipes, how to watch above all for any walls of earth collapsing on you, how to lay the length of pipe and then move on to the next part. Jim watched over and protected me on the job like I was his own son.

I was very happy there, taking inordinate pride in hanging out the 'Men at Work' sign every morning, learning to use a jackhammer with the best of them, and joining in the roughhouse culture of the construction trade. Alas, it was not to last. Even Jim's help could not forestall the day when, after a month, the owner, a decent Norwegian man, told me he could not keep me on because of lack of experience. I left, better off financially, but still desperate for a long-term job.

Chapter 13

ANIMAL HOUSE AND FALLING
IN LOVE

Change came unexpectedly. A member of the St Mel's football side, Billy McNulty, invited me to stay in his fraternity house near the campus of Loyola University on the shores of Lake Michigan on the northwest side of Chicago. It was summer time and most of the students had departed so I was able to share a room. Billy was the son of a West of Ireland man and had remained close to his roots all his life. Having not yet seen the movie 'Animal House', I had no idea what to expect when I moved into the TKE fraternity house on Kenmore Drive not far from the college. I didn't even know what a fraternity was or what the Greek letters signified, but didn't particularly care as long as I relieved Joe and Sally Gleeson of the burden of caring for their overstaying house guest. Paddy O'Leary, a good friend who had come over from Ireland, also moved in with me and we had a single room on the second floor of the house. Most importantly, there were two beds. After sleeping with poor Joe Gleeson it was a welcome change.

Because it was summer time, the house was only half full but that did not prevent the extraordinary culture shock that Paddy and I underwent. Many of the young men living in the fraternity house could not have been nicer to the new arrivals, but there were a few utter screwballs who, in hindsight, certainly would not have been out of place in 'Animal House'. It started the first night when sitting out on the porch.

One of the TKEs, as they called themselves, arrived outside with a BB gun to shoot at passing tow trucks. We all ducked for cover after his first shots rang out, but, fortunately, I think he missed. The next incident was much more serious. A group of us were walking home from Connolly's, the local Irish bar at the intersection of Devon and Sheridan streets, after a few drinks too many, when we came across an old drunk. He was lolling in the space between two parked cars, drinking some cheap wine. His face told of a lot of hardships and drunken nights, but he was harmless and not bothering anyone.

Without provocation, one of the TKEs hauled him to his feet and began punching him. The tramp was utterly unable to defend himself, having long since passed the point of sobriety. The TKE pummelled him furiously until we got ourselves together sufficiently to intervene and drag him off. The tramp collapsed on the ground, his nose a welter of blood. I blamed myself for not getting involved sooner. Every time I saw the old pug-faced drunk afterwards I felt gutted. It was clear that his nose had been broken in the assault and that his downward spiral had accentuated. The guy who did it was studying to be a medical doctor. It defied explanation. I came quickly to realise that a small number of the young men in the fraternity house were too rich and idle for their own good. It was a syndrome I saw many years later in Ireland when the Celtic Tiger minted millionaires by the barrel load. Aimless young men, bored to distraction with their lives, were fodder for all kinds of mindless behaviour.

It was a new experience for Paddy and me to witness the preening that went on before parties or nights out. In Ireland, a shower was still a luxury item. In Chicago, some of the TKEs spent what seemed like hours bathing and then standing in front of the mirror, looking at their hair and their profiles from every imaginable angle. Then there were the women who called around – beautiful but unattainable to an immigrant like me. I just didn't get it and the harder I tried the worse it seemed. At one house party, a young girl had already announced her intention to sleep with at least three members of the fraternity. I was invited along as an extra to watch. After some thought, I declined.

My best chances were after the Irish football games, when young Irish American women flocked to the Irish bars to meet Irish guys. Here I was a big man, the player out from Ireland, and it certainly made things easier, but I still felt incredibly shy.

'Say that again,' the American women would say when I said something completely mundane.

'God, I love your brogue.'

I loved them too, because they were open and not afraid to engage a man if they were interested in him. They could be wild, too. We went to a late night party where lots of drink and drugs were consumed. I found myself in a bedroom with an attractive blonde girl. We kissed and cuddled and she made it known that next time it could be a lot more interesting. Alas, I never caught up with her again. There is a massive culture gap between America and Ireland. Because we both speak the same language, that difference is often elided, but humour, politics, lifestyle are all quite different, as I soon found to my cost. Jokes considered hilarious in Ireland often fell flat. Ironic humour just didn't work and Americans mainly meant what they said, and were very direct. That was a culture shock to most Irish, who often have a far more roundabout way of expressing likes or dislikes. It didn't help with the fraternity women that I wasn't aspiring to be a millionaire; that my goal at that time was to just make any kind of a living. The women I met there wanted something more exciting, like an accountant. I couldn't blame them for that but I felt like I was speaking a different language.

It was often lonely there at the TKE house. To make matters worse, Paddy, my only mate, had a girlfriend in Milwaukee and I used to dread every Friday evening when he boarded the bus to meet her. The long weekend yawned, lonely and empty until the game on Sunday and the drunken revelry afterwards. This was not the American dream as I imagined it. I called Jennie a few times. Usually drunk, sometimes incoherent. She was always glad to hear from me. We discussed her coming over, but the conversation always seemed to lead nowhere. I had no money, while she was now holding down a job as a temporary teacher. She even offered to send me the fare home. I refused, my dignity greatly bruised. I had one opportunity to meet someone while at the fraternity house: a waitress in the nearby pizza place who paid me a lot of attention. I could never summon up the courage to ask her out, however. This did not go unnoticed by some of the TKE people, who wondered aloud if I was gay – worse than being a child killer in their eyes. I assured them I wasn't. I was just awkward and shy around their women. I came home one evening to find a large refrigerator blocking the entrance to my tiny room. This was a TKE's idea of a joke, to give me a hard time. Try as I might, I could not shift it. My relationship with the frat boys was going downhill fast. Paddy left to go back to Ireland, so it was pretty lonely. I was also barely working, an odd day here and there in construction.

I called home on a few occasions. My father was quite deaf and I could only talk to him in snatches. Often I just listened while he talked about the latest football games or how I was finding America. When I spoke, he mostly could not hear me. It was frustrating, but still wonderful to hear his voice. To my regret, I never wrote to him, satisfying his curiosity about what America was really like. In the last weeks of his life he communicated with me without being able to hear my responses.

My mother wanted me home. That was obvious from her phone calls, and there were times, especially after the refrigerator episode, that I felt like packing up. Two things stopped me. First, I had no money at all to buy a plane ticket, and secondly, the stubborn side of me was asserting itself. Left to myself, I have the instincts of a loner, particularly in a strange land, and I was quite content a lot of nights to be propping up the bar alone at Connolly's or smoking pot in my tiny room back at the house. My financial situation had again become dire to the point where I was existing on boiled potatoes. Talk about living a stereotype! Once, on a Sunday night I went to an 'all you can eat' place, gorged myself and then tried to slip out without paying. Outside I scarpered as fast as I could, only to run into a Chicago cop car. I was stopped and asked why I was running so fast. Unfortunately, a stranger driving past the restaurant had seen me bolt the building and told the officers where I had come from. I was brought back to the restaurant, where the waitress put me to shame by telling me in no uncertain terms that she was responsible for paying for my food if I didn't pay. I apologised and explained that I simply did not have the money, so the owner put me washing dishes in the back. After about an hour of this I slipped away again, this time taking care just to walk, even though every instinct told me to run as fast as I could.

The date by which I was officially due to return to Ireland was still a month or so off, and I was increasingly thinking of going back, even though that was not my original intent. I could have phoned home for money, of course, but that would have been an unbearable humiliation. The big man who had set out for America boasting about how he was going to make it there would be revealed as a complete idiot. Pride would always stop me making that call. Then it all changed. One of the guys on the football team told me about construction work with a man called Harry Johnston in Evanston, a suburb of Illinois. I called Johnston and he told me to start the following Monday. I practically cried tears of relief. I ran through my last money that weekend and was faced with trekking to Evanston on foot as there was no way I could afford the train fare. I walked seven miles or so to work on the Monday morning, rising at 5:30 in order to make the 8:00 start. The night before, I had plotted the route on a Chicago map, got lost several times, and was delighted to eventually find the coffee shop where

Johnston was waiting for me. He was a decent man, of Scandinavian origin, middle-aged, with a silver mane and keen blue eyes, and I will always be thankful to him. He saw right away that I was in need of a square meal. Without a word, he stood me breakfast, but was probably surprised when I ordered second portions of everything, and some soup besides. I was famished. He must have wondered what kind of new employee he had signed up. Seeing my need for food, he reached into his pocket and gave me a $50 loan. I will never forget him for that; it was the equivalent of being handed $1 million at that moment.

After the first day at work there I knew I was off the skids. Harry's son, Jeffrey, was in charge of the job and we got along famously. Jeffrey was wild and reckless and so was I on our frequent nights out, but he never failed to show up for work, no matter what. It was a good lesson for me, as I joined him on some of his expeditions to single bars. One night he brought me to Rush Street, the main night spot, to a bar where there seemed to be many single women. One of them, a real looker, approached me and asked if I would buy her a drink. Being the dumb immigrant, I was highly flattered and proceeded to buy drink for her all night. I could see the amusement on Jeffrey's face and began to wonder whether I was making a fool of myself. I followed Jeff to the men's room where he told me, 'That's a bar girl. She's there to get as much drink out of you for the establishment as she can. She's paid a percentage of every drink she gets.'

'Why didn't you tell me?'

'I thought you knew. Her vodka is 90 per cent water. Watch the bartender pour it and you'll see.'

'Fuck you.'

I went back, and sure enough, the bartender poured her drink out of my sight and charged me another $5 for it, a huge sum at the time. It was an expensive lesson in how many different ways there are in America to make a buck.

Jeff's friends were as wild as he was. Sometimes we would go back to his apartment in a Chicago suburb. One night, several women, high school friends of his, came around. After much boozing, what followed was as close to a 'love in' as I could define it, with old school friends pairing off all over the place, sometimes in couples, sometimes in trios, except me, of course. I was earnestly trying to expand my own dating horizons. It was difficult and I was not connecting. A peculiar, aching loneliness took hold. I have always found it difficult not to have a woman's touch in my life, but most American women seemed alien to me, didn't laugh at my jokes, or respond to my best pick-up lines. It didn't help that I was probably drunk on a good percentage of the occasions. It was a tough time and I kept harking back to my previous loves, way back to my childhood, and drawing sustenance from the pleasant memories they evoked. It eased the pain somewhat. I would sit in some Irish gin joint and dream about those days.

The first awakening for me was Eilish. She was about eleven at the time and I was younger, probably by a year. We used to sit in Stapleton's field behind my house in Tipperary and talk. We could often hear the corncrake, and once the cuckoo. It always seemed to be summer when I was with her. She loved flowers and I would go and pick them from near the bushes that ran close to the slaughter house. The grass was filled with daisies and she showed me how to make a daisy chain. She laughed, a lovely appealing laugh, when my chain kept breaking. It was hard not to feel a stirring. Once, I took her on a 'date' to the slaughter house that abutted the end of the field. She held my hand as we watched sheeps' throats being slit and cattle gunned down by a big rifle bolt. Then the men would skin the animals and cut the intestines out. We were kids and I was fascinated by this rawness of death.

It was hardly the most romantic of places. Thousands of flies buzzed around the sheep carcasses, the blood washed by us on its way to the nearby drain. The slaughter house men looked massive to me, their aprons stained with blood and grime. They knew me because I often watched them.

'Got yourself a girlfriend, then?' asked one of them as he held the water hose and swept the blood down the nearby gutter.

I went red. She wasn't my girlfriend; the very idea embarrassed me, but I sure was interested in her. She seemed to like me too, enough to go to the slaughter house one more time with me before she politely refused to go any more. It was hardly her idea of a dream date. When she was watching the soccer games that we played in the field, I was always in a lather trying to impress her. I took risks and tackled boys far older than myself. When I scored a goal, I told her it was for her. We sat in the field after the games and I told her about my dreams of America when I was older. She said she thought she might be a nun, because she felt so close to God and one of the sisters in school told her she'd be an excellent one. Once, when she sat cross-legged as we were with a group of friends, I saw up her dress. It was the first erotic moment in my life and I entered a whole new realm. I was confused with the feelings I had for her and there was little guidance or under-standing in Ireland at the time. Having bad thoughts was, at the least, a venial sin. So I desperately tried to banish the thoughts about girls, and specifically her, crowding in on me.

Of course our relationship was not meant to last. Her friends teased her mercilessly about me – that I was younger, and that girls needed to go with boys who were older. One Friday afternoon as we sat amid the daisies she told me she wanted to be with another boy 'older than you'. I felt my world collapse around me. It was the end of the affair.

A year later, I was in love again, this time with a nurse from the emergency room in the local hospital. I had hurt my knee playing soccer and she had to dress it. I took my pants off in front of her, the first woman outside of my mother that I had ever undressed for. She was kind and gentle, sensing my unease. She tousled my hair and told me everything was going to be all right. I loved her for it. She dressed my knee and I went home very much the wounded martyr. To my mother and father's exasperation, my knee refused to heal. I insisted that I still had pain, so I could go back to the nurse, which I did several times. She always met me with a mixture of good humour and feigned exasperation.

'Still here,' she'd say when she spotted me in the waiting room.

'Yes,' I'd lie. 'It's not getting any better.'

Sometimes I waited hours for her and refused any other nurse. I knew from their looks and smiles that they guessed I had a huge crush on Nurse Ryan. She had long, shiny black hair and looked like a bright pearl in her nurse's uniform. She was a shining star in my book. Finally, I think my mother realised about my burgeoning love interest – perhaps the nurse told her – and she dispatched me to the doctor, thereby bypassing the nurse. I made a miraculous recovery.

I next fell in love with a nun. I was eighteen years old and finishing secondary school. She was the nurse in the dispensary in the school, still in street clothes, still a novice, and still with questions about her vocation. I was repeating my final year in order to get enough honours to get a grant for college, which meant I was older than the other boys. There were lots of rumours and fantasies about her, as there will always be for any female in an all male environment. She was pretty and petite, with a lovely, kind face.On the first occasion, I went to see her for pills for a bad flu. We ended up sitting side by side for an hour in her cramped office. She told me that the doctor was known derisively as 'the vet' and I should only go to him as a last resort. I liked her. She had a quick sense of humour and a feisty air. She was unlike most of the nuns I knew. Many evenings after that I visited her and we sat in the darkened sick bay, talking about life. I think I was the last disembarkation stop on her way to the nunnery. She loved the idea of the contemplative life. She came from tough circumstances, with much turmoil, and she was looking forward to the calmer water inside the convent wall. Yet she had questions. By entering, she was drawing the veil on her chance of happiness, kids and a normal life.

She talked so softly that I usually had to reach closer to hear her. Once, her hair brushed my face. I could see by her startled reaction that she was taken aback by even that small intimacy. She blushed and I smiled at her. I had an overwhelming desire to put my arms around her and kiss her. It was really not sexual; it was more a protective force, to ward off the lonely life ahead if she was going to follow it. She got up and quickly moved away before I could act on it. As the school year passed it became evident that she was going to go to the nunnery and that the life behind convent walls was her true vocation. I urged her to reconsider. I thought that I might go away with her on an adventure if she agreed to it, perhaps to Dublin or even England. I was thinking of the boarding rooms on Talbot Street in Dublin where a friend had taken his first girlfriend while on a weekend trip to the city. It cost £6 a night, and included a cooked breakfast, he told me, and a landlady who asked no questions. It was the stuff of dreams in fundamentalist Ireland. It also sounded like an impossible dream, and it was. I never asked her.

Soon I was about to leave school for university. She was only months away from joining the enclosed order. On our last time together we walked down the long avenue from the school to the bus stop where I would catch the late night bus home to Drogheda, just seven miles away. It was dark on the avenue, a windy night, and the rustling of leaves made it eerie. On the left as we walked were the playing fields where she told me she walked on her own during the early morning hours. She said she felt closer to God watching the night disappear over the distant hills and feeling the first blush of warmth from the morning sun. On the right were the school walls. Tall and imposing, they ensured that no one could skip out after the front gates were locked. A strange world I lived in: one thousand boys cooped up together, no female teachers, just this solitary nun-to-be. I was afraid even to take her hand in the pitch blackness as we walked towards the road. We stopped under the street light and watched as the traffic whizzed past in a cacophony of sound.

It always seemed to me then that life was what happened somewhere else, somewhere far more important than where I was, and that the cars were rushing to that destination. I was stuck in some unknown place, where not much happened at all. Except her. We stood and talked and I said goodbye to her. Her eyes were soft with sorrow. She answered with a quick kiss, more a brushing of the cheek than anything. Nevertheless I got to feel her soft skin on mine and the touch alarmed me in its intensity. We stood, poised, for a moment. Then in the distance I saw the 11 o'clock bus to Drogheda rolling towards us. The destination was illuminated on the front of the bus, so it loomed larger every yard it drew closer. I was starting one new adventure and she another and the twain could never meet. It was a farewell I would never forget. I never heard from or about her again.

About six months later I lost my virginity. She was a science student, someone I had met at a party. I woke up in the morning to find her stretched across my chest, a mop of hair spread out like a golden star. I stroked her neck and she nuzzled me sleepily. I looked around the room as the sun came up. There had to be four other couples in various stages of undress sprawled around the room. She lived in a small town in the south of Ireland and she had a wonderful look about her, as if game for anything. I loved that wildness in her. She had a flat in Ballsbridge in Dublin. I will never forget the address, and it still causes a frisson when I walk by it all these years later. It was the top flat, which she shared with a college friend. It was just a single room with a shared bathroom down the hall. Like all Irish flats, it was infernally cold.

I was besotted. I would go to the science building and wait outside her lectures, then pretend I was just strolling past. She cooked for me and I stayed over several nights. I felt that I was finally an adult, and that this would last forever. One night, we went out to Howth Head, a mountain promontory just outside the city centre. We seemed to climb for hours until we stood triumphantly at the peak, masters of all we surveyed. The twinkling lights of Dublin lay beneath us. Overhead, an occasional plane roared, en route to Dublin airport. The Irish Sea stretched out into infinity and the reeds and the long grass swayed in the evening wind. In the distance, the Dublin mountains stretched towards Wicklow, the rays of the late evening sun glinting off them down on to Dublin city below.

Then we stretched out in the long grass and tumbled down a hill until we reached the bottom, where we lay, laughing. A man walking his dog came upon us and could not figure out why we were so hysterical. I looked up at the stars, the advancing sentinels of night, and felt this beautiful woman in the crook of my arm, and I thought that this was perfection. We stayed so long we had to walk home. We sang and talked and discussed our families. The road seemed short, despite the distance. I could see the love light in her eyes too. That night would stay with me forever.

I went away to London that summer, swearing undying love to her. After a month or so she came to see me, but, for some inexplicable reason, the love had died. I blamed her brother who had come to visit her while we were in Dublin and soon made it clear he did not warm to me. I thought little of it at the time. Now, however, she was staying with him and it was clear he did not consider me good enough for his adored kid sister. Little by little he succeeded in turning her against me. I fought back, but soon even I could see that his influence on her was greater than mine. I was going to lose her and it almost drove me crazy.

One day she left without a single word and went back to Ireland. It broke my heart. I went into a tailspin, drinking heavily, drowning my sorrows in hotel bars near Heathrow Airport where I was working. Some nights I never went home, just walked around the airport and went back in to my summer job as a baggage handler. For months I could think of nothing else but her. What finally did change everything was seeing her making out with a friend of mine in a corner one night at a party. A rage overtook me and I stalked out. It was the kind of cold shower I needed. I walked home, heartbroken, but nonetheless knowing I had to face the inevitable. I began to heal soon after, but was gun shy about relationships for years.

Chapter 14

GO WEST YOUNG MAN

There was no question about it, Chicago was defeating my best efforts to fit in, and day-dreaming about long lost loves wasn't helping me. Nights at the bar drinking alone only added to the sense of displacement. I longed for a female touch and some interaction. Finally I met an attractive young waitress at a local bar. She took pity on me, I think, as I was often hanging out alone in the corner, reading a book or just staring into space.

She was the typical waitress/acting student, trying to make it in the big city. We plugged in to our common loneliness and shared a love of Irish writing. She was about to play a role in a JM Synge play, 'Riders to the Sea' and in no time at all I was her voice coach. Most of our dates were about helping her with the proper pronunciation of the Irish syllables she was uttering. The play is a gloomy piece about young men lost at sea and the despair and grief of the surviving relatives. She was playing the part of Maurya, the mother of one of the men who is lost. We read the major piece she had to recite over and over. We spoke it aloud. I knew most of it. In a grief-stricken soliloquy in the play the mother realises all is lost: 'They're all gone now, and there isn't anything more the sea can do to me ... I'll have no call now to be up crying and praying when the wind breaks from the south, and you can hear the surf is in the east, and the surf is in the west, making a great stir with the two noises, and they hitting one on the other...'

Her accent was quite good except she didn't understand that the piece had to be read as poetry, not as prose, which is what I always thought Synge intended. I read it to her in a rhythmic way, over and over. She responded. So we sat there on several nights in her apartment, in our underwear, going over the piece again and again. Outside we could hear the busy hum of the city, the fire engines in the distance and the patter of falling rain.

On our last date, just as the play run finished, she kissed me and told me if she ever made it big she would never forget me. She gave me her card and told me to watch out for her name. For years after I looked at the acting credits for Tania Wozniak. I never saw it, though I'm sure she probably changed her name. Some nights, Harry Johnston would call around and drop me home from the job. We would always stop off in his local for a few drinks. When he had one too many, Harry would insist on playing Sinatra on the jukebox and we would listen over and over as the old crooner sang. The bar, full of oldtimers like Harry, would often join in as Sinatra sang, especially for the local anthem, 'Chicago, Chicago' and 'The Summer Wind'. I can never hear either of those songs without finding myself back in Harry's saloon, sitting up at the old oak bar with Sinatra blaring in the background. Johnston treated me so well over the next few months that I was almost embarrassed to take his pay cheques. It was another of the many acts of kindness done to me in America by total strangers like Johnson and Joe Gleeson.

I was officially illegal now, no longer having a valid work visa, working 'off the books', but being an illegal hardly bothered me. It was rarely in the national focus back then like it is now in America and I was just one of many Irish I knew in the same boat. My attraction to America was growing. I told Jennie I was starting to settle in, to call it home. She was upset, as I knew she would be. Ireland was becoming further away each day I grew closer to my adopted home. I loved the bustle of Chicago, the sense of being somewhere important, but winter was coming on, an ominous chill was in the air and I knew the construction work would finish up soon enough. Harry wanted me to stay on over the winter, on indoor work, but I knew it was just a kind gesture more than any particular need he had. My thoughts were turning to warmer climes.

By now, to my great relief, I had moved out of the fraternity house and was living in the apartment of an Irish carpenter named Cyril Power who had been recommended to me by Joe Higgins, a college classmate and friend who later became a fiery, left wing member of the Dáil and European Parliament. Cyril was that rare beast in America – a fully unreconstructed Communist, who believed in the people's right to revolution as much as Americans believed in their Stars and Stripes. This got him into some trouble in his local, where the prevailing sentiment was that Communists should be executed on sight. Because I often accompanied him into the bar, I got dragged into many of the disputes.

One night I got thoroughly drunk, managed to pick up the barmaid, and as we drove home in her car, confessed to her in a fit of bravado that I was a Communist too, despite the fact that I didn't have a political bone in my body at that time in my life. I could see by her shocked expression that I had made a major blunder, that far from impressing her, she was now deeply worried that this atheistic madman in the car with her would somehow infect her. Thus went my first real opportunity of a relationship in America outside the Irish scene. There was also a noticeably cooler reception for me among the bar regulars afterwards. As the winter closed in I began to think more and more of California. The regular work had meant that I was able to pay off the debts I had incurred through loans from friends in the GAA team when I was not working and put some money aside for a Greyhound bus trip. Patsy Mulkerrins, a Connemara man I had become friendly with, told me about his brother in California who would welcome me to play with the Connemara team, known as the San Francisco Gaels, out there. My form with St Mels had improved greatly after my first disastrous outing so clearly I would have some potential for a San Francisco team, especially one with Connemara connections.

That was the equivalent of finding gold dust. Connemara men were always well connected in the construction business and would look after anyone they signed up. Getting off to a good start in California would be half the battle, unlike what had happened in Chicago. Besides, wanderlust had set in, something almost embedded like a computer chip in every Irish person. To help matters along, another guy from Ireland, Pat Lyne, had told me he was going to go to California too. Pat and I had been good friends in college. I realised it was time to up stakes, cut my losses in Chicago and move on. I bade goodbye to Harry Johnston over an emotional few drinks in his local and soon I was on the bus heading west, my previous lives in Ireland and Chicago gone forever. I was now twenty-five years old.

Chapter 15

A DEATH IN THE FAMILY

The San Francisco Gaels were the local powerhouse football team and took good care of their players. Within a week I was working with Colie Gavin, the captain of the team, who owned his own painting company. A few good performances in practice had convinced them that I was a man worth hiring. The games were played in Golden Gate Park, the huge expanse of green which divides the Richmond District from the Sunset and is perhaps San Francisco's finest feature. The playing field was near Ocean Beach, a stone's throw from the Pacific. At night the famous fog rolled in off the ocean and blanketed the pitch, making playing Gaelic football hazardous. Visibility was often down to ten yards or so and collisions were frequent. We didn't care, we were playing our native game in a far flung field, 6,000 miles from home and it had rarely felt so enjoyable. The cool night air was like a healing balm after the sweat of Chicago. I liked nothing better than to walk from my apartment along the sea front which stretched for a few miles in both directions and listen to the foghorns out on San Francisco Bay.

My joy at my new location, however, would be fleeting. Back in Ireland, my father's health was fading. He had a heart attack while listening to his beloved Kerry play in a major Gaelic football game. My mother described how, as the emergency workers bundled him into the ambulance, he insisted on holding the transistor radio to his ear, and did so all the way to the hospital.

She had known he was not well. Earlier that week, on their way back from town, he had told her to run ahead and open the front door. He was on the verge of collapse when he finally got into the house. Try as she might, she could not get him to see a doctor. He was from a generation where men and women bore their burden stoically to the grave. His own father had lived to ninety-two and had worked every day of his life until he caught a fatal cold and was finally bedridden. From the hospital, my father wrote love notes to my mother. He signed them 'half a heart' which is how he was feeling about himself. She responded in kind. When he came home he could no longer climb the stairs, so he slept on the couch in the living room. She slept beside him on the floor, often holding his hand in the wee hours when the terror of the night and the unknown took hold.

Years later, when my mother was dying of cancer, she often called out to him during the long nights when it was her turn to be in the no-man's-land between life and death. As she lay dying, she said she felt him in the room and she spoke to him. That was nothing new. After his death I know she talked to him frequently. I often wondered what she said to him, probably in their bedroom, as she waited for sleep. It reminded me of the lines of a poem I had read.

> *'You are young, you two in loving*
> *Why should you wonder what endearments*
> *Old whisper still to old in bed*
> *Or what the one left will say aloud*
> *When nobody overhears, to the one*
> *Who irredeemably is dead.'*

'The living should speak to the dead', she told me once when I asked her if she felt his presence. As she commenced her own long journey after pancreatic cancer was diagnosed, I think she talked with him even more frequently. So I had hardly arrived in San Francisco when the news of my father's death from the second heart attack reached me. I had been out running that morning, a bright and beautiful day, with hardly a cloud in the sky. I had taken my familiar route, a loop around the lower half of Golden Gate Park, past the Polo Fields where the Irish games were often played, and back to the apartment. When I turned the key in the door I found a group of friends gathered, one of them holding the telegram. I knew it could mean only one thing. I felt faint at the knees. The next few hours were a daze. I had been sleeping on the couch, so there was nowhere to withdraw to, to spend time alone as I desperately wanted. Cup of tea followed cup of tea, but I couldn't face the strong whiskey they kept pouring and offering me. They were kind in the way all immigrants are at a time of trouble for one of their own, but I needed to be with my family. After the initial shock and the frantic phone calls, my father's death left me with a strangely empty feeling. Much of the point of my move abroad, I realised, had been to show him that I could get to make something of myself, after some layabout years. Now he was gone and so was a huge motivating force for me. Back home he had woken on the last night of his life and climbed out of his hospital bed to get assistance for a roommate who had taken ill. No nurse responded to his call button and he could find none on duty at the nurse's station some fifty yards down the hall. Exhausted, he had somehow made it back to his room and collapsed into his bed. The following morning the second heart attack felled him.

As the years have gone by, however, I realise that even though he is dead I am still changing towards him, understanding his own conflicts and insecurities better because many of them are mirrored in my own. Coming as he did from a family of fourteen, surviving on subsistence farming, to make it as a schoolteacher had been an extraordinary accomplishment, and whatever I achieved in my life would be measured against that. I went and sat on Ocean Beach for an hour or more, gazing at the Pacific Ocean, and thinking of the old man. I could not summon up any tears, they would come later.

Strangely, the night before, around the time of his death in Ireland, I had dreamed that he and my mother visited me in San Francisco. He had been dressed as I always remember him, in a tweed jacket, sweater and dark brown slacks. He looked younger than I remembered him and he told me, in between puffs on his ever-present pipe, that everything was fine and that Mom was fine. A message from beyond the grave? Perhaps.

I had to borrow the fare to get home. People were more than kind and I found myself on a British Airways flight to London from San Francisco that night. It was, perhaps, the loneliest night of my life. As we hurtled through the darkness I tried valium and cheap whiskey to settle my nerves, but nothing worked. Because the plane was bound for London, we passed the island of Ireland off to the left hand side. I could see the lights of Cork twinkling in the distance and I found them reassuring in a strange way. Soon I would be home, among those I loved at a time of great travail. I arrived in London groggy and hung over. The valium and drink appeared to be in a running contest as to which was affecting me more. I staggered over to the Aer Lingus terminal, only to be stopped getting on the plane by a British police officer. Just routine, he explained, because of the Troubles. I was so paranoid at that point that visions of being arrested and clapped in irons swam in my head. Fortunately, after I explained the circumstances, he let me go. Soon we were winging our way across the English Channel, the city of Dublin looming up just an hour after departure.

It seemed like I had never been away, but everything had changed in my brief absence. My brothers, Donal, Fergus and Michael met me. Jennie was with them. The men were sombre, dressed in dark suits with black ties. She wore black, too, and I knew she had loved him. They had spent many nights discussing the state of affairs in the North of Ireland, both unabashed republicans who had deeply influenced my own thinking. She had visited him in hospital and had warned me in a letter that he did not seem well. My brothers looked as hungover as I felt. Drink was the great Irish recourse in times of trouble. The sky was as grey as badger skin and rain threatened from the west. All over Ireland people were going about their mundane daily lives, but for us this day was very different. I thought of my mother and her last days with him, sleeping on the floor beside him, caressing him in the dark recesses of the night when he was afraid. She had just left his side at the hospital and returned home when the word came that he had suffered a massive heart attack. She was shocked beyond words.

She was waiting at the front door when we pulled up. She looked gaunt and pale, but her welcoming smile was as warm as ever.

'He talked about you the morning he died,' she told me. It was almost more than I could bear. My sisters, Derval, Triona and Orlaith looked shell-shocked and barely able to cope. It was hard to take it all in.

Later that day I went to pay my respects. His body lay stretched in the mortuary. I leant to kiss his cold forehead and yet found tears would not come. I still recognised this man, but he was now somewhere in a universe far away. I told him that I was blessed just by knowing him. I asked him to take care of my mother and to give us his strength when we faced the hour of our own death. Then they nailed the coffin shut. It was my mother's wish that we all went to confession before his funeral mass. She knew he would have wanted it that way. She had even enlisted the services of Father Peter, a local Franciscan friar, who was a family friend of long standing. I knew it was going to be a disaster. One part of my brain told me to fake it, but I couldn't do that in the old man's memory. To make it worse, it occurred in the living room of my house in the full daylight, so there was no place to hide the flush of physical embarrassment.

'How long since your last confession?'

'Sixteen years, Father.'

Startled, he looked at me. 'You were twelve?'

'Yes, for my Confirmation.'

He looked stunned. At the graveside, under the weight of a sullen, overcast sky, I looked at the six feet deep space my father would be buried in. It seemed so small, yet inviting because he would lie there. I knew my mother must have looked at it and known that this was where she would someday lie beside him for eternity. For a moment I lost my fear of death at the thought of the two of them back together. My mother stood over his grave almost imperiously. The final moment of physical communion between the living and the dead ended when the first clump of clay thudded against the coffin. She broke down for the only time. Still I had no tears. I flew back to San Francisco later that week.

Chapter 16

RETURN TO AMERICA

Painting, like the rest of construction, was a total mystery to me at the beginning. Colie Gavin, my new employer, took it easy on me, confining me to back fences and the rear of houses where I could do no damage. The pay was $5 an hour, enough to make a decent living. The memory of Redmond in Chicago died a quick death as I found myself working for an Irishman who treated me decently, even if he found it a real head scratcher that I could not drive. Nor could I really paint for the first few months. I had a few sorry episodes in that time. My first time trying to extend a 40-foot ladder ended in disaster when it crashed to the street. Luckily, there were no passers-by or they would surely have been killed. Indeed, a kindly old lady watching my antics came out of her house and offered me a cup of tea as a consolation.

'Well young man, you could certainly have done some damage there. You were very lucky. I was watching.'

'Yes, I'm sorry. The ladder got away from me,' I said, afraid she was going to call the cops to remove this incompetent young painter, who was a clear threat to life and limb in the neighbourhood.

'Well, it didn't hit anyone, or any power lines, so don't worry too much about it. Would you like a cup of tea?'

'Oh yes, please.'

I could have been back at home. Another time I was up a ladder when a 5.8 earthquake hit the Bay Area. As the wall seemed to move and the ladder shook, I thought I was suffering some kind of hangover flashback as I had been out very late the night before. It was only when I got to the ground that I realised what had happened and my knees started knocking. The painting allowed me to make a decent wage and to move out on my own. After a few months I moved from Martin Mulkerrin's house to another house on 24th Avenue and Geary, not coincidentally a few blocks from the Blarney Stone bar. The move meant I was now in the heart of the Richmond District, which was my favoured area to live. The Richmond District was later to become heavily Chinese, something that was a major culture shock to me when I returned after being away from San Francisco for a few years, but there was still a strong Irish presence. The neighbourhood ran right down to the Pacific Ocean and was as calm and serene as a country village. Most evenings the fogs rolled in off the sea and blanketed the Richmond in a cool embrace. I loved it; the clime reminded me of Ireland and I could see why so many Irish had come here. Indeed, San Francisco had a great Irish history. From the time of the Gold Rush, the Irish had flooded to the city by the Bay. For many of those Irish it was the last stop on the Continent and the last chance to make it in America. Many found that it was also easier to make a living there than on the East Coast. In the latter part of the twentieth century, the Irish had settled primarily in the Sunset and Richmond districts, built an Irish cultural centre and created their own image and likeness of the land they had never truly left behind.

Initially, there were four of us in the house on 24th Avenue, but then a new influx of emigrants started to arrive. It was the beginning of the exodus from Ireland that started in earnest in the early 1980s, and the immediate impact on us was that about ten people were suddenly living in a modest three bedroom house. Most were like myself – with college educations but no work worth speaking about in Ireland, and had left out of sheer economic necessity. Two had come from Northern Ireland, Catholics fleeing the Troubles. As I got to know these two, I finally got a sense of what it was like to try to live an ordinary life in a state where murder and mayhem were daily occurrences. Neither was political in the Northern Irish sense of the word, but just by their stories and experiences I built up a mental image of the discrimination practised against Catholics there. My father had been a staunch De Valera man all of his life and his trenchant views on partition influenced me. But the Troubles had become so bloody and heartbreaking that it was hard for me to carry the same certainty that he had. My siblings had gone their separate ways, politically speaking. My brothers Fergus and Michael went on to hold office for Fine Gael, one as a TD, the other as Mayor of Drogheda. My sister Derval also worked for candidates for that party. Triona was usually a staunch Fianna Fáil supporter, as was my brother Donal, for much of the time. My sister Orlaith, who had joined me in America, was a nationalist.

Back home in the Republic, while we had watched events unfold in Northern Ireland, we rarely felt part of the Northern Troubles, preferring to overlook the shocking events on our doorstep. Now, for the first time, 6,000 miles from the Troubles, I was experiencing second hand what they were really about. At this distance from Ireland, I noticed for the first time how we were being defined by the Troubles. Often the first topic of conversation when you were introduced to someone new was, 'Why are Catholics and Protestants killing each other?' It defined us every bit as much as the less lethal 'shillelagh and shamrock' stereotype. You found you had to focus on it. Certainly, when I decided to go into the newspaper business I recognised it would be a major part of my job to educate myself about it, as I was being frequently asked to comment on it – usually when there was an atrocity.

What really brought that home was the death of Lord Mountbatten, blown up by an IRA bomb in August 1979 just before I launched my newspaper. The commentary on the event was wall to wall and I realised once the newspaper started up, I would be a source of future interviews on the North.

We were a motley crew in the 24th Avenue house, and one that had their share of disagreements. Given the tightness of the space, that was hardly surprising. At least two of the women staying in the house swapped boyfriends, which led to its own tension. One night I came home to find a brawl going on between the two men and the two women. The cops were called by the neighbours and eventually everyone settled down. Every Friday night was party night. I started off drinking in the Abbey Tavern on Fifth and Geary, work clothes on, often bespeckled with paint, and then wound my way slowly up Geary Boulevard, stopping at every Irish local on the way – and there were several. By the time I got to the Blarney Stone I was usually well looped and liked nothing better than to play some country and western staples on the jukebox and regale everybody around me with sad tales of home. Then it was across the road to Tommy's, the Mexican restaurant, for the usual drunken dinner takeout before going home and falling into bed. As far as I was concerned, it couldn't get any better than that.

Some nights I would try and get a woman to come home with me. One evening I finally 'shifted', as the Irish say, at the Blarney Stone. She was a Jewish Southern California girl, confident in the way that only California women can be. We drove to Ocean Beach, which was deserted. A storm had come rolling in from the west and the rain ran in streamlets down the front of the car. It was also bitterly cold, but we were nice and cosy inside her sedan. Then it turned strange. I suddenly felt my backside heating up. I didn't say anything for a moment or two, but the heat continued to creep up my backside until I felt I was sitting on a hot griddle. I decided not to say anything, in case she felt I was some kind of fool. Was the car on fire somewhere? Not that I could see. And still the seat got hotter. I shifted uncomfortably and she looked over and asked me if I was warm enough now. I told her yes and she flicked a switch. The seat suddenly cooled down. I was immensely relieved and acted like nothing had happened. I would never have thought that a device to heat seats existed. I thought ruefully that they would go down well in Ireland where it is always cold.

We decided to brave the elements and took off down to the water's edge. We watched the wind blow across the waves until they became like white horses galloping to the shore. In the distance we could see the lights of the Cliff House, the famous restaurant which hangs on a promontory out over the ocean. Far away from out at sea the wind carried the sound of a foghorn from one of the many boats on the bay. It made a lonesome sound. Apart from that, only the sound of the passing traffic lanced the silence. What to do? Get wet and cold and embrace right there, or run back to the car? We decided on the former and we fell down on the wet sand. I lay flat and looked up at the angry sky as the rain continued to fall. I felt like joining hands with the black night, lying there forever and holding on to this perfect moment. We lay there for a few moments, kissing. Suddenly we heard voices and saw a flashlight as at least two other couples began to make their way in our direction. We jumped up and ran back to the car, giggling. Once back in the car I got her to heat up our seats again. We met several times after, but no other date had the sheer spontaneity and fun of that first one.

On another night the father of a roommate died and I happened to be at home when the phone call arrived from Ireland. Grimly, I went to fetch the young girl from the nearby bar. As I walked towards it, she rounded the corner with her boyfriend. I had the strangest sensation of watching from above as they walked towards me, laughing and talking. I knew that what I had to impart was about to destroy one person's happiness and end both their times in America. And so it proved. Distraught, she left for Ireland the next day, never to return.

I was drinking too much at the time, a combination of loneliness and giddiness at my new-found freedom. For the first time in my life I was living clear of all family and having to make new friends in a strange city. I had been away before, of course. I had essentially left home at eighteen to go to college and I had been in London and elsewhere, but only for a pre-determined time and always with the realisation that I was returning home. The drinking eased the pain of separation. Many of the Irish I drank with were unfinished souls. Some had spent tough years on the Alaskan pipeline, in a bleak existence and working eighteen-hour days until they made enough money to start a business in San Francisco. They did not scare easily and they had a well defined orthodoxy to their lives. If I cast any doubt whatever on any aspect of the greatness of America, it was bound to start an argument. So I did, quite frequently, with a few drinks in me. Surprisingly, it never really came to blows.

I was relatively well equipped for the task of emigration, despite the drinking, but if I needed any reminding of what happens to those who could not cope, I could find it every night at the bar in the Blarney Stone, or the Abbey Tavern. There grizzled veterans would endlessly play old Irish favourites on the jukebox and remember how good things had been in the old country, before they got falling down drunk. I had a hunch that they would find things very different from the dream if they were ever to return.

Chapter 17

STARTING A NEWSPAPER

My newspaper career started somewhat inauspiciously. I was still working for Colie Gavin, usually with a Cavan native, Mickey Freehill, painting all over San Francisco. Every few days I would accompany Mickey as he made the trek out to the Sunset district, looking for an Irish newspaper at the Irish Cultural Centre. In this day of internet access it is hard to imagine just how deprived we were of basic news from Ireland back then. If Mickey got an aged copy of the *Irish People*, the IRA support newspaper in the United States, he would be delighted because it had the sports scores. I would lap up all the news and information I could from it. Back then, Irish newspapers never made it as far as San Francisco, so the idea of setting up a local Irish newspaper seemed to me to be an obvious one. There was also a huge sea change coming in the community, with a new influx of Irish. Tim Pat Coogan, one of Ireland's leading authors, wrote a book about this period, called *Disillusioned Decades*. In it he explained how the entire Irish economy seemed to come to a shuddering halt after a brief expansion in the 70s. Indeed, between 1971 and 1981 there was net migration back to Ireland as a brief economic boom ensued. By 1981 however, it had all changed. Unemployment had risen to over 15 per cent. The emigrant boats and planes that most people hoped were phantoms from the past suddenly reappeared, like Banquo's ghost. The brief period of inward migration stopped as the planes and boats began filling up again. Heartrending scenes of separation were once more seen at airports and dockside. It was a time of deep gloom in many households throughout Ireland. The problems for the young immigrants who flooded into America in the 1980s, however, were significantly different to those of earlier generations. They were better educated, but changes in immigration law dating from a 1965 Act, ironically passed by Senator Edward Kennedy, ended most European immigration. It meant that most of the Irish who came were undocumented. Women and men with degrees and college educations were forced to take the same kind of work – as nannies, or in construction – as their forefathers. Because of their illegal status they also had no voice to speak to their concerns.It was a strange dichotomy. Though the best educated of all Irish immigrants to the US, they were as constrained as the previous generations in what work they could do because of their undocumented status. Still they came in their droves, seeing emigration as a kindly light amid the encircling gloom of the downfall in the Irish economy. Like homing pigeons, they repeated the traditional patterns of emigration. Galway and west of Ireland people went to Boston, Achill Island to Cleveland, Cork and Tipperary to San Francisco, Mayo and Connemara to Chicago and the Midwest and almost every county to New York, following tracks laid down by earlier generations. The influx into San Francisco revitalised many long moribund organizations. Irish games began to flourish and the original three football teams soon grew to seven. Irish bars began opening up in the old neighbourhoods and the Irish Cultural Centre underwent a transformation. It was in this context that I was thinking of a new newspaper.

I had started my own painting business, Sundance Painting, after learning some basics with Mickey Freehill and Colie Gavin, with my old Chicago friend, Tom McDonagh. Like me, he was keen to try something new. Our new business was barely holding together. Indeed, were it not for William Lu, the kindly Chinese landlord of our recently rented house on 40th Street in the Richmond District, we would have been utterly broke. For no good reason that we could fathom he engaged us to paint all his buildings. Otherwise we would have starved for lack of work. Without any certification or real background as painters we were really up against it. About six months in, I had a narrow escape when some scaffolding I was working on gave way and I very nearly plunged to my death. It was the final straw for me and house painting, and I was determined to build a better career. I needed to keep my feet on the ground.

Driving in the Sunset district with Tom one afternoon I spotted a store that sported the legend 'All Your Printing Needs'.

'What about this newspaper idea?' I asked Tom.

He looked at me quizzically. 'What newspaper idea?'

'The one I mentioned last week. With all the new Irish here maybe we should start a newspaper.' I said, pointing at the printing shop.

'Ok then,' he said.

Thus are careers in publishing begun. We went in and met a smooth-talking salesman who convinced us that we could start a newspaper for a couple of thousand dollars. We were delighted. I often think back and wonder if he had been honest would we ever have started down the road. Probably not. Between us we scraped together $952 exactly and decided we were going into the publishing business.I knew I wanted Jennie over with me to start the newspaper. She was a great writer and editor and there had been too many lonely nights for both of us. When I called her and asked her to come out, she agreed immediately. She knew, as I did, that this was our last best chance together. When she arrived at San Francisco International I took great pride in showing up in my twelve-year-old Audi, which I had just learned to drive. Things were awkward at first, but the pressure of putting out the newspaper soon consumed us all. I read that 90 per cent of new publications failed. In a fit of defiance I taped it on the wall over my typewriter. Real men didn't fail!

And it really wasn't as huge a risk as it seemed. We were young, unknown, and if we failed we'd probably move on to something else. This wasn't Ireland, where every business venture would be scrutinised, your family history analysed and any failure tantamount to a life sentence against ever starting a new business again. No, this was San Francisco, and if we failed here there was always Los Angeles, or New York, or some other point east or south or north. I think a little of the pioneer spirit of the city had infected us. Having made the decision to start the paper, I resolved to learn to type, not a bad idea for a budding editor. I bought an old typewriter and set to it, hammering out stories from the *San Francisco Chronicle* until I began making a fist of it. On my first night typing, a friend dropped over after football practice. An old construction hand, he seemed almost frightened of the machine, and viewed it with some alarm.

'What the fuck are you doing with that thing?'

'Learning to type. Tom and I are starting a newspaper.'

'Well, fuck me, if that isn't the daftest idea I've ever come across.'

'Thanks.'

I hardly needed to be reminded of the anti-intellectual bent in the older Irish community. The orthodox view was that such notions were better left to their children, and that their lot in life was the hard grind of eternal physical work. It was sad in a way, because many of those I had come to know were extremely bright and focused people who would have benefited greatly from further education. Most, however, had left school in their early teens and hit the pavements looking for work almost immediately afterwards. As a result they had little time in their lives to ponder further education. To a man they wanted their own children to have the benefits they never had, but they had major problems with anyone in their own peer group or younger getting above their station.

College educations were regarded with suspicion and any notion of putting pen to paper was viewed as strange. Indeed, our friend's reaction was one widely shared in the community, as we soon learnt. The notion of a new newspaper when one had not been started in decades seemed an impossible one. But we were willing to buck the odds. And I had form. I had been fascinated by newspapers and writing for them since I was a child. At the age of thirteen I became a horse racing tipster for a community publication in Drogheda. A few years later, I started a school newspaper and then wrote a television column for a new local paper. So it was in my blood, if not in my background, but I had never attempted anything on the San Francisco scale.

Chapter 18

PUBLISHER AND
CHIEF BOTTLEWASHER

The first edition of our newspaper appeared on 14 September 1979. It was all of twelve pages, yet it represented the totality of our dreams, hopes and ambitions. In the first editorial I wrote, 'This newspaper is born out of a hope that we can act as the link between the various strands in the community and strengthen the bond of birth and upbringing that we all can share.'

We called the paper *The Irishman*, after an old San Francisco Irish newspaper. We were, of course, labelled sexist for choosing such a name, but, to be honest, it never occurred to us that it would be an issue – until I went on a local Irish programme in Berkeley, California and spent the first half hour vainly defending it from a feminist presenter. I was young and naive at the time, and it was a fair cop. The newspaper came out at a tough time in Northern Ireland when the violence seemed to be peaking. By now I had spent many hours in conversation with Northern Irish exiles in San Francisco and had read extensively on the subject. I felt that there were no certainties any more, but that some realities had to be addressed and I intended to do that to the best of my ability in the newspaper. American politics had already begun to influence me; I had seen how parties such as the Republicans and Democrats could absorb opinions all the way from the extreme left and right to the centre in their philosophy.

I was also deeply influenced by another emigrant newspaper, the *Irish Post,* in London, whose editor, Brendan Mac Lua, maintained a strong nationalist line despite the mayhem in the North, refusing to demonise one side over the other, but always squarely pointing the finger at the political reality that, like in many other places in the world, such as Iraq, Pakistan, India and Sudan, the British policy of partition had created the problem to begin with.

Mac Lua's was a line I agreed with and I made it clear from my first editorial that we believed that partition was at the root of the problem in Northern Ireland, when 600,000 Catholics had been corralled into a state they did not want to be in and had then been ruthlessly kept out of power for decades. It had not, therefore, been surprising that when political change was not forthcoming, violence had erupted. It would only end with a decent settlement, fair to all sides, and there would be no military victories.

The newspaper launch coincided with my sister Derval's wedding, and I had to assure her in some protracted phone calls that I was really starting a business the same day and could not make it to the wedding. The easier choice might have been to go home and forget about the newspaper, but I had the bit between my teeth and was not about to spit it out. I had worked harder than I ever did in my life preparing the first issue. I found myself driven by a creative force I never knew existed in me. In the month of the launch it was nothing for us to work nineteen-hour days and get up after a few hours sleep and go at it again. It was a pattern that would become all too familiar. Every day brought a new crisis. Jennie was the type never to shirk a challenge and she performed Trojan work. She had the same level of conviction and commitment to *The Irishman* as the rest of us, and, despite the long hours, we were all looking forward to the launch when the day dawned. Then disaster almost struck.

On the way to the printers to collect the first edition, some thirty miles south of San Francisco in a town called Menlo Park, our car broke down and we were forced to try to hitchhike to the printing plant. Hitching on a California highway is extremely difficult, and as the clock crept forward and no ride was in the offing, I became very nervous. Finally a car stopped, driven by an American Indian who insisted on passing around a whisky bottle when we told him where we were headed. He was on his way to Los Angeles to a tribal council. He considered it a good omen to help somebody every day. We were just glad that he showed up.

We made it to the printer just in time to see the first issue going on the presses. I walked into the print room to hear the strains of the theme music from the film, *2001, A Space Odyssey* playing on the radio just before the presses started up. It seemed a harbinger of success. It is hard to describe what it is like seeing your own creation finally come to life for the first time. We had spent all of our $952 on the first issue and were already in debt, as the printer had insisted on being paid up front, but somehow it didn't seem to matter at that moment. As the paper rolled off the presses, with French, instead of Irish harps on both sides of the masthead, it felt like a unique personal creation. I was overcome with emotion and just wished that some of my family had been there to see it. In all the years since, I have never lost that thrill of the press rolling, the smell of printer's ink in the air and the hustling as a new edition of a newspaper flows off the presses.

We led our first issue with the Pope's visit to Ireland, which was just about to occur. It was a huge story back in Ireland but not covered very widely in the American press. Our second lead was the search for oil off the West Coast of Ireland, entitled 'Light of the Emerald Oil'. All in all, we were very happy with the edition. With bundles under our arms and proud as punch, we visited several of the Irish bars in San Francisco that night, showing off the newspaper like a new child. Then we ended up in the Blarney Stone, among our friends, getting drunk in celebration. We were finally on the road. We printed 5,000 copies and it sold for fifty cents. Irish immigrants, especially recent arrivals, were our target market. We distributed through newsagents and Irish bars.

The next morning, reality hit. Jennie and I were hopelessly hungover and we stared at our creation through drink-addled brains. Suddenly this little twelve-page paper didn't look like a very big deal, but we knew what it had taken to bring it out. And now we would have to do it all again, this time with no money. We were stone broke and would not be able to publish the second issue of the newspaper. It looked like we were going to have the shortest lived newspaper in the history of publishing. Then, one of those magical events occurred that made me feel that fate was on our side. Tom happened to have a passing acquaintance with the local doctor for the Irish community, Michael McFadden, a Scotsman who had a large practice in the Mission District. He went to see him, told him the story and brazenly asked for $5,000. Amazingly, Dr McFadden obliged. The death of our publishing venture was staved off and we even had some over to pay for a few staff and office equipment.

Today I marvel at McFadden's generosity to two young guys he hardly knew. Such acts of kindness were not unique to McFadden. Time and again when our venture ran into trouble we found a helping hand. Joe Finucane, a bar owner in the Sunset district, wrote a cheque for $1,000 when we were desperate for cash. Another time, five local businessmen gave us $2,000 each to keep the newspaper going. Kindest of all was a man called Bill Lewis, our typesetter, who had no Irish blood in him, but was one of those decent Americans who make the country a great place to live in. Each issue we would arrive at Bill's typesetting shop in downtown Oakland, not the greatest neighbourhood in the world, and Bill would treat us as if we were his children. He would help us with design and layout, endlessly correcting our typing mistakes, which were many, and even standing us dinner on several occasions when the paper ran late. We were often unable to pay him on time but it never seemed to matter to him or his wife, Elsa, a German native, who also treated us like family. Often she would leave and arrive back with pizza and French fries for us. It was the kind of generosity that became familiar to us. There is an essential decency in Americans that is actually their best trait. They genuinely wish people well, especially those starting out in business, and there is none of the begrudgery often found in other countries. Perhaps because the country is so vast and sprawling, there is little of that.

An example of this magnanimity happened a few weeks into the newspaper when I secured an interview with the then San Francisco Mayor, Dianne Feinstein (later Senator Feinstein), who had done significant work with Irish organisations. To my chagrin, my tape recorder did not work and my cheap camera refused to flash. She never batted an eyelid at this display of rank amateurism. I eventually ended up taking her photograph without the flash by standing on a chair a few feet from her, and then laboriously hand writing down all her responses, forcing her to pause every few seconds. She must have wondered who let this idiot in, but she never betrayed any annoyance. It is very hard to glimpse this side to Americans from the popular culture which shows up on television or in the movies. After you experience it, however, you understand why they became the greatest power on earth.

With much local support from the Irish community too, it was clear that the new newspaper was striking a chord. As young immigrants began to stream into San Francisco, our fledgling newspaper found its feet like a once shaky young foal. Soon after we started, we received a major boost when local *San Francisco Examiner* columnist Kevin Starr wrote a column praising the newspaper. He wrote, 'The book reviews, essays and editorials assert once again that passionate love of life and language that is characteristic of the Irish wherever they are.'

Two stories got us major attention during our first year. Our big scoop was an interview with mass murderer Charles Manson, which came about in a serendipitous fashion. I owed the unlikely interview to three Catholic priests. I was doing a feature on Catholic prison chaplains in California and had visited the California Youth Authority prison where the worst young offenders were held, as well as Folsom and Vacaville prisons, profiling three brave padres who often put their lives in danger to help inmates. The sights and sounds of Folsom, not far from Sacramento, and made famous in the Johnny Cash prison concert anthem 'I'm Stuck in Folsom Prison', will always be with me. The prison seemed like a huge warehouse, with cells piled on top of each other like cattle pens. It was stiflingly hot and not a breath of fresh air seemed to permeate the building. There was no question in my mind that incarceration in this place could quickly drive a man mad. Father Keaney, from Leitrim, a big bluff man with a thatch of blonde hair turning grey, was one of the few human touches to the prison. On our way across the exercise yard, where prisoner after prisoner was working on buffing his muscles, he was greeted like an old friend by many of them. Still, it was hard not to be frightened by the undercurrent of menace that was in the air.

Vaccaville in Central California seemed little better. This was where Charles Manson was confined at the time, and the chaplain, Father Pat Leslie from County Louth, had struck up a relationship with him. He asked me to come down and see him, and I readily agreed. On a white hot day in midsummer, a friend, Colm McCann, and I made the trek down. The outer gates of Vaccaville were imposing, and once inside one gate you were in an airlock until the guard decided to open the second one. An atmosphere of paranoia reigned. Dante's lines 'Abandon hope all ye who enter here' flashed into my head. I had read all about Manson in Victor Bugliosi's book *Helter Skelter* which chronicled the insane killing spree by members of Manson's gang in the Los

Angeles area in the early 1970s. Although Manson himself did not carry out the killings, his robot-like followers seemed to respond to his every whim. Although there were far worse mass murderers than Manson, few seemed to plumb the depth of horror and revulsion that Manson did among the general American populace. His followers had murdered Sharon Tate, the eight months' pregnant wife of Roman Polanski, as well as several other innocent people, in a drug-filled orgy of horror. In many ways, Manson was the perfect contrast to the flower power movement and the summer of love in San Francisco. Middle America had looked askance at that movement, with its emphasis on free love and sex, and Manson provided the necessary vehicle to attack such new fangled concepts.

Pat Leslie was a quiet man, with the slim build of a marathoner, which indeed he was. He had a low key manner and hardly seemed to know much about Manson's notoriety, or more likely, not to be affected by it. Manson's job in Vaccaville was helping out in the church, quite a change to his life on the outside. I assumed that Father Leslie would stay with me during the interview, but he dropped me off in a little courtyard behind the church where Manson and another man, who I later learned had murdered his parents, sat. I almost froze with fear when Father Leslie suddenly disappeared. Manson was much smaller than I had expected, a tiny man really, and he had a swastika emblazoned on his forehead. A few sentences into our conversation I found him quite mad and rambling, and definitely a complete socio-path. He was a man who could stab you with a knife or hold a pleasant conversation with you and not know the difference. His language was incredibly violent.

Years later I got to know a notorious Loyalist paramilitary in North-ern Ireland who was part of the Irish peace process. This man reminded me of Manson in the violence of his language and the con-stant hate-filled assertions. From whatever dungeons of his mind

Manson dragged up his fevered cants, it was clear that here was a deeply disturbed person. What was extraordinary to me was how he had held power over so many people. What seemed mostly gobbledy-gook to me had deeply impacted many of his followers to the point where they were prepared to kill for him. Manson strummed idly on a guitar during our conversation. Visions of being clubbed over the head with the instrument raced through my mind. I watched every move he made intently. He fancied himself as a songwriter and sang his latest composition to me: something about the damage being done to the birds and the environment by big oil companies. Coming from a man who hadn't hesitated to direct the savage taking of human life, it was quite an irony. I remained deathly afraid throughout the meeting that he would swing the guitar at me, as it would certainly garner him the headlines he clearly loved. In fact, I was working out my moves if he tried to do it. These mostly included running away as fast as I could, but seeing as we were locked into a small courtyard, that may have been quite difficult. In retrospect, the sight of Manson chasing me around the courtyard might have been funny, but it didn't strike me as remotely humorous at the time. Meanwhile, the guy who had killed his parents seemed unhappy that I wasn't interviewing him. He cleared his throat a few times and tried to get into the middle of our conversation. Manson fixed him with what I presumed was his allegedly hypnotic stare, which looked to me more like a cross- eyed grimace.

'Stay out of this, man,' he said, 'me and the dude have it going.'

The mother and father murderer promptly shut up. I was never as relieved when an interview ended and Father Leslie returned.

Leslie took me to lunch in the prison cafeteria and introduced me around. The sense I had from all the prisoners I met was of essentially weak human beings, unable to control impulses the rest of us are able to keep buried. Almost without exception, they had horrific early lives – Manson was the son of a prostitute and was beaten continuously as a child – and had little chance at life compared to others. Yet there was no excusing the horrific crimes. One rapist explained how he felt unable to stop himself doing it, yet he hardly seemed to regret that he had. It gave him that fleeting moment of power, he explained, that he did not have in the rest of his life. So it was about power, not sex, he explained. Another man, a murderer, thought of himself as an essentially useless individual, but with a gun in his hand felt a surge of power that gave him a deep sense of entitlement to go out and get what he wanted by whatever means. Sitting talking to those men in the cafeteria, I was struck by how there was nothing normal about them. They continued to justify their actions all those years later. It was clear that California has a penal system, not a rehabilitative one, and that the prisoners would be likely to re-offend if released at whatever point in the future.

The tension and fear in that prison were infectious. It was only in the car with Colm driving back to San Francisco that I finally relaxed. I had met the craziest man alive, by many people's estimation, and lived to tell the tale .When writing the article in *The Irishman*, I opened with some lines from a poem, quoted in Norman Mailer's *The Executioner's Song*, that summed up Manson to me:

> 'Deep in my dungeon
> I welcome you here
> Deep in my dungeon
> I worship your fear
> Deep in my dungeon I dwell
> I do not know if I wish you well.'

Although Manson had told me I would become famous for publishing the interview with him, I found it very hard to sell. He was still too violent, too extreme for most publications. Eventually the *Sunday Press* newspaper in Dublin and a German magazine bought the rights.

If Manson was bizarre and strange, the California Youth Authority prison was downright sad. Father Liam McSweeney, who had been a next door neighbour of ours in Ireland, was the chaplain, and as he took me on his appointed rounds it was impossible not to feel depressed by the number of young people who had already thrown their lives away. All under eighteen, many were from very tough and deprived backgrounds that gave them very little chance of a normal future. Now they would spend the formative years of their life behind bars.

The three chaplains I met were remarkable men. A rural Irish upbringing could hardly have prepared them for their mission – saving souls in perhaps the toughest environment on earth. In some ways, though, I believe that their Irish background, with its focus on family and on viewing the whole person in religious terms, helped. Seeing them with the lost and damned souls in California's toughest prisons was a remarkable sight. The gentleness with which they dealt with even the most hardened inmates was a rare touch of balm in an incredibly hostile world. I walked away from the prisons counting my own blessings.

Chapter 19

IRISH 1, MOONIES 0

The second major story we broke was about a young Irish girl named Mary Canning who got caught up in the Moonies when visiting friends in San Francisco. Despite the best efforts of her relatives, she was whipped away to the Moonies residence, some sixty miles outside of San Francisco, near the wine country. It was a common enough occurrence for idealistic young Irish to get snared by the Moonies, who were very active in the Bay Area. I had witnessed on a number of occasions the devastation this caused for families in Ireland. To have a child snatched away thousands of miles from home was a horrific experience. Many never saw their kids again; some returned to their families years later, but were permanently changed. Often we would get frantic calls at the newspaper to publish details of a young Irish man or woman who had suddenly dropped out of sight and not reported in to their families. Many times parents feared the worst: they had been mugged and were in hospital, or even killed. In several instances, however, they had joined the Moonies or one of the other sects that dotted the Bay area. According to one expert on cults, the Irish seemed particularly vulnerable to their influence. Dr Lowell Streiker, author of *The Cults are Coming*, told us that Irish and Dutch kids were particularly susceptible to them.

In this case, Jim Canning, Mary's father, came out from Donegal to search for his daughter. A farmer and a big bluff man, clearly ill at ease in the spotlight, he cut a very sympathetic figure when he appeared on news shows calling for his daughter's return. He was a man out of his element in a city like San Francisco. Yet he had an unshakeable conviction that he would win his daughter back, and his confidence spread to all of us. All the literature stated that the best and perhaps only time to get a kid out from under the Moonie clutches was early on in the process before the indoctrination took full hold. It was also clear to me that the weight of continuing publicity was very important. The Moonies did not relish the constant questions they were getting from the media, and the hope was that Mary would be shaken loose by them, rather than have the bad publicity continue.

The story of Mary Canning had spread like wildfire through the Irish community and there was an immediate consensus that an all-out effort should be made to free her. I chaired a meeting of over 300 people where various schemes to win her back were discussed, many of them not legal. The case had become a leading story on all the San Francisco networks and indeed, further afield, and, because of my newspaper expertise, I was handling the media. I argued for a major demonstration outside the Moonie headquarters in Sonoma County, some sixty miles from the city. I believed that taking the fight to their headquarters and the resultant publicity would be a powerful incentive for them to release her. There were a fair few dissenters from this strategy, some of whom questioned whether I knew what I was talking about. Mutterings about this newcomer to town telling the settled community how to handle things reached my ears. Not for the first time, I learnt to trust my own counsel and ignore the naysayers.

The following Saturday, a motley group responded to my urging and undertook the journey to the Moonie headquarters. Included in the gallant band were several nuns and one priest who had seen the television coverage and had decided to join up. Some of the men, totally unbidden, carried hurley sticks, which, for those who are unfamiliar with hurling, Ireland's oldest native game, are rather like ice hockey sticks. Arriving outside the Moonie compound, about forty of us gathered in a circle and began to chant 'We Want Mary'. After half an hour a large number of Moonies came down to the gate and silently observed the chanting. They were like peas in a pod: preppy young men, dressed in conservative tones, and with neatly clipped short hair, the young women in sensible skirts and blouses. Before long, however, as we raised the decibel level, their smooth facade began to crack. Insults were exchanged, and before we knew it, an all-out altercation began. In the middle of it all were the nuns and the priest, belting about them with a will.

It was probably one of the most surreal moments of my life, and the media clearly thought so too as it led all the news bulletins that night. No one was injured in the fracas and we eventually returned to San Francisco with a deep sense of satisfaction at the media coverage and a feeling that we had struck an important blow. So it proved. The Moonies released Mary Canning the following day and her relatives immediately employed a deprogrammer to help her reconnect with her family. Soon afterwards, they returned to Ireland, where, as far as I know, she picked up the threads of her old life. Our headline that week said it all: 'Irish 1, Moonies O'. It is rare to get such satisfaction from covering a story.

Chapter 20

FAREWELL TO JENNIE

Jennie and I decided to break up. The warning signs had been obvious. She was deeply unhappy because she was out of Ireland. We had some pitched arguments: the lack of any extended family and the relentless focus on the newspaper, which was barely surviving, led to a sense of crushing pressure. She was working in a local Dunkin' Donuts and I was jealous of the attention she was getting from some of the customers. Several police officers asked her out, and I'm sure she was tempted. For her part, she was annoyed with my frequent late nights and my workaholic behaviour when it came to the newspaper, but most of all, she missed Ireland. There are some who can never make the adjustment to strange shores and Jennie was one such person. She loved her native Donegal, to go romping on the beach with her dogs and to come home flushed by the brisk wind, with her excited dogs lapping in her wake. She loved Dublin, too, and she just missed Ireland, period.

Early one morning I woke up and realised that we could not continue as we were. She lay in the bed beside me. I stretched out my right hand and let it fall on her soft shoulder. She stirred and came awake. We lay there in silence for a few moments. She lit a cigarette and the only sound was the soft sough of her breath as she drew the smoke in. She spoke first.

'This can't go on.'

At first I denied that this was the case, even though I knew it to be the truth. It was my typical reaction: trying to smooth everything on the surface and letting the hidden emotions continue to roil away. She was insistent.

'I'm heading back to Ireland.'

Despite myself, a deep sense of relief flooded through me. She had the balls to make the call, not me.

'I suppose it would be best.'

'This is not the same relationship we had in Ireland. I'm like a fish out of water here.'

'I know. But I want to stay here; there is some hunger in me that won't let me go back.'

I reached over and kissed her. She looked at me with those big blue eyes and said, 'I'll always love you.'

'I'll always love you too.'

Thus it ended, with a whimper. She left on the plane a few weeks later and there were many agonising phone calls for several months after. But she thrived back in Ireland, becoming a journalist, and later a highly successful lawyer. She had made the right move.

Chapter 21

FRIENDS OR LOVERS?

With my business partner, Tom McDonagh, I eventually moved into a house in the Richmond District, just a few blocks from Ocean Beach. It was a wonderful place to live. The tang of sea salt in the air, the wonderful cooling fog rolling in off the Bay, and the endlessly perfect San Francisco days. We had a dog now, too. We called him Pub Spy, after a famous newspaper character in Ireland, and I liked nothing better than to take him down to the beach as the sun set and sit on the wall and watch the golden rays descend over the horizon. Pub Spy loved to hunt along the beach. He was a small dog, but seemingly fearless, loving to converse and play with dogs of every shape and size and always having that knowing look after we returned home, as if some important information had been transmitted.

We had created an office in the lower part of the house and we lived in the two bedrooms upstairs. Our little business had expanded to the point where we needed a secretary. That was how we met Julia. She was English and impossibly beautiful – high cheekbones, classic English rose features. She was older than us, at least thirty-two, which seemed ancient at the time. She had come over after a broken romance and had spotted our newspaper ad for a secretary. She came to the interview wearing a sleeveless black dress, which also happened to be low cut. We were bowled over from the start. She had that charming London accent, so different to the upper class, toffee-nosed Britspeak. No other candidate came close. I knew right away we were going to hire her – and that I would fall for her. Her resumé was superb and we were both a little in awe. Where had this vision come from?

She told us briefly about her years working in some of the top law firms in England, the broken romance with a married partner and the flight to America and her determination to start again. She needed the break, she told us, her large eyes welling up with tears. In retrospect, it was a good performance, and one designed to capture the hearts of two young Irish lads making their first ever hire. Because she didn't have a work visa either, the job suited her fine, but she was clearly capable of getting much better. Now she was with two Paddys who still spent part of their days running up ladders and painting houses. Despite my resolution to abandon house painting, I still very reluctantly lent a hand when Tom desperately needed help. It was an interesting contrast.

By the time Julia was with us a week we both knew we had made the right choice. She simply swept in like a whirlwind, reorganised our bookkeeping, even physically cleaned out the office space and the rest of the downstairs area, which hadn't seen a feather duster for aeons. I suddenly found myself looking in the mirror before she arrived in the mornings, checking my breath after breakfast, making sure I picked the cleanest clothes, even making more frequent trips to the laundry. I tried to act cool and casual around her, but more and more my feelings were starting to show. I know she caught me looking at her once or twice, and I wondered what she was thinking. She seemed to encourage the flirting with both Tom and me. She wore the low cut dress a lot, often sat with her legs crossed and her skirt riding high on her thighs. It took great willpower not to stare from where I was, just a few feet away. She had a lovely way of tossing her head and pulling her hair back from her forehead. There was nothing about her I didn't like.

When she talked to her family in England she would speak in hushed tones. Once or twice I saw the glisten of a tear in her eye. She hadn't been away much in her life and this was a difficult move because her father was ill. Every day she would take her lunch to the nearby park and sit basking in the sunshine, sometimes applying suntan lotion to her arms and face. I drove by deliberately two or three times just to see her, but I couldn't pluck up the courage to ask her if I could come along. Tom and I did not discuss it directly, but I sensed that he liked her a lot too. There was a lot to like. We had never been rivals over women before; he preferred the big busty California kind – the ones he could say goodbye to the next day. I liked European or Irish women mainly; I hadn't quite adjusted to the brash American approach yet.

One night, Julia and I went to dinner and I brought her home afterwards. I was hoping she might say something to me as I stopped outside her door, maybe 'come upstairs for a coffee', but there was nothing. I could see why she probably didn't want anyone to come inside. The house looked dingy and was in a very bad neighbourhood – it was certainly a long way from London's West End. Her poor circumstances only made me want her more. It came to a head on a Friday night when she told us she wanted to go for a drink after work. The sexual tension crackled. We almost knocked her down in our eagerness to go with her. Neither of us was going to step back from an invitation like that. Soon we were cruising down Geary Boulevard in Tom's pickup truck. She wanted a quiet place, somewhere where we all could talk. We found it in, of all places, a Polynesian Bar called Trader Vic's close by the Russian Orthodox Cathedral on Geary Street and 24th Avenue. It had a seedy but exotic feel to it, a faux Polynesian hut with a circular bar and lots of leis and grass hoops about the place.

There were just a few stragglers at the bar and we sat on either side of her. Tonight was going to be *the* night for one of us. A few drinks later and we were carefree with each other. Her skirt was riding high on her thighs again and she regaled us with funny stories about

London nightlife and the creeps she regularly met. 'Not at all like you guys,' she said, batting her eyes. Tom and I had reached an awkward juncture. It was time for one of us to leave, but neither of us could bring ourselves to. We didn't know which of us she wanted to be with and she had given no indication of who she favoured. We pondered that for a few more drinks until Tom finally screwed up the courage to ask her.

'Well, Julia, which of us do you really like?'

'I like both of you very much, Tom.'

'Yes, but if you had to pick one of us, who would it be?'

She looked first at him, then at me. 'I couldn't decide. You are both very good people and I like you both a lot. I wouldn't hurt anyone's feeling, but if you want to make that decision between you, that is fine with me.'

It was quite a statement .With that, she went to go to the ladies and make a phone call. Tom and I stared into our drinks for a moment. He spoke first.

'You go with her. She's more your type.'

'No,' I said, 'you go with her. I think it's you she likes.'

It struck me that the conversation had gone off in a very strange direction. Instead of two bulls circling, we were like two sheep waiting for directions. Tom declared that he wouldn't take her.

'I wouldn't want to leave you here alone at the bar,' he said.

It was a very touching moment for me, a statement that friendship was more important to him that just a casual relationship. I, on the other hand, thought I was in love. But even with that, I couldn't cross my friend Tom, especially as he was so generous to me in so many ways. I realised then that neither of us was going to go home with Julia. She came back, sat on the bar stool and waited for one of us to speak.

Tom began. 'Well, Julia, we both like you very much, but we don't think it would be fair...'

She stopped him. 'I understand,' she said. 'I want you both to know you mean an awful lot to me... but I better go.'

I can't remember ever being as disappointed as I watched that beautiful body walk away from me, perhaps forever. But Tom and I had stuck it out together, in a strange ritual of male solidarity that surprised both of us. It was time to get drunk, share a Mexican meal on the way home and fall into bed, dreaming of Julia's perfect body, which I would only ever touch with my mind, as Leonard Cohen might say.

Chapter 22

A POLITICAL AWAKENING

The longer I lived in San Francisco, the more interested I became in Californian politics. I came from a very political household, where my father, an unredeemed follower of Eamon de Valera, who founded Ireland's largest political party, Fianna Fáil, indoctrinated us very young on the importance of politics. I was soon looking to make a contribution in America. My first lesson in the black art of American politics came in 1981. The Richmond and Sunset districts were represented in Congress by Phil Burton, an old bull of the party who was then No. 2 to succeed the ageing Tip O' Neill. Because the nature of the two neighbourhoods had grown more conservative, his district was suddenly shaky and he had been targeted by Republicans.

The major political machine in San Francisco was run by John Maher, an ex-heroin addict and one of the most remarkable men I had ever come to befriend. He had achieved quite a bit of fame, being the subject of numerous articles, a TV film and a full length biography. Maher had founded Delancey Street – what was then and quite possibly still is probably the best drug rehabilitation centre in America. It began when Maher, a convicted felon and heroin addict, went straight, and began bringing some fellow addicts home to his apartment in an attempt to help them. From that small beginning grew Delancey Street. It was enormously successful. Since its founding, over 10,000 men and women have graduated into society as taxpaying citizens leading successful lives. They include lawyers, truck drivers, sales people, medical professionals, realtors, mechanics and contractors. It was all based on an 'up from the bootstraps' approach. Addicts were often sent to Delancey Street by judges instead of serving prison terms. John also took in many of the lost and troubled souls, such as the homeless and hookers, that no other programme would even try to rehabilitate.

Maher reckoned that Congressman Burton was in trouble and that our newspaper was the perfect antidote for the problem. His analysis showed the Irish in the Sunset and Richmond districts to be the swing vote. The Irish vote was trending conservative, but still grateful to Burton for all the services he had delivered. John believed that an endorsement from *The Irishman* would make a big difference. Suddenly I went from being an utterly obscure editor to centre stage in one of the most hard fought political campaigns in San Francisco history, one that was being watched closely nationwide, because if Burton was defeated it would be a big scalp for the Republicans. It reached its climax for me at a major fundraiser for Burton held in a mansion in the posh Pacific Heights district. On the night, the house was chock-a-block with beautiful people: celebrities, media and other political powerhouses. I was starting to feel distinctly out of place, especially when I bumped into the hors d'oeuvres waiter and he spilled the contents on the floor.

The guest of honour was Senator Edward Kennedy, who, regardless of his currency elsewhere, was still a hero in the liberal enclaves of the United States, and, as the most liberal of all, San Francisco adored him. I was very excited by the opportunity to meet him.When Kennedy's imminent arrival was signalled, all the movers and shakers rushed from the house to line up on the driveway to greet him. I was hanging back until I suddenly felt a strong pair of hands on my shoulders, and Congressman Burton propelled me through the gathering crowd to the place of honour right outside the passenger door of the arriving limousine. As US senators, congressmen and the San Francisco Mayor looked on, Kennedy stepped out, grasped my hand and wheeled to face the clicking cameras and news reporters. What he made of the shaggy-haired, long-bearded young man, clearly uncomfortable in a cheap suit he had bought the previous day at a secondhand thrift shop called the Blind Baby's Bazaar, he never said.

'How are things in San Francisco,' he asked.

'Fine,' I said.

'How is your race going?'

'Very well,' I lied.

'Well, keep it up. You are a shoo-in.' he said. 'How is Tom doing?' I had no idea who he was talking about.'Very well,' I said.

'Great. Tell him I will call him.'

I never did find out who Tom was. This exchange was followed by an awkward silence. By now I was hoping someone would come and rescue me. Just then, Phil Burton, having given me my moment in the sun, reached in, followed by a scrum of other politicians. My time in the spotlight was gone, but it was a very convincing lesson that all politics are local.Phil Burton won in a gallop and we endorsed him.

John Maher told me I'd done some good, which was more than most newsmen he knew. I got to know Senator Kennedy well subsequently and he laughed when I told him about our first encounter. I was just happy to experience American politics first hand, an arena that had fascinated me much of my life from a distance. Now that it was up close, it didn't seem all that different from Irish politics in some ways. John Maher could have been a party supremo in any major Irish city, and the experience had shown me that national races turned on minute local issues and that loyalty to the machine was paramount, not just in Ireland, but alive and well in America too. Phil Burton died suddenly a few years later, on the cusp of power, just as he was about to become Speaker of the House.

I became a close friend of John Maher and visited him often in 1982 and 1983 at his office in the converted Russian Consulate residence on Pacific Heights. There, this former skid row drug addict would gaze out at some of San Francisco's most beautiful views as he expounded his always trenchantly held opinions. He could hold forth for hours on an endless array of topics, including Ireland, New York, politics and rehabilitating addicts. Through it all, he would drink cup after cup of coffee, rarely allowing any interruptions. He still walked and talked like the old New York hood he was, and it was fascinating. He was an unreconstructed Irish Republican. When Princess Margaret visited San Francisco a few years after referring to the Irish as 'pigs' during a Chicago dinner in 1977, he arranged for several squealing piglets to be released into the area near where she was staying. I was one of the people roped in to help hold the pigs. Having never spent time on a farm I didn't have a clue; neither did anyone else present. The one I was holding began to squirm, alarmed by the bright lights and flashbulbs. I felt my grip slipping, but everyone else was in the same boat. As the media watched, the piglets took off running down the street, with the cameras in hot pursuit. We never did find out where they ended up.

When the Queen visited San Francisco in 1984, Maher organised 10,000 people to march in protest at her government's policies in Northern Ireland .When the hunger strike deaths occurred in 1981, he had a group of Irish Americans carry mock coffins outside the British consulate in a 'made for television' event that brought huge attention. It was a typical gambit by the media-savvy Maher. He was an extraordinary political powerhouse. On any given day you would find judges, contractors and city officials at his office, all waiting for appointments. He was an Irish boss almost as powerful as a Daly in Chicago, and he relished it. He had major ties to Willie Brown, the black son of a Texas sharecropper who was then the Speaker of the California Assembly, the second most powerful job in the state. Later, Brown, forced out of office because of term limits which did not allow him to run again, became Mayor of San Francisco. Between them, Maher and Brown pretty much controlled politics in the Bay area. A lesser relationship he had was with the Mitchell Brothers, porn pioneers who ran a porn theatre in downtown San Francisco, called the O'Farrell Theatre. Jim and Artie Mitchell were involved in every Irish cause that Maher got them into. It was strange sometimes to see the makers of 'Behind the Green Door' – one of the first smash porn films – side by side with nuns and priests planning Irish protest activities. One major meeting was held in the parlour of the theatre while men in brown raincoats hurried inside. When they were given the location of the meeting, many of the attendees, pargons of the Irish community, knew little of what the O'Farrell Theatre stood for. It was an uncomfortable crowd, to say the least. Strippers and hookers wandered in as pillars of the Irish community blessed themselves. Fortunately, no nun or priest showed up and none of the others went home.

After it was over, Jim invited me to take the tour. The Mitchell boys had a touch of whimsy about them that dulled the hard edge of the porn connection. With some of the girls, we previewed a new porn film they had prepared. The male lead was clearly having problems maintaining his manhood. 'Ah, God help him. I'd love to give him a hand,' said one of the ladies, while the others nodded. It was all I could do not to burst out laughing. The Mitchell Brother saga ended very badly when Jim shot his brother dead after a drug induced frenzy. What had seemed a relatively benign porn empire became instead an ugly mess as huge recriminations followed. However, the theatre remains open to this day.

Maher took me to Fresno, California, to meet one of his heroes, and soon mine: Cesar Chavez, head of the United Farmworkers' Union, at their annual convention. Chavez had been described by Robert Kennedy as 'one of the heroic figures of our time'. When he died, over 40,000 showed up to pay their respects as he was laid to rest on a remote hillside where he had often gone to watch the sunrise. Chavez was born the son of a migrant worker in Arizona. In 1975, Cesar Chavez rallied millions across the US in a boycott of grape growers who were nakedly exploiting their migrant workforce. He insisted on tactics of non-violence and is considered a saintly figure still in the Hispanic community in California. In 1968 he conducted a twenty-five day fast to show his support for non violence. Through it all, he never took more than $6,000 a year in wages.

The first time I met Chavez was on one of the hottest afternoons I have ever experienced. The central California town of Fresno was festooned with Latino flags and emblems as the farm workers gathered. In the great meeting hall I sat spellbound as speaker after speaker railed against the grape growers and called for support of the boycott. John took me upstairs to meet the great man. When Chavez entered the room he did it so quietly that I hardly knew he had arrived. There was no entourage or trappings of greatness. Yet, after a few moments, I knew that he had an extraordinary, quiet presence. Maher asked me to brief him on Northern Ireland. Chavez listened quietly for over an hour, never once interrupting. At the end he told me he had studied the history of the Irish hunger strikes and asked me two questions: would non-violence work in the context of the North, and was there anything he should do to help? My answers were that non-violence was the siren song of John Hume, one of the great leaders in Northern Ireland politics, and that he could help by just maintaining an interest and contacting Hume.

The second time I met Chavez was in John Maher's apartment in San Francisco in 1985 just when John was beginning to go downhill. I sensed that Chavez knew that and had come to offer advice and counsel. Alas, even the great Cesar Chavez could not help a man bent on destroying himself. John Maher began drinking again, for reasons all too clear to his closest friends. His relationship was not going well and the ghosts that often bubbled to the surface during our conversations were clearly back haunting him. He moved to New York. I will always believe the reason for this was so that he could malinger and die far away from the institution he had created and which depended so much on his inspiration. In New York he began floundering like a star-fish thrown on a rocky shore. I met him frequently, as by then I, too, had moved to New York. He got drunk a lot. He became maudlin and sentimental, remembering his mother and speaking in pain-filled tones about the mental illness that dogged his family, and clearly him too. John was friendless in New York save for a small cadre of ex-San Franciscans who protected him as best we could. It was no easy task. He was often incoherently drunk, and, despite everyone's best efforts, the man who saved so many people could not save himself.

He began sleeping in a construction trailer owned by a friend and had his first heart attack, brought on by the sheer dint of his drinking, soon after that. Even after that warning, his death wish continued. It was a particularly slow and painful suicide by a man who had brought back so many others from a similar fate. Back in San Francisco, John was not so subtly being written out of the script at Delancey Street. After their best efforts to win him back to sobriety failed, they simply jettisoned him. To his eternal credit, he never embarrassed them, even as they seemed to give up on him and forget him. I believe he made a determination that however he was going to end his life it would never reflect on his brainchild or on the people whose lives he had helped save. I had one long and intense conversation with him shortly before he died. It was on one of his good nights and he was talking of the old days in San Francisco. I interrupted him.

'Why are you doing this, fellah?'

'Doing what?'

'Killing yourself from drinking.'

He blustered for a moment, but then he gave in. 'Too much pain.'

'John, you have so many people who love you, so many you have saved.'

'Yeah, but you know what happened to Elvis Presley?'

'What?'

'They protected him from everyone but himself. That's me. I can help the world but I have to destroy myself.'

Those words came back to me when John finally died of the inevitable second heart attack, a young man, still in his forties. When I heard the news I felt as many others did – that it was a merciful release for a man who was clearly experiencing massive pain in his life. I believe that there are some people, such as writer Brendan Behan, and my friend John Maher, who find it too painful to be alive and are unable to shake the dark clouds over them that lead to unfettered drinking.

His funeral was one of the saddest I have witnessed. Where there should have been thousands from the ranks of the great and the good across America, there was only a handful of us, and a cheap white coffin, little better than a cardboard box. He went into the ground unlamented by those whose lives he had saved, but I wept at his grave, as did many of his San Francisco friends. I know some who still visit that windswept hill where his body lies. Today, Delancey Street lives on as a monument to his memory that even his detractors can never erase. In the end he did not rage against the dying of the light, but he left behind a beacon of hope for which he will be forever remembered.

Chapter 23

TOUGH TIMES IN SAN FRANCISCO

As Willie Sutton said when asked why he robbed banks, 'It's because that's where the money is at.' In my case, New York and Boston was where the Irish Americans were at. Small newspapers are not good economic investments in San Francisco, especially ones started with less than $1,000. Despite the kindness of friends and benefactors, we ran into crushing cash flow problems about a year into our existence. It became a race against the bank at times, cashing cheques in bars in order to find enough money to cover cheques already written. It was the kind of stressful weekly pressure that made life very difficult. Publishing was the type of business where you never knew when you went to the bank on Friday if your pay cheque would clear. Often times it didn't, and I spent many a sleepless night worrying about the finances. Rent was often in arrears, and much needed office equipment went not bought because of the cash crunch. It was a shame, because the newspaper itself was finding its stride.

We were breaking Irish American stories that few of the other papers, mainly based in New York, bothered to cover. The 1980 Census, with its finding that there were 40.7 million Irish Americans in the US, was an extraordinary fillip to the community. Yet it had gone pretty much unremarked upon until we revealed the story behind the figures. Likewise, the slow but inexorable growth of Irish American political organizations dedicated to achieving progress in Northern Ireland was missed at first. Because many of these had their rubric outside New York, they were ignored in the Big Apple, centre of most Irish activity. By covering them I saw the beginning of a grassroots community outreach that could and did eventually have considerable political impact. Much of this time, from 1982 on, I was also keeping myself going by freelancing outside the newspaper, mainly for the *Irish Press* newspaper in Ireland, covering whatever I could for them.

I will never forget one news editor there, Paul Muldowney, who gently gave me the only tutoring I ever received in writing journalism. He had infinite patience with the stories I sent him and always conspired to give me big play in the newspaper, even when the story didn't deserve it, because he knew my financial plight. My first story for the *Irish Press* almost landed me in trouble with Irish libel laws, which are much stricter than American ones. It involved an Irish priest who was moved by his order out of his parish house. He alleged that it was because another priest in the house was having an affair with the housekeeper. It all ended in tears, with a court action featuring the priest, Father Liam O' Byrne, now deceased, suing his own order, an extraordinary action by a man who I found to be as traditional in his outlook as the most conservative members of his Church.

I got to know him well during the case and we had little in common. Because of a heavy-handed upbringing where beatings by Christian Brothers in school were a regular feature, I had little enough respect for the traditional Church. O'Byrne loved his vocation unquestioningly and would not have a word said against the old mores. Despite our differences, I fully believed that he was telling the truth. There was something I saw in him that deeply impressed me. There is in the Irish character a trait which bridles at the misuse of moral authority, perhaps because the British sought to abuse it for centuries in relation to their country. Liam O'Byrne was experiencing such a rebellion late in his life. Like many Irish, I have always believed that authority has to be earned, not just handed down by edict. The latter was the case on this occasion and O'Byrne was not about to allow his life's work to be steamrolled under by a church organisation fixated on avoiding a scandal. They had picked on the wrong man to jettison. Where other faithful members of his profession would have bowed the knee and accepted the edict, not O'Byrne. For a man like him to have given his life to an order and then to be treated so shoddily seemed to me an extraordinary miscarriage of justice. He was eventually vindicated when a court found in his favour, but the damage was done to him and his order.

For years afterwards he would rehash the case with me again and again, and it was clear that he had been permanently impacted. For the first time, I saw the havoc that institutions could wreak on an individual who did not blindly follow their edict. The very roots of his religion had been shaken but in the end he was the better for speaking out; to have bottled it up would have utterly destroyed him. Years later, Father Byrne was the prison pastor for Dan White, the man who shot the Mayor of San Francisco, George Moscone, and gay City Supervisor Harvey Milk, in 1978. The story was told in the Oscar-nominated movie 'Milk' starring Sean Penn. I received a few letters from White, who subscribed to the newspaper, requesting a meeting, but I never responded, as it was an inflamed issue, with gay quite rightly up in arms that the man who shot their icon had gotten a wrist slap of a sentence. White committed suicide after getting out of prison.

Despite our ability to break stories, the newspaper continued in dire straits. We would have been in even more financial problems if Tom had not continued with the painting business, without which we could never have survived. Often times I had to turn from editor to house painter to help out on the bigger jobs. This sometimes led to a 'Superman' type existence, starting the day as a house painter in some Mission District Victorian and ending it transformed into a (paint splattered) editor sitting at a typewriter until the wee hours, trying to get a newspaper out. I have several photos of me at the time, taken at Irish events, where it is clear that there is paint stuck to my hair! This must have made an interesting talking point for the local community who knew nothing of my secret life as a housepainter. It was also a time when I was drinking too much. The weekly pressure of keeping home and business together was too much.

One of our mislaid plans at *The Irishman* was to start a Los Angeles section of the newspaper and eventually a Los Angeles bureau. It seemed a good idea at the time; there were large pockets of Irish in L.A. who could provide an extra focus and sales for the newspapers. In pursuit of this ambition, I drove down several times to L.A. during 1983 and 1984 to set up the necessary arrangements. The six hours or so drive down Highway Five was always an interesting experience. Often I got off the highway and travelled through small rural towns which seemed to belong as much to John Steinbeck's era of *The Grapes of Wrath* as to the modern day. There was another route to Los Angeles, far more tortuous, but incredibly beautiful, down the coastal route known as Highway One. The vistas were stunning in many places and the names, such as Half Moon Bay, Santa Cruz, Santa Barbara, conjured up the old Spanish and Indian heritage of the Golden State.

The sprawling city of angels was never my favourite place; getting from one part to another proved to be a nightmare as a missed exit on the massive highways could set you caroming off into unknown territory for an hour or two. It was also too spread out for any cohesiveness in the Irish American community. I quickly learned that Irish radio was really the only way for the community to interact and that a newspaper had almost no chance. Whereas in San Francisco I could frequently walk through the two major Irish neighbourhoods and see vending machines for my paper, there was no such possibility in Los Angeles where the Irish areas were so far flung and disparate that there was no sense of community. There were a few radio shows, a thriving Irish games scene, and many Irish social events that provided some focus for the locals, but, as with New York and Boston, there was a healthy disrespect and suspicion of the other city, and an Irish newspaper from San Francisco was always going to be viewed with doubt in Los Angeles.

However, I did have some extraordinary experiences during my trips to Los Angeles. Once, I attended a Gaelic games tournament and was asked to play with one of the sides in a hurling match as they were short a player. I lined up as goalkeeper because I had a bad back at the time and could not have handled an outfield position. The game, like so many in America, was bad tempered and there were many controversial decisions, yet my side, the Wild Geese, were well ahead at the half time whistle. When I returned in the second half I saw some supporters of the opposition team, St Brendan's, standing behind my goals, but thought little of it. As I watched the game being played out, mostly at the other end, I suddenly heard a sawing sound and turned around to see the supporters hacking down the goalposts.

'What the fuck are you doing?' I asked the bigger one who was swinging away with abandon while I tried to keep an eye on the play on the field.

'Fuck off,' he said before running away with the posts.

This was clearly their way of expressing disapproval with the game's inevitable outcome. I hardly had time to react when the St Brendan's side mounted one of their infrequent attacks, and I will always remember the face of the forward on their team who bore down on goal, looked up to shoot, then suddenly realised there were no longer any goalposts to shoot at, except for two small wooden stumps. The referee wisely abandoned proceedings right after that. Irish newspapers got hold of it and it made huge headlines. That same night I went to a post game dance where I had to take some painkillers for back pain. This should have warned me off the drink for the evening. Unfortunately it didn't and I was soon slugging back the pints and watching some Irish dancers perform before the dance proper started. I always found Irish dances in California very enjoyable: a mix of old songs and dances like the Siege of Ennis and the Walls of Limerick, some country and western airs and a good dose of patriotic Irish ballads. In contrast, the young ladies present were thoroughly modern Californian women, often with high paying jobs and careers. The dances straddled the generations. Older Irish men and women who hadn't seen 'the old country' in thirty years would dance the sets side by side with Valley Girls singing along to 'Don't Cry for me Argentina' which was big at the time. There was always a raffle to benefit some immigrant without health insurance who had landed in hospital. Often times the older Irish brought their daughters along, hoping they could make an introduction for them to some nice young Irishman. As one father told me, he and his wife were 'petrified with all the drugs and all that' about who their daughter would end up with. If only they knew how much casual drug use there was among the immigrant Irish community, they would hardly have been as anxious to pair up their daughter with an Irish man. In San Francisco in particular the hangover from the Hippy 60s was all too evident, even in the Irish community where pot and cocaine were freely available.

On this particular night, I was apparently in flying form for much of the evening. I say 'apparently' because I don't remember any of it. The first thing I recall is waking up on the floor in my friend Frank's apartment in Santa Ana with the sun shining directly on my throbbing head and realising that there was someone lying beside me dressed in bright colours. Through the fog of an almighty hangover I barely dared to look. When I did finally lift my head I saw a beautiful Irish dancer, in her mid-twenties, still in her full regalia – all bright buttons and shimmers and even the hair piece intact – sleeping soundly on my crooked arm. Draped over us both was a large white table cloth. 'Oh Jesus,' I said. She moaned and turned over, but thankfully did not wake. How she and I got there I will never know and I have no idea what transpired between us. I never got to find out either. I carefully extracted my arm from under her neck, leaped up and bolted into the bedroom where my friend lay sleeping. Soon afterwards I heard a banging and shuffling and realised that she had woken up and gone home.

Another night while on a Los Angeles trip I went to a céilí in Orange County. I danced with a young woman whose parents came from Clare. I told her that my mother was also a Clare woman. Within ten minutes her parents were over, inviting me to their table. When we sat down they regaled me with stories of the old country and what the old days were like in California. The young girl looked on, and it seemed to me she was sizing up a potential suitor. Next came the invitation to visit the house the following night for some dinner. I went along with this, for reasons of loneliness as much as anything. Three thousand miles from Ireland it was nice to get Irish hospitality as I remembered it and occasionally longed for. The mother took over on the second evening, plying me with food and drink until she had squeezed every available iota of information out of me, including whether I did my own laundry. I must have failed the test of the mother as I was not invited back.

The old time waltzes and Irish set dances in an age of disco and loud music must have appeared passing strange to the young girls at these dances, but in a way it was exotic and was as close as they would get to recreating their parents' world. Native-born Irishmen, still relatively thin on the ground, were very popular with such women, and the more countrified the better, it seemed. I saw some strange marriages in my time between West of Ireland men and Valley Girls, not to mention Belfast men, who were very popular for political reasons, to aspiring actresses and models. Athletes were also popular and the then annual visit of the Irish All Star hurling and football teams to San Francisco and

Los Angeles were occasions of wonderful sin. Many marriages came out of brief liaisons between Irish football and hurling stars and local women in the two cities. Strapping country Irishmen and the perfectly tanned California girls proved irresistible to each other. After my Irish dancer experience I never mixed booze and painkillers again.

In 1982, I began another relationship, this time with a journalist from the *Washington Post* who had been covering Irish issues from the capitol for the *Irish Press*, the same newspaper in Ireland that I worked for. We carried on a long distance friendship for many months before I flew to Washington to meet her. She brought me to the newsroom of the *Washington Post* and introduced me to legendary reporter Bob Woodward, the equivalent of meeting Muhammad Ali for an aspiring boxer. The *Post* newsroom looked just like the movie set from *All The President's Men* and it was one of those rare times that I had to pinch myself to make sure I was really standing there talking to Woodward. Even then I was not easily impressed with 'celebrity', but Woodward and Carl Bernstein had exposed an extraordinarily corrupt web spun by Richard Nixon, the president of the United States, and forced him out of office in the process. The problem, however, was that within months they had imitators everywhere in the US, all of them looking for the next great breaking story. The long term impact was that journalism became more and more a game of 'gotcha', to the detriment of solid fact-based reporting.

She also brought me to the White House on a VIP tour and it was a very special moment to gaze at the unoccupied Oval Office and meet some key members of President Reagan's staff. I even got to witness the president arriving on the South Lawn. He looked just as tall and leathered as he did on television. She visited me in San Francisco, and, once again, I found myself strolling on Ocean Beach with a beautiful and interesting girl. We were very keen on each other but it was proving too difficult because of the distance involved. She wanted me to move to Washington but I could not see any future there, and besides, New York interested me far more. We broke up with little recriminations on either side.

Soon afterwards, I met Patricia Harty, who became the rock in my life in San Francisco. There were no fewer than fourteen kids in her family from outside Nenagh in Tipperary, and most of them had ended up in California. She had come via the Bronx where she had written part of an unpublished memoir called 'The Only Other Virgin in the Bronx' which accurately described life in the early 1970s in the most Irish borough in America. She was a typesetter and very good one, so before long she began working for *The Irishman*. Her value to the newspaper was immense. Soon we were playing house together, in a two-storey dwelling we rented in the Sunset District within sight of the ocean. I loved it there and look back on it as among the happiest times of my life. At night I would run down to the breakers and jog back, taking in the sheer calming beauty of the most delightful city on earth. I remember once, after taking my usual run, lying in the back garden on a bench and saying to myself, 'This is as good as it gets.' I was delighted at what I had built in California: a stable relationship, my own company and a lifestyle far removed from what I had at home.

I went back to Ireland in 1983 for my brother Fergus's wedding. On the surface, it all seemed the same as when I had left, four years earlier, but, of course, people's lives had moved on. Friends had got married and were distant. The hometown, apart from the family gatherings, was full of old ghosts and remembered times. Seeing my father's grave for the first time in four years was also a shock. Instead of his presence, there was a stone slab with his name in Irish and a space for my mother when she passed over in the future. It shocked me to see his name emblazoned on the headstone. Somehow a part of me expected him to be waiting by the front door when the cab from the train station arrived, excited to hear all the news of America. Instead there was a grey stone in a cold graveyard on a driving wet Irish day. A host of memories came flooding back and I cried more on seeing his grave than I did upon learning of his death. During the visit, I took my first trip in many years to West Kerry, his native place. Because I had no immediate memories of the place, it was the best part of the visit, to walk the roads that generations of my father's family walked, to sit in the local pub and listen to the musicians, to walk up by the Three Sisters, headlands that reach out into the hungry Atlantic to form a natural promontory that provide one of the most beautiful vistas in the world.

As we sat in the local pub, my first cousin told me the family story of the Famine and the young woman who died. The family was half-starved and too weak to carry her to the graveyard so she was buried in a field on the land where my father grew up. Padraig made it sound like it had happened just a few weeks previously, so vivid was his account, and it was hard not to be emotionally affected. I also had a personal memory of the lasting impact of the Famine, a fact that often made me realise just how close an event it was to all of us in Ireland, even though it was 150 years ago. My grandmother, my father's mother, who was born in 1871 and died, aged 92, in 1963, lived with us when I was a child. She habitually wore a shawl, and I remember how she would always hoard potatoes under the shawl, as though they were gold dust. No other food seemed to occupy her mind as she slipped into senility, but the potato was a powerful talisman for her, to be protected at all costs.

My father, too, was full of the old superstitions about the Famine. Once a year he would break bread off the jamb of the door while reciting an Irish prayer called 'Fograim an Ghorta' which he took with him from his native West Kerry which, roughly translated, began: 'I banish the Famine forever from my door, tonight and every night with the help of God.'

On other days in West Kerry I just sat in Begley's pub and gazed out at the harbour where the fishing boats bobbed in the distance and on a clear day the locals told visiting Yanks you could see Boston if you really tried – and some even went outside to look. This was one of the last parishes before America and the townland was full of stories of those who had emigrated there. The back streets of Boston or the boroughs of New York were more familiar to them than many of the finest streets in Dublin, their capital. At a dance one night, a girl caught my American inflection and asked me what part of the States I was in, so used was she to having returned emigrants chat her up. It was the first time I became conscious of the many Americanisms I had picked up. One local told me that as soon as I left my money on the counter after buying a drink it was clear I was from over there, even if they never spoke a word to me. Years later, in a strange ritual of transference, everyone in Ireland was leaving their money on the counter as they drank, learned no doubt from returning emigrants.

At night as I walked from the pubs back to the bed and breakfast where I was staying, I could feel the looming presence of the great mountains that act as natural barriers to the rest of the world in that part of Ireland. It was because of them that the Irish language survived, as the foreigners found it so hard to gain a foothold. I could feel, rather than see, Eagle Mountain to my right, and off in the darkness, Mount Brandon, where St Brendan supposedly planned his sea voyage to America. I found the area enormously charged. I loved to hear the Irish language spoken and when I engaged young women in the local bars in Irish I found it an incredibly sensual experience. Two of my brothers came down to visit and we spent a hectic few days travelling around the Gaeltacht and out as far as the Blasket islands, some miles off the coast, where the bare, ruined buildings of the community that abandoned the island in the 1950s still survive.

Chapter 24

A TEXAS FRIEND IN NEED

Back in California, seemingly a million miles from West Kerry, I was encountering more problems. The newspaper, thanks to an obliging bank manager, stuttered from one loan to another. I had one friend in my hour of need, who invested $10,000 in the newspaper, a Texan named Jim Delaney, who was a dead ringer for John Wayne. Jim was almost too good to be true: a wealthy developer who, relatively late in his life, had developed a passion for all things Irish. He founded an organisation called the Irish American Unity Conference, which, in retrospect, was a forerunner of the kind of intelligent and committed Irish organisations that transformed the Irish American scene in the 1990s. I had given Jim significant publicity in Ireland and America through my stories about him and, on St Patrick's Day 1984, he invited me down to San Antonio, Texas, where he lived. On my first day there, he took me to see the site of The Alamo and it was deeply affecting to see the Irish tricolour flying proudly at the site where thirty-three Irish Americans, including Davy Crockett, fell. The Alamo is perhaps the most famous battle in American history when 189 men faced the Mexican Army of over 4,000 and held them at bay for weeks.

San Antonio is an untypical Texas city. The San Antonio River winds its way through the city, splitting it in two, and the beautiful river walk would equal anything one could see in Europe. I met Henry Cisneros, the mayor of San Antonio, then a promising Hispanic politician, who later became a member of President Clinton's cabinet before resigning over the fallout from a long time affair he had. He discussed Irish patriot Robert Emmett with me for over half an hour and proudly showed me Emmett's portrait in his office. He was just one of several Texans I met who had a knowledge and sense of Irish history that was truly impressive.

After St Patrick's Day, I travelled to Dallas where an Irish festival was being held. I experienced one of the most remarkable moments of my time in America when seated at the Makem and Clancy concert during the festival. Behind me, I heard several people conversing in what I was sure was Irish. I turned around and began talking to them. It transpired that they were out and out Texans for several generations and that the language they were speaking was not Gaelic but an Irish form of the gypsy dialect. I listened, fascinated, as they told me they were descended from Irish gypsies who had gone to Newfoundland in Canada over a century before, and had eventually made their way to Texas. Generations later, their children, though by now widely scattered, retained the language and spoke it amongst each other.

As my financial state in California showed no signs of improving, I finally decided I was going to move to New York. Two events sealed my determination. The first was a Christmas day I spent alone in the most beautiful yet loneliest city in the world. Midway through the meal I became aware of how profoundly I missed home, hearth and family. Even Ireland in midwinter, with gales blowing, was more attractive to me. At that moment, I realised that I needed to be closer to Ireland, still 6000 miles away. My resolve to move east was firmed up shortly after. One Friday, when I came home after spending almost 24 hours at my printers, putting out an issue essentially single handedly, I dragged myself down to cash my cheque at the local bank because I had another weekend planned away in the Gold Country. To my horror, the teller told me the account was overdrawn and there would be no funds available to help me.

At that moment, everything I had done to keep the show on the road seemed useless. No matter how hard we all worked, there seemed no chance whatever that we would ever turn a profit. It was clear that the incessant cash crunch was beginning to impact my relationship with Tom as he found himself more and more subsidising the newspaper from the painting business. During this time I had talked several times to Brendan Mac Lua, founder of the *Irish Post* newspaper in England, the leading Irish emigrant paper in the world. He had encouraged me at key times and now I asked him if he would subsidise to some extent a move to New York to start an Irish American magazine. After some hesitation he agreed to loan me $40,000, a fortune for me at the time. I soon began putting a plan in place to move east.

Chapter 25

GO EAST YOUNG MAN

I left San Francisco on a grey, overcast day in April 1985. I said goodbye to my trim little two-bedroom house in the Sunset district, to my cat Tinker and to my girlfriend Patricia who was joining me later. As I pulled away from the house in my old brown Oldsmobile I was aware of a great sadness mixed in with excitement about the future ahead. I had only been to New York once, for a dinner held for the Irish Prime Minister. I had immediately fallen in love with the city, however. Perhaps because of my small town upbringing and my close family, I always loved the feeling of anonymity large cities had, and you didn't come more anonymous than in New York. It was while walking along near Central Park with Patricia on that first visit that the idea of a New York Irish magazine first struck me. I picked up an Italian American publication called *Attenzione* and was immediately struck by the opportunity to do the same with an Irish American product. I would miss California, though – the fact that in seven years there I had never to wear an overcoat or worry too much about the weather, the fact that I had made so many close friends that I would now leave behind, the fact that it was in the city by the bay that I had launched my first business and career.

I had $10,000 in my pocket, the proceeds from the sale of my half of the newspaper to my partner Tom. We had ended up at odds with each other, inevitably perhaps, given the crushing pressure of trying to keep a small company alive in the teeth of huge obstacles. Many years later we would talk and become friendly again. As San Francisco slipped away I faced some tough realities. I had no place to live in New York, nor did I have any office space; the city was a giant question mark to me and I was starting all over again from scratch. I also had no knowledge of the city apart from that one trip there. I was going to have to get up to speed very fast. For the first ten days I stayed in a hotel called the Pickwick Arms which had been recommended by several friends. It was small but functional and I was close to the Irish strip – the bars of Second Avenue where much of the Irish activity took place. But it was not the city I knew in America and it was incredibly lonely. Each night I would return to the cramped hotel room and call friends or Patricia in San Francisco, expressing enormous doubts that I had done the right thing. I remember vividly making the first calls about the magazine to potential advertisers and clients and getting a universally puzzled response.

'You're starting a what?'

'A magazine.'

'Oh, I haven't seen an Irish one of those.'

'I know, but it is time there was.'

The *Irish Echo* was the leading Irish newspaper in New York and essentially their only frame of reference, so I understood their reaction. There had never to my knowledge been the kind of glossy magazine for Irish Americans that I had planned. Also, I was a complete unknown in New York. San Francisco might as well have been on the moon as far as any achievements there were concerned. Soon after I arrived, one of my few contacts in New York – Bill Burke, a banker friend – held a lunch for me with some Irish American leaders. When I see the photos now I can't help but laugh. I am still in full California mode: long hair, straggly beard, waistcoat and boots. All the Irish American leaders are sober and suited and gazing with ill-disguised curiosity at this West Coast apparition. I wonder what they were saying after I left.

New Yorkers have very specific opinions of where they stand in the great scheme of things. A few years later, when I was better known, I started a newspaper to compete with the *Irish Echo* and there was an immediate understanding of the task we were undertaking because the frame of reference was there. On the living front, I was luckier. I sublet a two-bedroom apartment from an advertisement in the *Village Voice* near the Brooklyn Heights area, not far over the Brooklyn Bridge. I persuaded Sheenagh O'Rourke, who had been the best advertising director I had on *The Irishman,* to come back from Ireland to take the job with the fledgling company. She could stay in the second bedroom for now before finding her own place. On office space we were ripped off. I answered an ad in the *New York Times* for what seemed like a very reasonable space near midtown. The man we met showed off the finely polished floors, the airy windows and the beautiful lobby entrance. Patricia, who had joined me by then, and I took it on the spot. He asked for a deposit of $3,000 by the next day, and I duly rushed it down to him in the morning. It was the last I would ever see of it or him. I had fallen for a classic New York scam, where he had somehow obtained the keys for the space, passed himself off as a broker and probably 'rented' the same space half a dozen times to other gullible marks. Strangely enough, he had given me his correct business card, and I reported him to the District Attorney's office, where I got brushed off by an Assistant DA who looked young enough to be in High School. I was incensed at what the scammer had done and still am to this day. Nothing gets me angrier than someone taking advantage of someone new to town. For years afterwards Patricia would call him and berate him a few times a year, and he was always apologetic.

Meanwhile, back at the magazine, which we decided to call *Irish America* because it was the most obvious name, we had begun our uphill climb. Slowly but surely we began to find our feet in New York. However, our entire future would depend on a direct mail shot for the magazine. Throughout that first summer in New York, we worked day and night on getting lists and framing the direct mail piece. I was operating purely on a gut instinct that there was market out there for our publication, that people were tired of the shamrocks and green beer image which seemed to define Irish Americans for so many. I felt it was time for a profound change and I just hoped that I was right. We had simply no money for market research. We sent solicitations to over 250,000 Irish Americans, and if that had failed, our $20,000 or so would have gone down with it. It was a long, hot summer, made worse by the fact that there was no central air conditioning in the sublet, merely a few fans that re-circulated warm air. Many nights I lay awake, dreaming of a cool San Francisco evening, and wondering what on earth I had done by moving to this strange town. But New York energised all of us, too. We were at our best in planning the new publication. The day that Sheenagh came back from Allied Irish Banks having sold her first advertisement we broke out the champagne and cake. Then, when the first direct mail responses started to trickle in we were at Grand Central Post Office first thing every morning to see how were faring.

The news was very good. We were pulling about three and a half per cent, very high for a direct mail shot. It was clear we had struck a deep chord with up to 10,000 Irish Americans across the States. Each day we would arrive back with the bulging mail sacks and transcribe the names and addresses laboriously into our files. Each subscription was a labour of love, however; our dream was unfolding before our eyes. We would be staying in New York, not limping back to California after all. I had some mixed feelings about that.

The first issue of *Irish America* came rolling off the presses on 5 November 1985. We were in Lancaster, Pennsylvania – Amish country

– at the printers to see it come hot from the presses. That night, we officially launched the magazine at the Halloran House Hotel in Manhattan. We had good friends in from Ireland and California and it was a
festive occasion. Our English-based benefactor, Brendan Mac Lua, also
came over for the first night. It was a proud occasion for all of us – the
first ever Irish American magazine, as far as we could determine. A
week or so later, the initial euphoria had died down and we knew we
were facing a tough battle to put out a second issue as successful as
our first. It was a hard time for everyone. I was drinking too much, a
function of the need to wine and dine potential advertisers, as well as
my own fondness for it. Worse, Patricia and I had left Brooklyn and
moved into a tiny one-bedroom apartment on the West Side of Manhattan, at 54th and Eighth, which proved a huge mistake.

Again, it was New York inexperience. We never factored in the
noise from the busy Eight Avenue which the apartment overlooked.
Every night was like Times Square as traffic roared by. Even on Christmas Day there was little respite. Over time, it entered every membrane
of your brain. You learned to time the deep-throated roar of the buses
as they steamed up the avenue, their brakes screeching as they
stopped outside the apartment. Your mind became a medley of different horns blaring, exhausts crackling and above all, the noise from the
construction crews who always seemed to be repairing one part or
another of the road. It was a cacophony of sound. Even the deepest
sleeper had to have problems in this neighbourhood.

I would stand and watch the traffic at four in the morning. Sleep
became a remembered pleasure. I suffered dreadfully, having always
been able to shut my eyes no matter where in the world I landed. But I
soon learned that I needed near total silence to do so. The apartment
on Eight Avenue was my single worst mistake in America. To this day,
that easy passage from bed to merciful sleep has eluded me. The lack
of sleep, the drinking and the pressure of the job was beginning to

take a toll. Patricia, too, seemed preoccupied, driven by the same awful combination of sleeplessness and pressure to keep the fledgling magazine going. She missed her family in San Francisco terribly and I realised I had taken her away from a life so relaxed and laid back that it seemed criminal now to be shoehorned into a tiny apartment on the second floor of a building that overlooked one of New York's busiest avenues. Patricia and I had got married very soon after we made the move to New York. It was a small affair, just the two of us, but that was the way we wanted it. We had been through a lot together with the start-up of the magazine; now things were about to get even worse.

Chapter 26

INTO THE DARKNESS

My depression began with a series of pains and shortness of breath for which the doctor could find no physical reason. Despite exhaustive tests that showed up nothing, I was certain that I was suffering from some terminal illness. A dark, almost impenetrable gloom settled over me. The only way I could relieve it was to drink myself into a stupour, which I often did several nights a week. But when I awoke it was even worse than the day before. Later, I understood that, of course, alcohol fuels a depression, and far from helping, makes it worse. It is hard to explain what a profound depression can do to a person. It gnaws at the centre of your being to the point where horizons in every direction are dark and no sun breaks through. When it continues day after day it can leave you feeling the most extraordinary sense of helplessness.

In my case it took a physical form where I seriously doubted I could even get up, while walking was an arduous task. After a few weeks of this you wish yourself oblivious. Days were passed in a haze, desperately trying to make it through to the evening and the blessed thought of being able to lie down in a bed. Then, of course, there was the awful din of the traffic which made a full night's sleep impossible. Lying there, every ache and pain was hugely magnified to the point where I convinced myself I was coming down with cancer or some truly terrifying disease. Repeated visits to different doctors who assured me such was not the case failed to change my conviction that I was dying. The awful, despairing feeling of a driving depression in full flight is difficult to describe to anyone who hasn't experienced it. Night after night of lying awake, and then, the following morning, trying to rouse myself for the day and getting the magazine out while dealing with the leaden weight of hopelessness. Years later I read *Darkness Visible*, the extraordinary work on his depression by author William Styron, and it truly resonated with me. In the Irish culture, depression used to be regarded with suspicion as a made-up illness, but I have learned firsthand how genuinely devastating it can be. My work, and my relationship, of course, suffered badly. I was withdrawn and unreachable and seemed to stay that way for months. There was one awful night when Patricia did not come home. I went down to the office thinking she might be working late. In the elevator I set off the alarm and the door would not open. Eventually the owner came and released me. I went home and paced the floor until there was almost a trough in it. I called the police and gazed pleadingly at the apartment door for hours. The cops told me that they could not do anything until it was confirmed that she was missing. At 8am she called. She told me she had left a note that she was staying in a hotel and that she just had to have one night out of the apartment to sleep. I had completely missed it. I felt worse than ever. No doubt my depression helped end our marriage. That and the dramatic shift from California to New York pulled us apart. The break-up was done quietly, as we both preferred it, and we continued to work very well together. We had invested money, time and our lives in the magazine and wanted desperately for it to succeed.

Health-wise, things finally came to a head one day when walking down Second Avenue. I did not trust myself to keep on going and several times felt on the verge of collapsing. I seemed to be trapped inside some dark glass and could not properly comprehend what was going on around me. I didn't trust my feet to carry me and the ground seemed unsteady. I was in a cold sweat and was convinced that people were noticing me. The line from the Pink Floyd song pounded in my head: 'There's someone in my head and it's not me'. Anything would be better than this, I thought. I had finally hit bottom and it brought about salvation. I went to my doctor, Kevin Cahill, and told him I could not go on. He had been worried about me and recommended that a psychiatrist colleague see me right away.

That was how I met Dr Mortimer Shapiro. He was a wonderful old Jewish doctor with a shock of white hair, a beard and a red Ferrari coupe with which he drove his neighbours to distraction. When asked, he told them it was his grandson's, though he had no children. His office was on the Upper East Side, and, as luck would have it, the Irish doorman knew me well. I could see by his questioning stare that he was wondering what the hell an Irish lad was doing going to see some kind of shrink. Shapiro's office was on a ground floor, dark and intimate with only a small desk light. On the floor, rather incongruously, was a tiger skin. I learnt later that in his spare time he was a big game hunter in Africa. It was one of many surprises he had for me.

On the first day he met me, he carefully noted my symptoms and told me the problem was very likely Catholic guilt. I was very sceptical, but the more I discussed it with him, the more I became convinced that he was right. As he took me through the early years of my life, it all fell into place. He was, he said, 'shining a light on the back of my head' and slowly but surely the light pierced the dark and gloom. He asked me to retrace one of the most traumatic days of my young life, to pick a violent incident that still lingered with me all these years later. I lay on the couch and he turned the lights down lower. He stayed seated behind his desk as the memories came flooding back.

'I was late,' I told Shapiro, as I relived the experience. 'The large clock over the door into the school read 9.15....'

I was supposed to be there by nine but a desperate attempt to finish a math paper before I made it in had forced me to run late. It was cold, bitterly so, the frost-topped pavements were slippery and the biting wind of an Irish winter's day swept across the townland. I shivered as I walked, not just because of the cold but what I could be facing because I was late. There was still time, though, I thought, if I sneaked in the back entrance, to slip into class and avoid the headmaster, a Christian Brother who often patrolled the corridors waiting for late-comers. He scared me. I never learned his first name, as everyone called him 'Gog', a colloquial term for an egg. It was not hard to see why. His bald, completely hairless pate dominated his face. It was as smooth as a baby's backside and occasionally he would rub his hands over his scalp as if looking for that stray errant hair that might be left. He was the principal and his remit strayed far beyond the schoolmas-terly duties. He was essentially the enforcer, the man who made sure the rules were kept. He made up those rules, usually in a totally capri-cious and arbitrary manner. They changed from day to day, from boy to boy.

His word was law and some of the others teachers were as afraid of him as the boys were. If he was smiling, which was rare, they were smiling too. If his face was like thunder, they tried to shelter from the storm. He was whip thin, a bag of bones really. He prowled rather than walked the corridor, always on the lookout for some likely prey. You dare not be late, wear hair oil, chew gum, have laces untied, a dirty shirt or any number of indiscretions. Sometimes it didn't matter whether you had done something or not. He just wanted to hit you. Everyone was wary of him. He was the boss. He was a sadistic bastard. He had the reputation of being a bully who picked on the weaker boys in the classes and delighted in thumping them around the classroom.

He usually used some made up pretext to do it – a misspelt word or a math problem gone wrong. He seemed to glory in spotting the mistakes and petrifying some child half his size. The groans that went up when a class found out that he would be one of their teachers in a new term were loud. No one wanted him. He seemed to know it. He was never my teacher so I had avoided him up to this point. I had caught him glaring at me once or twice during recess but had thought little of it – his permanent feature was that scowl and glare and a look of sheer hatred. He was a misanthrope. He had lost his humanity somewhere along the line.

Like thousands of other boys of his era, he was probably forced into the brotherhood in his early teens. Cut off from normal life, only in the company of other young men, he developed a sour and twisted personality. In the Brothers any kind of physical expression or acknowledgement of sexuality would have been utterly prohibited. Impure thoughts were to be confessed. The natural development of the body was to be hidden and obsessed about in silence. There was nothing natural about his life, or eventually about him. By the time he came to our school he was an embittered man of uncertain age – his bald pate made him look older. There were many rumours about him, mainly about his drinking. One rumour alleged that he had been found unconscious in the men's room of local hotel, that he had been seen staggering and falling after emerging from a pub downtown. Such rumours took flight among thirteen-year-old boys like me, fuelled by the fear he evinced everywhere he walked.

This was my adversary this morning. I didn't know if he was on the prowl or not, merely that I had to somehow slip in the back door and walk the thirty or so steps to my classroom. I was perhaps a little too relaxed. I had pulled off this late stunt several times before. I would probably get a talking to from the brother whose class I was late for, but he was no sadist, rather a gentle soul, my English teacher, Brother Nolan.

School photo,
aged 10, in
Drogheda CBS.

Above: Graduation day from University College Dublin in 1977 with sister Triona, mother Kathleen and father Donal.

Below: Hurling days, with the San Francisco Gaels in 1978.

Above: With partner Tom McDonagh (on right) during my days as co-boss of Sundance Painting in San Francisco.

Right top: My first meeting with Senator Edward Kennedy in 1980 at a Democratic Party fundraiser.

Right bottom: In my San Francisco apartment in the early 1980s.

Above: On the presses, literally, with the *Irish Voice* in the early days.

Below: A moment in history. Gerry Adams (far left) at the Waldorf Astoria during his historic visit in February 1994. John Hume (third from left), who did so much to achieve peace in Northern Ireland, is ignored by the media.

Above: With Tony O'Reilly, the late Niall Millar, head of Tourism Ireland, and O'Reilly's wife, Chryss Goulandris, at an *Irish America* Magazine Top 100 event in 1994.

Below: At Ardmore Studios in Wicklow in 1994 with actor Mel Gibson during the filming of *Braveheart*. A group of Irish American business leaders, led by Don Keough (third from left), president of Coca Cola, had come to Ireland. I am directly behind Gibson.

Above: With New York Mayor Rudy Giuliani and my brother, Fergus O'Dowd, TD on the set of the Adrian Flannelly show.

Below: The family got together when *Irish America* magazine hosted President Clinton at the Plaza Hotel in 1996 as Irish American of the Year. From left: Agatha Taylor, cousin, wife Debbie, sister Triona, me, mother Kathleen, brother Donal, sister Orlaith and her husband Ciaran Staunton.

Above: With Hillary Clinton, President Clinton and my wife, Debbie, at the White House, Christmas 1999.

Below: With Hillary and Bill, Debbie and our daughter Alana at a fundraiser we hosted in March 2000.

Above: With Hillary at an event in 2007.
Left: Playing snowman with Alana at our home in Syosset, New York in 2004.
Below: With British Prime Minister Tony Blair after a discussion with him on Northern Ireland in New York in 2007.

I knew the routine. Slip in the door, keep to the left so that someone at the far end of the hall could not see round the corner, slide along that wall, walking softly … gently does it … safe so far, now only a few yards to go, the door handle on the classroom so close, so inviting.

'O'Dowd!'

It was a snarl rather than a shout. My mind froze. I looked up and saw a frenzied 'Gog'. He ran down the corridor, a swishing bundle of black robes topped by a slowly foaming mouth and reddening face. He was a truly scary sight, looking to me like a large mad dog. He didn't stop when he reached me, and as we collided, his wiry frame pushed me back against the wall. Dimly, I felt my head crack against it and for a moment I felt dizzy and weak. He saw my knees buckle and grabbed my cheeks with both hands and pulled me upright.

'You're late,' he hissed, spittle hitting me on the face.

I could feel my cheeks redden. I struggled a little but he just grabbed me harder. His hand came up and struck me flush across the face. He grabbed my lapels and pulled me away from the walls. Then he balled his hand in a fist and began punching me, rocking me backwards. He forced me back along the corridor as I put my hands to my face to pro-tect myself. He brushed them aside and began punching me harder, first his right fist, then his left.

'You're late, and you were playing soccer in the football field,' he hissed through clenched teeth.

The reference to soccer was true. I had, indeed, played soccer in the playing field, which was the equivalent of a mortal sin at the time, as soccer was banned because it was a 'British game'. I remembered the Saturday afternoon we had played soccer, about a dozen of us. We put down two coats as goalposts at either end and played six a side. We knew no Brothers went near the field on Saturday so we were safe – or thought we were. I wondered who had snitched on me to 'Gog'. I knew he had spies throughout the school. It didn't bear thinking about that one of my playmates that day had shopped all the other players.

'Playing soccer, and your father a great Irishman,' he hissed, still punching me.

That was another sore point with him. My father was known for his love of the Irish language and his strong political convictions about a united Ireland. Now here was his son caught playing 'the British game', what a perfect opportunity to wreak revenge on my father's behalf. He had pummeled me around the corner. The long, empty school corridor yawned in front of me. He drove me down it like a man demented, his fists knocking me on the chest and on my face. I was bright red and burning now, vainly trying to defend myself. A door opened along the corridor and another Christian Brother emerged. He saw the beating and quickly withdrew behind the door and slammed it shut. He would see no evil. We had, mercifully, reached the end of the corridor by now and there was nowhere else for him to beat me. He grabbed my hair and pulled my face close to his, so close I could smell the bad breath.

'O'Dowd, you will never make anything of yourself. Mark my words; you're a useless idiot, someone who will cause trouble for your parents the rest of your life.'

Incongruously, he smiled at me and then walked away. It was almost a leer, I thought, a message that he had sated himself in beating me. In hindsight, and with the shocking revelations that have since surfaced about clerical sexual abuse, I wonder if he took pleasure in beating up barely teenage kids. I feel that there was probably a large sexual element in such cruelty. He was at a place and a life where sexuality and violence intersected, and young boys were unwilling vessels, as later became clear, for the worst kind of child abuse. Suffice to say, I was not surprised when the dam burst years later and the horrific tales of this period came to light.

Atonement by suffering was a fair comment on the Ireland I grew up in. There were many heavy beatings administered by Christian Brothers and others. There was a relentless moral landscape that punished even the smallest indiscretions unmercifully. We lived in fear of this all-punishing God who would damn us to Hellfire if we did not follow the one and true path, no and ifs or buts. But there were also many fine religious like Brother Nolan who inspired me to be a writer. He had us study American literature: Walt Whitman, Hemingway etc. He opened the imagination as only the best teachers can.

I later spent a year at Gormanston College and found the Franciscans caring in a way I almost found hard to accept.

⚜

The punishing, not the loving God, was the source of my troubles, Shapiro explained. The doctrine had been set in concrete in my brain. Guilt and shame were outgrowths of it, as was low self-esteem. Getting it all out of my head was a major excavation job, he told me, the equivalent of taking a jackhammer to a slab of concrete. On my twice-weekly visits over the following months, he slowly but surely succeeded in recasting a large part of me, giving me new self-esteem and knowledge about myself that I had never possessed.

Shapiro was a contrarian, utterly atheistic himself, who examined every perceived truth and dismissed most of them, and he was hard on me, constantly probing my certainties and peeling away layer after layer of self deception. It was the healthiest intellectual exercise of my life. I looked forward immensely to our sessions as he worked hard to rearrange me until I was fully sane again.

The fact that he succeeded was a massive surprise to me. Suddenly, the drinking, the covering up, the small lies and the massive insecurity all hit home and seemed such obvious cop outs to me. I realised why I had gone practically nuts when I first went to college on finding the first vestige of freedom after the oppressive moral climate of my upbringing. The drinking, the partying and the huge insecurities about

163

myself were framed in a different context.

I felt as if a giant key had been turned on a door and I was able to enter a completely different space. For the first time, I was able to close the door, albeit softly at first, on so much that had gone wrong for me and put it behind me.

Chapter 27

A MAN OF TWO COUNTRIES

T he depression had forced me to a crossroads. I was a man of two countries, one the land of my birth which I still hankered after, and yet somehow rejected. The other was my adopted home of the United States where I was happy but never fully a part, forever camped outside the mainstream. An immigrant is a stranger in both cultures. When I returned to Ireland on vacations it had all changed, still recognisable enough for me to be at home, yet an outsider there. When I returned to the US I was from somewhere else, no matter how much I tried to fit in. Emigration forces you to think about who you are but also to regret who you might have been if you had stayed behind. Such thoughts breed a strange loneliness at times, as if you have a separate self that remained when you came over. The collision of the two realities has been the cause of much of the depression, drinking and drug use for millions of Irish emigrants over the years. No country in the western world has exported so many of its people, so it is hardly surprising that displacement sometimes causes major problems. Ralph McTell, observing Irish emigrants in London many years ago, caught it very well in lines from his moving ballad 'From Clare to Here' about the pain of forced migration.

'The only time I feel all right is when I'm into drinking. It sort of eases the pain of it and levels out my thinking.'

After my bout of depression, I thought long and hard about returning to Ireland, even though I was in the throes of a new business venture in New York. Somehow, the notion of home and hearth and family was increasingly attractive. The sadness in the eyes of my mother every time I left her to return to America impacted me deeply. I learned to close the door softly when I left, to ease the pain she felt a little. I know she feared each time I would never return. I went so far as to apply for a job in Ireland, running the news magazine *Magill*. For weeks my head was full of ideas and plans for living at home and jumping into the mainstream. However, no call came for an interview and I realised I was just too long out of the country to be considered for the job. I received a form letter thanking me for my interest. It was one of the hottest days in a particularly grim New York summer. Despite the heat, I felt myself blush with embarrassment. To not even get an interview was a real kick in the pants.

But that failed job application steadied me and I realised more and more that my future lay in the US. It all crystalised for me on a plane flight back from Ireland soon after. The lights of New York had just hove into view off the right side of the plane and for the first time ever I thought, 'I'm home now'. It was an involuntary thought. It was the moment, after almost a decade in America, that something fundamental had changed in my psyche. Ireland was no longer home. I had reached the tipping point. Yes, there would always be special places there, especially in Ballydavid, in Kerry, just a few miles from where my father was born and where I would later purchase a small cottage for the then princely sum of $18,000. My father, his father and his grandfather had walked those roads and I felt enormously comforted by the fact that I could walk the same roads now. I also loved that I could view the same incomparable vista of sweeping mountains and dashing sea, linger over a sunset out by the Blasket Islands like they had done and contemplate the beauty of this most western outpost of Europe. But those would be stolen moments from now on. It was no longer practical to imagine that my life could be spent there.

New York and America was home. *Irish America* magazine was going very well. We had tapped into a ready market among the 44 million Americans of Irish descent. We were helped greatly when Maureen Dowd, later a top columnist at the *New York Times*, wrote a front page article about us, saying we signalled a rebirth of Irish American pride in heritage. Both Maureen and Jim Dwyer, also a Pulitzer-winning writer for the *New York Times,* were constantly helpful to us as we started our publishing life in New York and both remain firm friends today. Another soldier in our cause was radio host Adrian Flannelly from Mayo, who regularly featured me in the critical beginning years.

Though we were only a handful of people, four in all, working on it, the magazine came to exert an influence far beyond its circulation numbers, which had settled at around 50,000. Suddenly I found that my own influence was becoming significant. It was flattering. Politicians courted us, newspapers, especially in Ireland, picked up our stories, and our views on issues such as Northern Ireland suddenly attracted major interest. Our success was based on the fact that we published several lists, such as the Top 100 Irish Americans, that were very popular. Each March we hosted a black tie dinner at the Plaza Hotel in New York honouring our Irish American of the year. Over the years, people such as Senator Edward Kennedy, President Bill Clinton and Gregory Peck accepted our award, as did Hillary Clinton, Jean Kennedy Smith, who became a forceful ambassador to Ireland, and actress Maureen O'Hara. The event became a centrepiece of Irish celebrations around St Patrick's Day, received widespread television and newspaper coverage, and became well known in Ireland after several Irish Prime Ministers also attended. The magazine was becoming very widely known.

I also became close to some remarkable people who shaped my life. I found top American businessmen and women to be fascinating –

much more grounded and real in outlook than many politicians, who spent an inordinate amount of time wondering where the next move was and how you might help them get there. Business leaders were more pragmatic and focused. Most were Republicans; the best ones, as well as being extraordinary leaders, were deeply involved in philanthropy and giving back. The lesson from the best Americans I knew was never to forget where you came from or to what you owed your good fortune. Don Keough exemplified that to me.

At the time that I walked into his office in Atlanta in 1991 to interview him he was President of Coca Cola. He looked at me quizzically, smiled and said, 'Where have you been'? It was his way of saying he was ready to talk about his Irish heritage which began when his great grandfather, Michael Keough, left Wexford around the same time as the Kennedys in the famine times. No one had ever asked him about it until we did at *Irish America* magazine.

Keough grew up in the Great Depression during which time his family lost their farm when it burned down. From such unpromising beginnings, he began an incredible journey that ended as top man in the world's best-known company. The Iowa farm boy, homeless for a period in the Depression, had made it very big.

But he never forgot where he came from or who he was. He was also the first Irish Catholic to make it to the top of Coca Cola and his heritage was deeply important to him. After our interview he invited me to stay in touch and we have been best friends ever since.

He exemplified all that was best about America and I learned a tremendous amount from him. Keough also brought Warren Buffet and Bill Gates to Ireland to try and help with economic development there and I'm sure had a large say in the siting of the Coca Coal plant in Ireland. He had an extraordinary way of accomplishing what he wanted. He never cajoled or threatened, or seemed to lose his temper, but somehow it always got done in that easy Irish way of his. He was a wonderful family man as well, with six kids and almost a score of grandchildren. I was very happy to work with him on his book *The Ten Commandments for Business Failure*, a title typical of Keough's no-nonsense approach, which reached the *New York Times* business best seller list.

Warren Buffet, the legendary stock trader from Nebraska, was one of Keough's best friends. The two men had lived in the same street in Omaha for several years, and Johnny Carson of the 'Tonight Show' fame was also a near neighbour. Keough had told me that he couldn't quite figure out what Buffet was up to back in the Sixties, and when Warren came over one night and suggested that Don might invest in his new company, Don passed. It was a mistake that cost him hundreds of millions, as Buffett was starting up the forerunner of Berkshire Hathaway, which became the premier investment stock on the US stock market. Nonetheless the two became firm friends.

Don suggested I meet Warren Buffet, and I gladly took up the idea. I arrived at his decidedly underwhelming downtown office in Omaha. There was a lone security guard on the entrance to the building and he hardly cast me a glance. I thought about all the fabulously wealthy people who surround themselves with security and scurrying employees. Buffet had none of that. As it turned out, we actually met in the bathroom. I was at the urinal when the door opened and the richest man in the world was suddenly standing beside me. He chatted like I was a long time acquaintance.

His office was staffed by only twelve people, and his inner sanctum was an unremarkable space with no view worth talking about or any fancy paintings on the wall. I asked him what it felt like to be the richest man in the world. 'I don't think about it,' he retorted simply. And I believed him. There was no computer on his desk, no fax, no cell phone, just an old-fashioned dial tone phone, which never rang while we talked for almost two hours.

I often think of men like Buffett and billionaire Charles Feeney when I find people trying to impress me with their wealth and fortune. Both men have kept in touch with their inner core, accepted the simplicity of life, the need for old friends, and a lack of pretension. It is a rare gift in a world rife with narcissism and obsession with image.

Like Don Keough, Denis Kelleher had come from tough times, but in his case it was the little village of Gneeveguilla near Killarney. A shoe-makers' son, he left at eighteen for America in the late Fifties and never looked back. He began work as a messenger boy on Wall Street but soon figured out the business there as well as anyone on the street. His company, Wall Street Access, was eventually valued at over a billion dollars, not bad for a Kerry emigrant who left with nothing but spare change in his pocket.

Denis too, was a rock of advice on very many occasions. Like Keough, he was a quiet philanthropist who gave many millions away to good causes but never sought the limelight. I was heavily influenced in both business dealings and in life itself by both men.

Dr Kevin Cahill was not a businessman but a great doctor who had treated Pope John Paul 11 after he was shot and Ronald Reagan when he was president. Originally from the Bronx and of Kerry ancestry, he was an incredible humanitarian who spent many years in Africa and South America battling on the front line against Third World diseases. I got to know him in his capacity as Director General of the American Irish Historical Society which owned a stunning Fifth Avenue building opposite the Metropolitan Museum and where a treasure trove of Irish American history and scholarship lies in their archives.

Kevin never refused a patient and I sent him many undocumented Irish who had no way of paying. He and another doctor, Paddy Boland, a cancer specialist, originally from Kildare and now a top sur-geon at Sloan Kettering – among the top cancer facilities in the world – did untold good work for Irish people who were unable to pay their bills or afford cost-prohibitive health insurance. Through these men and their example, I learned that giving back should be an important part of my life.

By now I had also stopped drinking, which was no mean feat. I had been considering it for some time, not because I thought I drank too much, but because the hangovers were so potent that I could hardly work the next day. In my business booze was everywhere – at the receptions, the dinners and the gala events. It was far too easy to think I had a god-given right to the free booze which flowed so easily. And it was tough to resist when drinks were being pressed into your hands and were topped up at every opportunity. I was an all-or-nothing drinker. If I started, I rarely stopped until the old familiar buzz was ringing in my head and the pleasant feeling of heightened awareness took over. The problem was that I never stopped at that. Relentlessly I would continue to down the beer until I had become an incoherent version of myself, occasionally ready to pick drunken arguments.

There was an Irish strip on Second Avenue in Manhattan, and every Friday night was a not so solemn procession from Eamon Doran's to the Green Derby, to Joyces. I usually ended up in Joyces, and Philip, the barman, became familiar with my late night meanderings. Oftentimes the barmaids and bartenders from other Irish pubs joined us as the night drew on, as Joyces was known as a late house. Then the singsongs could start, the flirting followed and it was usually dawn by the time I left. I loved Manhattan in the early morning, the dramatic silhouettes of the tall buildings against the brightening sky, the sleeping city about to stir itself awake, stopping for breakfast in one of the many coffee shops, shooting the breeze until the booze or tiredness finally wore me down. I was becoming addicted to the life-style. There were nights, however, when I did not want to touch the stuff and survived quite easily without it. I also rarely drank during the day or when I had been drinking the night before. I played mind games with that, believing that this was a sure indication that I did not have a problem. To this day I don't know if I did or not. Culturally, drinking is a far greater part of the Irish make-up than it is in other countries. For an Irishman I didn't drink that much. For an American I certainly did. I still loved the buzz and the bullshit every Friday night on the Manhattan night scene and wasting away so many hours on nothing important except arguing with the other members of the 'tribe' as we sometimes called ourselves. But it was not a lifestyle I could continue.

It came to a head on the opening day of the baseball season in 1992. I went to the Mets opener and started drinking around mid-morning. The last two innings of the game were seen though a drunken haze. We went back into Manhattan and immediately commenced drinking again. As the day passed, a group of women and their friends from my office came by, celebrating a birthday. Around 11 o'clock that night, I lost all memory of what transpired. I know I made it home at about 5am. I woke at eleven to the sound of a ringing phone. I was mortified by the number of people who called to see if I was alright. Apparently I had made a total idiot of myself. My face was burning with embarrassment the next day. Right there and then I made a vow that I would not drink again, and all these years later I have stuck rigidly to that promise. It didn't take AA, just one bad night too many.

Chapter 28

THE IRISH VOICE

By the mid to late 1980s, the number of young emigrants from Ireland flowing into America increased sharply. It was the return of the bad old times, as the Irish economy floundered and the emigrant plane became the fastest way off the island. It was a troubling development, as just a few years earlier hopes had been high that hard times had been left behind permanently. It was not to be, but the exodus represented an opportunity for us. We realised that the young Irish were poorly served by existing Irish American newspapers, many of which were caught in a time warp. I made the decision to start a new newspaper and to call it the *Irish Voice*, in order to stand in sharp contrast to the leading Irish newspaper, the *Irish Echo*. The new paper would be bright and breezy, would not depend on rewrites from Ireland as the other papers did, but reflect the lives, loves, hopes and dreams of the burgeoning Irish community in New York.

Looking back on the start-up, I was hopelessly optimistic, believing that we could get into profitability in less than a year. Unlike with the magazine, the newspaper was well funded. Jefferson Smurfit, our magazine partner, had put in $1 million but it was still an inadequate amount given the huge start-up costs. In late November 1987, just two years after launching *Irish America*, the *Irish Voice* hit the newsstands. We had worked like dogs over that long hot summer putting the model together. We decided, much to the chagrin of our newsstand consultants, to go with a blue masthead, not green, the colour they seemed to think everything Irish had to be. There were also other major innovations; stories on issues like sex and drugs, where relevant, were to be allowed, and we would follow up on local stories, no matter what the cost. The premier issue led with the first ever survey of Irish undocumented working in New York. This was a story everyone else ignored, as if even talking about such matters would tarnish the wholesome image of the community. We discovered, however, that many of the young immigrants were in dire shape, in deep need of professional services such as counselling, job placement and overall guidance. They also said, overwhelmingly, that they would not go back home because things were so bad there.

It was the third publication I had launched, but also the toughest. Adjusting to a weekly schedule was very difficult and I had greatly underestimated the staff needs and the cost structure in getting it off the ground. After six months we were hopelessly mired. We needed more investors and the future looked bleak. I was working night and day and weekends too, as were many of the staff, and the newspaper was selling well, but we were still in a very deep hole and money was running out. My major investors summoned me back to Ireland to face the music. We met at the Jefferson Smurfit headquarters in Dublin. The big multinational company was Ireland's most successful firm, but this upstart newspaper in New York already looked like it was more trouble than it was worth. A pow-wow of most of the senior officers of the company, including Chairman and Chief Executive Michael Smurfit, was held to discuss the future of the newspaper. It was an unnerving experience. I had been very nervous going in to the meeting to begin with and I soon learned that every hand was against us. The overwhelming consensus was to pull out and effectively shut the newspaper down.

I was having none of it. I had learnt in America that when the pressure came on, you could not yield to managers and professional buck passers. I told them the paper would not shut down under any circumstances, that even if they pulled out they would be replaced, and the decision on whether or not the newspaper could continue was not theirs. They listened in silence. Then Michael Smurfit spoke up. Against the flow of the meeting he suddenly supported me wholeheartedly. He said that, as a founder himself of several companies, he understood what I was trying to do. Suddenly the atmosphere changed dramatically. All the managers nodded in assent, as if the previous conversations had never taken place. It was a valuable lesson in leadership and I was forever indebted to Smurfit for exercising it.

Soon afterwards, the newspaper turned the corner, thanks to a dedicated staff and the addition of a business manager named Ashley Balbirnie from the Smurfit group. He made a profound difference as I began fully to understand my inadequacies on the financial side of the company. The newspaper eventually went from strength to strength, mainly because of one person. Debbie McGoldrick had worked with the *Irish Echo* and I had hired her away from them because she was an immensely talented and hard working editor. She was the child of Irish emigrants, Peggy Ryan from Kerry and Jim McGoldrick from Sligo, and had retained an incredible connection with her roots and Irish heritage.

Her work on the newspaper was extraordinary, including her own column, 'Green Card', an immigration enquiry forum that became the best read article week in and week out. She remains the heart and soul of the newspaper to this day, an incredibly hard worker who has the savvy and skill to keep the newspaper ticking over and profitable even in these very tough times for media.

I liked her so much we fell in love and were married in August of 1996 in Glen Cove, Long Island, near her home town of Syosett. Three years later, on 25 July 1999, our beautiful daughter Alana arrived – the greatest days of my life.

Debbie helped make the *Irish Voice* the successful publication it became, as did Financial Controller Kevin Mangan, who has been with me from the start. And with it came a major degree of influence in Irish America. Politicians sought us out, endorsements were eagerly looked for. We became the benchmark in the community and quite literally, along with the magazine, the voice of the Irish in America. I realised it one night when an ad for David Dinkins, who was running for Mayor of New York, came on television. It touted our endorsement, a very important one by an Irish newspaper for a black candidate. Dinkins went on to win, becoming New York's first black mayor, and it was nice to be a small part of it.

Ironically, we could not publish the biggest story we ever came across. I was sitting in my office in July 1992 when the phone rang. It was a source who wanted to tell me that Ben Dunne, one of Ireland's premier businessmen, had just been arrested in Florida after threatening to jump off a hotel balcony while he was high on drugs and with a call girl. I made enquiries and found out that the story was true, that he had been staying at the Hyatt Regency Grand Cypress in Orlando and had been found in a distraught state on the balcony of his 17th floor hotel room, screaming for help.

My source made one stipulation: *Irish Voice* could not be the ones to publish the story because it would identify him. Reluctantly, I agreed. I called in the then editor of the newspaper, Maura Crowe, who suggested we give it to a journalist she knew in Dublin whose job was on the line in a series of staff cuts at the *Sunday Tribune*. We did, and the *Tribune* had the exclusive. As a result of the arrest, Ben Dunne's personal finances came under investigation and the trail led to the door of leading Irish politicians. The McCracken Tribunal was set up in Ireland when it became clear that payment to politicians had been involved.

One of those politicians was Charles Haughey, and the Dunne episode began his long fall from grace when it was discovered that he had been paid $1.3 million. I knew Haughey and considered him one of the smartest politicians I had ever met, but obviously there was grand corruption there, too. Another politician snared in the story was Michael Lowry, a leading figure in Fine Gael, who was heavily involved with Dunne on a business level. In retrospect, the incident and its exposure may have helped Ben Dunne turn his life around, as he has since succeeded in rehabilitating himself in impressive style.

I have seen many versions of how that story first broke, including erroneous accounts that U2 were staying at the same hotel, but the truth of it is just what I have written.

Chapter 29

TACKLING THE NORTHERN
QUESTION

By now, I had enough stature to be able to exert influence on issues such as illegal immigration and new laws to help the Irish undocumented, and a raft of other areas of importance in the community.

My 'alien' status was also changing. From about 1983 on, I had been accredited as a foreign journalist working in America and eventually got a green card. It was a blessed relief after years on the outside looking in. To this day I have contempt for people who speak out against illegals or try and demonise them. I believe the overwhelming majority of whatever ethnic background are deeply committed people, trying to make better lives for themselves and their families.

Irish Voice was at the heart of the strategy that brought about the Morrison and Donnelly visas, called after Congressman Bruce Morrison and Congressman Brian Donnelly, which allowed tens of thousands of undocumented Irish to get the coveted green card.

There was one issue, however, which had continued to hold my interest and in which I believed the Irish American community needed to play a leading role. Though Northern Ireland was regarded by many as a 'basket case' situation, I had a feeling that Irish America could make all the difference. I was determined to see how far we could go. Northern Ireland had been a constant during my formative years.

Living just twenty-five miles south of the border inevitably meant that the issue impinged on my life. My father was an old style Republican who remembered the War of Independence and had bitter memories of the civil war in his native Kerry also. He sided with De Valera and stayed with him after the split. In the 1930s he had briefly joined a Gaelic nationalist party called Aiseirí, but by the time I was growing up he was safely back in the Fianna Fáil camp. He was an unrepentant united Irelander, and the renewed violence in the North merely pushed him further down that path. It was hard to blame him and that generation. Their families still had memories of the Famine; they had seen the Black and Tans, and later the travesty of partition.

My own political thinking only really began when I left Ireland. But I quickly learnt when I went into the newspaper business that the free speech that journalists and politicians enjoyed in America could not be taken for granted anywhere else in the world. This came home to me forcefully when I met Gerry Adams for the first time in Belfast in 1983 when I interviewed him for my newspaper.

Adams had been elected to the Northern Ireland Assembly in 1982, but was banned from entering Britain until after he was elected as MP – member of the British parliament – for West Belfast, in 1983. Imagine a US state senator being banned from going to Washington from his home state! He was also banned from the airwaves.

The censorship of Sinn Féin's views in general, in my opinion, had tragic consequences, as the lack of sustained information and analysis about the North meant that there was little or no understanding of the situation on the ground there. Some commentators even referred to West Belfast residents as 'the terrorist community'.

Adams, of course, was also not allowed into the United States, and in the era of Reagan/Thatcher cooperation the likelihood of an American audience ever getting to hear or see him seemed hopelessly remote. The view propagated about him by the British back then was as a fanatical terrorist who would stop at nothing to achieve his bloody aims.

But the Gerry Adams I interviewed in 1983 hardly lived up to the British stereotype of a terrorist. He had a very nice line in self deprecatory wit, and, unlike many politicians, was neither pompous nor self-important. He was also very curious in the interview, asking many questions about America, indeed at one point he turned the tables on me, becoming effectively the interviewer as he quizzed me for some twenty minutes on the Irish American dimension, asking where Irish American opinion really stood on the North.

In my introduction to that 1983 interview, I said, 'One could ask the question, does he take himself as seriously as everyone else does?' Having got to know him subsequently, the answer is, no, he doesn't. It is perhaps his most appealing quality. It's a lesson many self-absorbed politicians everywhere could learn.

In the years that followed, I, like many others, kept an eye on his career. I read his book, *The Politics of Irish Freedom,* on a flight back from Ireland in 1986. What was startling to me was the amount of fresh analysis and perspective the book contained on the Northern Ireland issue. It was my first inkling that the overwhelming view that Sinn Féin had little to offer in terms of new thinking was well wide of the mark.

Generally, the Irish establishment and media felt that the North had sunk into a deep well of despond from which it could never be rescued. The combined decades of violence begetting violence and failed political initiatives had left most people worn out and despairing. I remember reading *Uncivil Wars* by Padraig O'Malley around that time, with its ultimate conclusion that all we could do was suffer on as best we could. The lack of critical thinking on the issue was perhaps far more apparent to someone outside than to people stuck in the middle of it.

Perhaps I had become infected with the American 'can do' mentality, but I never believed that the situation was hopeless. History clearly showed that when constitutional nationalism and Irish republicanism stood together and America became involved, remarkable things could happen. Parnell almost used that troika to bring about Home Rule. However, for most of the American media, Northern Ireland was akin to a fly stuck in amber. Nothing ever seemed to change there and the cycle of violence seemed endlessly repetitive.

A few years later, Gerry Adams asked me if he could write a column in the *Irish Voice*. I immediately agreed. After all, I had lauded the American tradition of free speech for long enough. Here was my chance to show that I truly believed in it. For balance, I took on a column which contained contributions from a variety of unionist voices including Gary McMichael of the UDA's political wing, Ian Paisley Junior of the Democratic Unionist Party and Chris McGimpsey of the Ulster Unionist Party. I later helped McMichael write a book based on his columns in *Irish Voice*.

I struck up an easy relationship with Adams, who was always interested in the latest news from America. The closed public image of him seemed ever more at odds to me with the private man, who I found more than willing to listen and learn about where Irish America was heading.

I had been deeply impacted by the Irish hunger strikes of 1981, when ten young Irishmen, led by Bobby Sands, starved themselves to death in pursuit of political status in the Maze prison outside Belfast where they were being held. All were members of the IRA or related factions. Margaret Thatcher denied the men the Special Category Status and rights as political prisoners that they had previously enjoyed, explaining simplistically that it was part of her new criminalisation procedure where 'crime is crime is crime', as if the centuries of political struggle between Ireland and Britain had never happened.

Prior to the hunger strikes, I had thought a lot about the North but never got fully involved in understanding it. Following the deaths of Sands and the others, I found myself incensed that young Irishmen were dying half a world away over an issue that, it seemed to me, could easily have been resolved. There were, I suspect, thousands like me around the world, who never viewed the Northern Irish situation in the same way again. The hunger strikes had brought that change about.

Now the Troubles were costing thousands of lives lost and tens of thousands injured in an area smaller than Connecticut. It was Europe's longest running war and seemingly intractable and insoluble. The IRA, who were fighting for Irish unification after Ireland had been divided in 1921, were involved in a struggle to the death with the British Army who were upholding the status quo for the Unionist majority. The Unionists also had their paramilitaries, the Ulster Volunteer Force (UVF) and the Ulster Defence Association (UDA). In many ways, I found that the Troubles defined me in America. Whenever I met someone new, inevitably the first thing they would ask about was the violence in Ireland. For years I gave cursory answers, but more and more I was forced to ask myself questions about where I really stood on the issue. There was an Irish tendency to emphasise the difficulty rather than to try and solve the question. To many Irish it seemed so intractable that any attempt to do anything about it was doomed. I felt differently. America and my own modest success there had infused me with a spirit of optimism. I came to the realisation that the Irish and British notion of exclusion was almost every bit as damaging as anything the warring parties were doing. As I later wrote in the *Guardian* newspaper, 'The acceptance of violence continuing while a peace strategy is worked out was a critical factor in Sinn Féin joining the Irish process and making it successful.' While that may seem contradictory to some, that was the reality. Appeals to end violence were futile without a thoughtful strategy to bring that violence to an end and replace it with a political process. Simply put, a solution had to be based on inclusion rather than exclusion, bringing the extremes to the middle and making them part of the process, rather than leaving them outside it. I thought Irish America would be a good place to try to get the ball rolling.

Over forty million Americans trace their roots to Ireland and the Northern Irish. The mainstream American media invariably presented them as out of touch with what was happening in Northern Ireland and as clinging to an outmoded and outdated concept of Ireland that relied as much on leprechauns as reality. Not for the first time, I found the stereotype very wide of the mark. The success of my publications was based on taking the real temperature as against the perceived wisdom about Irish Americans. On Northern Ireland there were, of course, the extremists, but there were also a far larger number, including myself, who felt that a dose of American know-how and inclusion politics might work wonders. For us it was not a case of winners or losers, merely of finding a way that both sides could claim enough of a victory to make peace happen.

I had a close friend in the Irish Embassy in Washington. Brendan Scannell was a native of Kerry and had many of the characteristics that people from that country are famed for: shrewdness, a far seeing vision and a no-nonsense sense of himself. I had roomed with Scannell's brother, Gerard, in college in Dublin in many years before. I had cemented my relationship with Brendan by appearing as a 'ringer' for the Department of Foreign Affairs in a few rugby matches they had been involved in. Brendan would call around to our hovel of a flat early on Saturday morning and drag us out to the games, hangover or not. He amply repaid us afterwards with pints and good food as he was earning a decent living and we were penniless students.

Now he was the political counsellor at the Irish embassy and many of the same questions about Northern Ireland had been occupying him. He was trusted implicitly by men like Senator Edward Kennedy and he worked closely with Nancy Soderberg, who was Kennedy's point person on Ireland, and later with her successor, Trina Vargo. Unlike most diplomats before him, Scannell saw that Irish America was not a force to be opposed, but rather a strength that should be harnessed. He was fond of citing the Jewish lobby as an analogy, where a determined group had made themselves indispensable on an issue, and now had superb access to the powers that be. There was also an ambassador in Washington, Dermot Gallagher, who broadly shared that view, as did Sean Ó hUiginn, the head of the Anglo Irish Division in Dublin.

I consulted one other player. Ciaran Staunton, a young Irish immigrant living in Boston, who had an unsurpassed knowledge of and insight into what Sinn Féin and the IRA were thinking from years of contact with them through Republican support groups in America. He was one of the few people I ever met who was able to read the runes when it came to Irish Republicanism. Like Scannell, he was articulate and shrewd, and we had become friends when he volunteered to help launch my newspaper in Boston. Later, he became my brother-in-law, married to my sister Orlaith. Staunton told me he felt there was a major discussion going on within Irish republicanism about their future course of action. There was a definite sense that a small, imperceptible movement was underway. Was there a way that America could get involved that would be helpful? I discussed it at length with both Staunton and Scannell. Scannell suggested we approach Senator Edward Kennedy's office. Kennedy was the Irish chieftain in America and nothing on this issue got through without his approval. He had been muted on the Irish issue for many years, even though I felt his instincts were to speak out more loudly. Initially he had been outspoken. After the Bloody Sunday massacre in Derry in 1970, when fourteen unarmed nationalists were killed by the British Army, he had unleashed a very angry speech which called on the British to get out of

Ireland. However, over the years, the Irish and British governments had succeeded in toning down the rhetoric of leading Irish American figures in their quest to take control of the issue themselves. Kennedy had no choice but to row in behind the governments, even when their policies were plainly not working.But the topic remained very important to him and his staff was razor sharp on the subject, as I found out when I finally made contact with his Foreign Affairs person, Trina Vargo. We met in Boston in 1991 when President Mary Robinson was visiting. After our first conversation, I knew not to expect an easy ride. Vargo was very anti-IRA and their record. I tried to convey that something fundamental might be changing and that her boss should be interested. I knew she had a direct line to the Clinton team via Nancy Soderberg, soon to be the Deputy National Security Advisor and a former Kennedy staffer herself. Soderberg was also formidable and well versed on the topic because of her time with Kennedy. She was writing the Irish statements for Bill Clinton during the 1992 campaign. But she would never accept a phone call or pick up the phone to me. I was still seen as way too Irish Republican and my scheme as harebrained.

It was not at all clear who was going to win the election at that moment in 1991. After the Kuwait war, George Bush looked unbeatable. The Democratic field was being derided as 'the seven dwarves' but both I and diplomat Brendan Scannell had a feeling that the Governor of Arkansas, Bill Clinton, was the most likely of the bunch to make an impact. Scannell was adamant that President George Bush could never deliver anything because he was far too close to the British government. The only chance was to reach out to Clinton, who might be likely to take an interest in the issue and hitch our star to his wagon. Clinton was a smart, moderate Democrat from the south, the only combination that had won the White House for the Democrats since Lyndon Johnson. Another plus, and a big one for us, was that he had

an interest in Ireland from his time in Oxford University at the outbreak of violence and the civil rights movement in Northern Ireland in
the beginning of the 1970s. But we would have to have something special to offer a candidate if he was to get involved. After all, the US had
essentially taken the British side on the issue of Ireland for over 200
years. Why was there any reason to change now?

As we discussed it, Scannell and I came to an emphatic conclusion.
The only prize worth offering would be a dramatic movement from the
IRA, some kind of ceasefire, in effect, which would galvanise the
Americans into getting involved. It seemed a forlorn hope. The IRA
had one disastrous ceasefire in the 1970s, and apart from a brief cessation every Christmas, never repeated that experience, which had
almost finished them off.

A large penny dropped for me in a conversation with an IBM senior
executive named Jim Reilly who had become my friend. I had met Jim
when pursuing candidates for inclusion in the 'Business 100' issue of
Irish America. Jim, whose father came from Killarney, County Kerry,
had been featured on the cover of *Advertising Age* magazine as one of
the best minds in the business. He had been one of the men responsible for the 'Little Tramp' series of advertisements for IBM personal
computers – one of the greatest advertising campaigns of all times, that
convinced ordinary users that they could manage PCs by showing that
even Charlie Chaplin's hapless creation could work one. Lean and
angular, and without a hair on his head, Jim was known as the 'Bald
Eagle' at IBM. As our friendship grew, I had come to share many fascinating discussions on Ireland with him. One of the greatest creative
thinkers I had ever met, in his spare time he was an avid bagpiper who
liked nothing better than leading his band off to the nearest Irish
parade on weekends. Over dinner at the Kinsale restaurant on the
Upper East Side of Manhattan, I outlined my thinking to him: Clinton
could be elected, Irish America would then have leverage in both

directions on Sinn Féin and the White House, and I was looking for a way to really make it count. I told him that this was the best opportunity ever for American influence on Northern Ireland to bear fruit. We discussed the possible scenarios for a half hour or so, and then Reilly produced a pen from his suit pocket, grabbed a napkin and began drawing. He drew a box in which all the various parties involved in Northern Ireland were lined up opposite each other – Nationalists, including the Irish government, on one side; Unionists, including the British government, on the other. Across from each he drew an arrow to the other.

'All frozen in place for nearly a quarter century,' he said. 'Every move from one is matched or checkmated by a move from the other. They are all "inside the box". Destined to always checkmate each other.'

He then wrote 'US' outside the box and pointed an arrow from Sinn Féin to the US.

'You change the equation when you introduce an outside force. If Sinn Féin responds to that force it changes the entire equation. Suddenly, all the other players have to change their stance as well, because there is a new player from outside the box. Whoever responds to that outside force will make a dramatic breakthrough,' he predicted. 'The universe of possibilities is suddenly expanded for them many times. It is completely in their interest to do it.'

He explained that this was a common IBM management technique to help in problem solving, but that he had long felt it had potential impact for solving issues on a much wider plane. The application to Northern Ireland was immediately apparent to me. Jim and I discussed other ways in which U.S. intervention could be helpful if it was managed properly, but none made anything like the impression the 'outside the box' scenario made for me. I told Jim I wanted to keep in touch on the issue. He was more than happy to do this, and in the weeks and months leading up to the election I would often find Jim taking time out from a hectic schedule to throw some more ideas into the pot. We both agreed that once Clinton was elected there would be even more reason to sit down in discussion. He was right, of course, and I often smiled in later years when I heard everyone from Gerry Adams to President Clinton use the same 'outside the box' analogy. I lost touch with Jim soon after and wonder if he ever knew just how influential his little tutorial had been. But for now, the next step was to get access to Clinton. Through my contacts with Vargo and Soderberg I had established a line, no matter how tentative, to the people who would influence the next president, if he was a Democrat. It was time to set the wheels in motion.

Chapter 30

GETTING BILL CLINTON ON BOARD

C hris Hyland, a New York interior designer, was Bill Clinton's Deputy National Political Director. A former classmate of Clinton at Georgetown and a successful businessman, he was one of the first FOBs ('Friends of Bill') to sign up for the candidate. Hyland was part of a vast network of FOBs who rallied to the candidate's side once he began his White House run. While Clinton's Rhodes scholars classmates from Oxford were the most high profile, men like Hyland readily took to the hustings in support of the Southern governor. Balding, with a permanently fussy air and little or no campaign experience, Hyland did not easily fit the profile of a political operative. But, like so many other FOBs, he pitched in, and what he lacked in skills he made up for with a boyish enthusiasm. As part of his task he set about galvanising ethnic support for Bill Clinton who had just come off a major success in New Hampshire, where, despite finishing second to Paul Tsongas, he was widely accepted as the real winner of the primary, after revelations of the Gennifer Flowers episode had almost scuttled his campaign. The results in New England had set up the rest of the primary season as a ding-dong battle between Clinton, now the frontrunner for the Democratic nomination, and his rivals, who believed that the issue of his moral character could still undermine him.

Hyland's job was a complex one. The 'Reagan Democrats' – the white, ethnic Catholic constituency which had long been solid Democratic until Ronald Reagan swung them behind him – would be a crucial swing vote in the 1992 election. It was Hyland's task to gather financial and political support from those bases. His call to me was direct and to the point. Could an organisation supporting Clinton be set up in the Irish American community? I told him it could and that it was already under active consideration. I said that there was a deep well of support for any candidate who would pay attention to the Irish issue. I had been expecting such a call. Several Irish groups had made efforts to contact the Clinton campaign with an outline of an Irish programme for the presidential candidate. Like any campaign in its formative stage, it was still by no means certain who was handling the ethnic vote, and specifically the Irish issue. Obviously, Hyland had now been detailed the job.

He asked me about the best way in which to energise this new constituency for the presidential candidate. I told him that there was broad-based support for any candidate but Bush, who had delivered nothing to the Irish American constituency. We discussed ways of motivating the support base. I told him that, as a first step, I would place an article in my weekly *Irish Voice* inviting those interested to come along to an inaugural meeting. I expected that a few dozen or more core Irish activists would show up for such an evening because there was considerable interest in the community in the candidate from Arkansas. His second question was, who should chair a new group for Clinton? I didn't need to give it much thought. Former Congressman Bruce Morrison, a hero to Irish Americans for his work on immigration reform, and who also had extensive knowledge of Northern Ireland, and Boston Mayor Ray Flynn, a longtime leader on Irish issues, were two outstanding candidates for that job. I told him they would make excellent co-chairs. Hyland and I agreed to meet and discuss the 'Irish Americans for Clinton' organisation further. I was impressed with the shrewdness Hyland displayed. He had done his homework on the community and was, in my memory, the first political operative from any major presidential candidate to actually begin directly working with the Irish. We met a week later and agreed that an 'Irish Americans for Clinton' event would be held at Fitzpatrick's Hotel in Manhattan in late January. I ran an article in the *Irish Voice* and about thirty people attended – though the number of people who have since claimed to be there has quadrupled, at least. Hyland wanted us to raise several tables for a Clinton fundraiser which was being held in February at a New York hotel. In the event, I was only able to fill two tables. I was, in fact, turned down by some who would later claim to the heavens that they were there. The dinner itself, held at the Hilton Hotel, was a typical rubber chicken affair, notable only for the large number of Indian Americans who showed up in comparison to the Irish.

Halfway through the meal, Clinton entered the room, surrounded by a phalanx of aides. It was my first opportunity to view Clinton in the flesh. He made his way painstakingly around the room, stopping for lengthy periods at every table. He had an easy familiarity with people and was clearly at home pressing the flesh. He came to our table and Hyland introduced me. He nodded hello and fixed me with that intense stare. For that brief moment he gave you his undivided attention.

'We'd love to see you involved in bringing peace to Ireland,' I told him.

'I would love to do that,' he said. 'It's an issue I have followed.'

That was it. We posed for the obligatory photograph and he looked like he was gone. Suddenly he turned on his heel and came back.

'Niall, tell your friends Ireland is on my radar screen,' he said. 'I think we can do something.'

His brief words gave me hope. This was a time when American politicians stayed clear of the Irish issue. This guy was sending signals that he was different. A few months later, in late September, all had changed utterly. Now Clinton was the frontrunner for the presidency, essentially on the cusp of throwing George Bush out of office. The rank outsider had suddenly become the favourite as Bush foundered in debates and revealed himself out of touch on the economy. The longshot was suddenly leading the field.

All summer long, we worked with the Clinton campaign, which drew up supportive statements on Ireland that were causing severe heartburn on the British side. We knew there was a tiny gap opening up and we were determined to exploit it to the full. But we were in unknown territory. Every presidential candidate in known history had ultimately essentially toed the British 'no interference' line on Northern Ireland in the end because of the special relationship. Yet here we had a man who might throw all that history overboard. It was an exhilarating prospect. Clinton had appeared at an Irish issues forum in Manhattan and energised the crowd with a series of promises which included a US visa for Gerry Adams. Most dismissed it as electioneering. Some of us were not so sure.

I met with Clinton in late September, along with Paul O'Dwyer, the happy warrior of Irish politics in New York and a former City Council president, his wife Pat and Boston Mayor Ray Flynn. The meeting took place deep in the bowels of the Sheraton Hotel in the city, in a large room entered through several sets of doors. Unlike at the fundraising dinner a few months before, secret service were everywhere. The change in status was very evident. Clinton walked in after about fifteen minutes of waiting. Incongruously, the first thing I noticed was a large white paint stain on his left shoe. He seemed oblivious to it. He was carrying a large portable phone and dictating a message of condolence for a senior Democratic Party figure, Paul Kirk, who had just died. At the same time he was studying a schedule for the rest of his day and eyeing us up and down. Multitasking could have been invented for him. Right away we found out that he was on top of his brief. Usually when you talk with a senior political figure on the issue of Ireland there is a staffer present to correct and sometimes even answer all the questions. I have conducted some 'interviews' with senior American political figures in which they have done a good imitation of a ventriloquist's dummy, parroting the answers suggested by their aides. Clinton, however, had no difficulty fielding our questions. It was clear that he was involved, that his campaign was interested and that the issue of Northern Ireland was on the table like never before. It was an exciting time. As he left, Paul O'Dwyer, who had seen every president since Hoover, turned to me and said, 'If that fellah gets elected he'll make history on Ireland'. Coming from Paul, it was quite a statement.

The time was right for another meeting with Ciaran Staunton. He came to my office on Park Avenue South in Manhattan and we went to a nearby coffee shop. Over coffee and bagels, I outlined the bare bones of where I felt the strategy might lie. The idea of bringing America into play in the North, and how that might be achieved, either through a special envoy if Clinton was elected, or following up on the campaign promise from Clinton for a visa for Gerry Adams was the goal. There would have to be some quid pro quo, I told him, some type of gesture from the IRA which would help convince the Americans. I also felt that a core number of Irish Americans could be brought together to, in effect, mediate between the Provisional IRA and the White House, in the event that the project went ahead. I would hand-pick the people in the group, who would represent a significant strata of Irish American business and political clout and would be unlike any previous group that had gone over to Ireland. The more I thought about it, the more such a group seemed a definite priority to me.

The US government would not officially sanction any direct contact with the IRA, but the group could do informally and unofficially what a government appointed advisor could not do. The indirect connection through 'Irish Americans for Clinton/Gore' could give it credibility. I told him how the 'Irish Americans for Clinton/Gore' group had fared since its inception and that we now had more input into this presidential contender than any in living memory. A major new strategy could be worked out if Clinton was elected and the Republican movement in Ireland were prepared to listen to the new scenario.

'It's still a long shot,' I said, 'but we may be on the verge of a huge breakthrough over here. I think your people in Ireland should be very aware of this.'

I talked about the context for such an opportunity, the growing sense that a time and a tide had washed up on Irish shores and that it was time to do something fundamental about the North.

'People are looking at South Africa and the Middle East,' I told him, 'and are saying "Why not Ireland?"'

To my profound relief he didn't dismiss the notion; in fact he completely agreed with me.

'We've been looking to make something big happen over here for some time, as you know,' he said. 'I think they will be very interested in this back in Belfast.'

In order to set the game in motion, I asked him to arrange an appointment with a senior member of the Provisionals when I would be home at Christmas 1992. I had no idea who I would meet or who they would decide to have deal with me. I knew some of the top men like Gerry Adams from interviewing them over the years, but had no established links with them. I would have to trust Ciaran to link me in at the right level.

Chapter 31

CLINTON WINS THE WHITE HOUSE

E lection day, November 1992. Although all the polls showed Clinton well ahead before the big day I was still racked with doubts. Bush, after all, was the incumbent and could prove difficult to beat. Ross Perot, running as an anti tax candidate, was also polling very well and was an unpredictable factor. That afternoon, Jim Dwyer, a journalistic colleague at *Newsday* who later won a Pulitzer Prize and moved to *The New York Times*, called to tell me that the exit polls all over the country showed our man well ahead. It seemed we had finally backed a winner.

I had been involved in fundraising for the campaign and founded the Irish support group. At one point in the election we received a call from a senior figure at the Clinton headquarters asking for a conversation about the Irish American vote. I had handy a map we had created showing the number of Irish Americans in each state totalling, 40 million in the US overall. Clinton told me later that it made a big impression on him. At the Democratic convention held in New York that summer, Clinton met with his Irish supporters, assuring us all that he would take Northern Ireland on as an issue in his administration. We were beginning to overcome our own scepticism at that point. We also polled our readers at *Irish Voice* in the first ever Irish American survey, and the results were mirrored on polling day, with the Catholic vote going by a nine points margin to Clinton. Our first priority after the election results had settled was to secure a meeting with members of the Clinton transition team. As could have been anticipated, it turned out to be no easy task, and the Little Rock headquarters itself proved to be bedlam. Chris Hyland, our ethnic outreach coordinator, was now ensconced there as a top member of the transition team, but reaching him by phone was proving tougher than calling Clinton himself, as every interest group in the country seemed to focus its attention on Little Rock. Eventually we reached Hyland who set up a meeting with the transition group for a few weeks later. He told us that we were one of only ten or so groups who would get access.

The 'Irish Americans for Clinton/Gore' group had now outlived its usefulness and a decision was made to rename it 'Americans for a New Irish Agenda' and to involve as broad a network of Irish activists as possible. The only agenda would be to see through the Clinton campaign promises. On the appointed day, on a bitterly cold winter morning, a small group of us left for Little Rock. On the flight down to Nashville, where we were to change planes, I spoke to Paul O'Dwyer, then reaching the end of his career and confined to a wheelchair, about his hopes and dreams for the new man. He spoke about the many politicians over the years who had tried to deliver something on Ireland. In all cases, he told me, the ambition foundered because of the closeness of the British/US relationship. Would this be different now, I asked him?

'I'm old enough to be cynical,' he replied. 'But not old enough to stop believing that some US president will take this issue in hand. The Irish contribution to this country deserves a president who cares about the people back there. I'm convinced to the bottom of my soul that this is the man.'

Those were strong and emotional words, coming from a man like Paul, and I felt a great sense of history as we neared our destination. When had any Irish American group had so much influence on a US president? Even when Eamon de Valera was leader of the Provisional

Irish Republic during the Irish War of Independence in 1919, Irish American leaders could not get this founding father of the modern Irish state an audience at the Warren Harding White House. In fact, they were not even able to get him a meeting with any senior administration official at the time, so strong was the bond with the British. Paul O'Dwyer had arrived in America a mere six years after those events and had heard the political activists recalling them angrily as a lost opportunity for Irish American influence, which had been allowed to dissipate because of personal animosities. Over the next half century there would be many more efforts made by Irish Americans to engage the higher levels of the US government on the issue of Ireland, all of them unsuccessful. Now, however, it all seemed different.

As we changed planes in Nashville to fly on to Little Rock, our sense of expectation heightened. Already the vendors in the Nashville airport had 'Bill Clinton, our 41st President' tee shirts and coffee mugs for sale and in the newsstand his face was on every newspaper from around the South. It seemed the whole region was embracing him. The flight attendant announced our destination, prefacing it by saying proudly 'Home city of our new President'.

The city of Little Rock, where the Clinton transition team was located, was somewhat of a disappointment to me, looking very like the small provincial capital it was before the Clinton hurricane hit town. The downtown area, where the transition team was based, looked threadbare and ill-worn, with buildings poorly maintained. The Clinton headquarters was in an anonymous office block, in an area populated by car parks and cheap shot and beer joints. Inside, the headquarters was hardly an improvement. The impression was one of complete chaos, as if a hurricane had blown through town and no one was quite sure how to pick up all the pieces. Names and faces that had dominated the nation's TV screens in the weeks after the election were huddled in small, box-like offices; everywhere cardboard boxes were stacked almost ceiling high, entire future government departments waiting to be picked up and bundled away to Washington.

'Is this what it is always like?' I asked a staffer.

'We don't know. It's our first time in twelve years,' he responded. 'We are all new to this.'

I thought of that comment subsequently when the Clinton White House got off to such a stumbling start on a range of issues. Judging by the brief tour of the chaotic transition office, perhaps it was not too surprising. Our first meeting was with David Wilhelm, the Democratic National Committee Chairman from Chicago, who looked impossibly young for such a responsible position. In fact, one of the abiding realities of the visit to the transition team was just how young all the baby boomers who would shortly run the country were. Most seemed barely out of short pants. Wilhelm thanked us for our efforts on the Clinton election and took us through the broad sweep of the Democratic strategy once they gained the White House. He explained that he was not an expert on Irish issues, but that the president-elect had made clear his commitment to the Irish question.

Chris Hyland accompanied us on our tour of the headquarters. When we entered his office he had waved cheerily at us, while trying to disentangle himself from at least five phone lines at once. Despite the pressure, he was clearly in his element; all his hard work had resulted in his elevation to the transition team and to membership of the exclusive club which contained the inner circle of the next president. Hyland had bad news for us: Nancy Soderberg, who was due to meet with the delegation, had been called away by the president-elect because of a breaking foreign policy crisis involving Libya. However, we were happy to hear that Mayor Ray Flynn, who had travelled separately to Little Rock as part of our delegation, had apparently managed to meet both Soderberg and Clinton for a brief meeting at the governor's mansion.

Our meeting went ahead, with Hyland chairing. Bruce Morrison had missed his connection in Nashville and participated by speaker phone. In all, about twelve members of Americans for a New Irish Agenda had made the trip. Several of them used the occasion to sound off about the lack of attention the Irish issue had received under previous Democratic administrations and expressed the strong wish that Clinton would be different and would live up to his stated promises. During the opening hour of the meeting there was a tremendous sense of a community getting a festering complaint off their chest. Dr Bob Linnon, Chairman of the Irish American Unity Conference, broke down in tears when talking about the indignity of strip searches on women prisoners in Armagh prison in Northern Ireland. He complained bitterly about the lack of American concern for such issues.

I viewed the session as very healthy, and as the first in a number of necessary encounters between a community that had long felt aggrieved and locked out of any influence on Irish issues by successive administrations and a new administration which was promising a new start. Irish Americans had looked on with envy at the success of other ethnic groups, particularly the Jewish lobby, and their decisive role in influencing US policy on the Middle East. Now, after almost a quarter century, they were hopeful that they might at last have a more of a say. Hyland remained cool throughout the session despite some of the heated rhetoric being aimed in his direction. He had learned a lot about the Irish issue in the months since we had first met and handled questions with aplomb. The Irish issue is not one that is easy to waffle on about, so Hyland impressed those present with his knowledge. What he was saying, in effect, was that the new president intended to deliver on each of the campaign promises he had made.

Paul O'Dwyer made the most impassioned speech of the meeting. He traced the history of the Irish conflict in the modern era and talked about the abdication of leading Irish American figures, including senior politicians, from responsibility for what was happening in Northern Ireland.

'Your president,' he concluded, addressing Hyland, 'can make the difference in Northern Ireland. I have spent a lifetime trying to help bring about a just and lasting peace. I am at the end of my time now. This is our greatest opportunity. Please don't let us down.'

I would often think of Paul's words in the following months. But for the physical difficulties he laboured under, he would have been the key member of the Irish American team. Yet there was a deep sense of personal satisfaction that he was living to see what he always wanted to witness: Irish America and a US president finally playing a major role in Northern Ireland.

Following the meeting, a number of us regrouped at a Little Rock restaurant. The mood oscillated between optimism and a healthy cynicism about what exactly the new president would deliver. Some of the group embraced wildly optimistic scenarios. I was less effusive. The words of Brendan Scannell in the Irish embassy were ringing in my head: 'Remember, a candidate is a very different animal to a president. There will be huge pressure on Clinton to bow to the same old line – that the British and the State department decide Irish policy.' Just before we boarded the plane back to New York, we ran into the groups from Boston who were also awaiting their flight. In the course of our conversation I learnt, from an inadvertent remark, that Mayor Flynn had not met Clinton that day, despite what he had told us. It was a strange claim from a man who was obviously close enough to the President based on the fact that the President had personally campaigned with him in several key Catholic states. It was not the last time I would run into a credibility problem with Ray Flynn.

Chapter 32

SETTING THE SCENE

J ust after Christmas in 1992 I was at last able to begin my overtures to the IRA and Sinn Féin, their political wing. Ciaran Staunton had set up the first direct line of contact. It would take place in Dublin, at Wynns Hotel, just off O'Connell Street. Wynns hotel is one of Dublin's most loved landmarks. Though not itself an impressive building, its history and clientele make it unique. Located just a few short steps away from Dublin's main thoroughfare, it is perhaps the least fashionable of all the city centre hotels. It was outside Wynns that a young writer called James Joyce met a young servant girl called Nora Barnacle and it changed the course of literary history. The hotel was burned down during the events of the Easter 1916 Rising, the headquarters of which was the General Post Office, just across the road. It seemed an ideal place to make first contact, as it was not far from the railway line linking Dublin to Belfast, and it allowed ease of access to any Northern visitor.

I had spoken with Ted Howell, director of Sinn Féin's overseas department, a few days after Christmas, after we had missed each other on the phone a couple of times. As with all communication with Sinn Féin, messages were cryptic and conversations short. The meeting place was picked out in advance and the time, exact location and a brief description of who I would be meeting was delivered to me in a brief handwritten note. Spies, as well as tapped phones, were everywhere, it seemed.

I was quite nervous making my way to the hotel on the morning of the meeting. Being in Ireland for any extended length of time made me aware of the extraordinary resistance to anything ever changing in the North. The twenty-five years of conflict had left a war weariness that was palpable and a sense that nothing would ever be different. Earlier that year, yet another attempt to fashion a solution had collapsed when talks between the political parties in the North, mediated by Sir Ninian Stephen, an Australian intermediary, had ended inconclusively. As had been the case over all the years, Sinn Féin were pointedly excluded. There had been high hopes for the talks at one point, but, once again, the deep divisions evident between the parties on opposite sides prevented any significant progress. Yet here I was over from America, presuming that huge change could come about if the US got involved. I was careful to hide such sentiments in case they were laughed at openly. I made the mistake of asking a Dublin cab driver his opinion on the issue. 'Dig a ditch across the border and let them fight it out among themselves,' was his succinct reply.

Many Irish viewed their countrymen who lived in America with a mixture of bewilderment and distrust. The perception had become widespread that they – particularly those who had been in the US for many years – were stuck in some kind of a time warp and did not really understand what was happening in Northern Ireland. Some Irish commentators even went so far as to blame Irish Americans for causing the Troubles by their financial support of the IRA. While there was undoubted support for the IRA among a section of Irish Americans, as there was among some Irish, North and South, to tar all with the same brush was totally misleading. It was true to say that Irish Americans, for their part, did view the Northern Irish conflict in somewhat simpler term, but that in itself was not a bad thing in my opinion. After all, it had become clear as day that the Troubles had no hope of ending unless the violence was stopped first, to allow what the poet Seamus

Heaney had called 'a space for hope to grow'. Yet every solution tried in Northern Ireland had fallen apart because it did not address the fundamental issue of stopping the violence before moving to the politics. Like badly knit sweaters, the 'solutions' always unravelled once the violence began fraying the threads. It is a lesson that holds for conflicts worldwide. To many Irish Americans, both sides in the conflict had retreated behind mutual walls of recrimination and what was being termed 'whataboutery' in which every atrocity on one side was met with a statement of 'what about ...' in which a similar atrocity on the other side was recalled.

During Christmas 1992 things looked bleaker than ever. The traditional IRA Christmas ceasefire had been brief and the killings resumed soon after. The Irish media, north and south, seemed just as tired of the conflict as those involved. The general air of cynicism in the reporting and the demonisation of those at the extremes continued daily. There was a palpable air in much of the media in the South that the North was best forgotten about. So was I on a fool's errand? No more so than when I started my first newspaper with $952, I thought. I had an inner confidence now because of my success in America.

The great American gift to the world is optimism, expressed best in the Founding Fathers and their absurd notion in the Declaration of Independence that the divine right of king's writ did not run in their country and that people could actually rule themselves. I found that optimism at every level in American life, like the waitress dreaming about her Broadway break in the coffee shop I frequented near my apartment. She couldn't sing a note as far as I could tell, as she was always humming songs off key, but that didn't deter her. She had her arms around the dream and would not let go. Then there was the dog walker who lived in my building who saw himself building an empire based on the needs of tens of thousands of Americans to have someone walk their dog and clean up after them. He had even picked out a name for his company, the 'Doggy Can Do' Company. He asked me to invest, which was surely very optimistic. Men like Don Keough and Denis Kelleher, who had made it from nothing to the top of the business pyramid, inspired me too that dreams were possible. I knew I would need all that optimism now.

As events would have it, I was late reaching Wynns Hotel, after finding it almost impossible to find a parking spot in central Dublin. It was raining now, a great cloudburst that drenched every living soul in its path, including me. At 11.50am, wet and bedraggled and twenty minutes after the appointed time, I finally went in the hotel entrance and took a left into the bar. The place was half empty, one or two locals at the bar, and a scattering of shoppers, clergy and visitors. I had feared I wouldn't be able to pick him out in a crowd, but I needn't have worried. Ted Howell was reading *The Irish Times*, as arranged, with a pint of Guinness in front of him. Tall, bearded, with thick greying hair, and dressed in the Sinn Féin 'uniform' of jeans and a casual jacket, he looked for all the world like a Dublin working man enjoying a lunchtime pint. The introductions were brief, first names only, but I could feel his keen eyes boring into me. This was a man who was used to making vital decisions based on his own gut feelings about someone. He set about ordering me a pint, which I had to refuse, having sworn off it a few months previously, and I settled for a mineral water instead. I made some small talk about the weather and the trip over from the States. He smoked continuously and made little effort to make conversation. This, I found out, was not a try-on for his first meeting, but his usual phlegmatic personality, much better suited to listening than talking. But to me it felt like a scene from a Le Carré novel.

After a brief interlude of pleasantries, I launched into my outline. Even as I heard myself speak it, it seemed more absurd by the minute – the negative atmosphere in Ireland about the North was really having its effect. I told him that I felt there was a tremendous opportunity developing in America, that we had excellent access to the new president and that Sinn Féin had a unique opportunity to broaden the whole discourse and force the issue of Northern Ireland to near the top of the international agenda in the US. I explained that by involving the US, Sinn Féin could force a fundamental change in how all the other parties related to the conflict. I outlined how I felt that all the parties were frozen in place by twenty-five years of the current situation and that for the permafrost to melt there needed to be some new thinking by Sinn Féin.

'The international isolation is like a wall around Sinn Féin,' I told him. 'Your message can never reach outside or win an international hearing, and the British control most of the media access anyway. You have got to somehow break through that international isolation.'

He nodded. 'We consider it vital that we engage outside forces, particularly the United States, in the issue,' he said. 'Part of our objective is to ensure that our movement is not isolated.'

But that was precisely what had a happened to them. Because of the grinding violence, year in and year out, and the work of the British spin masters in Washington, they had been demonised all over the world. Most people, if asked, would identify the IRA as the only perpetrators of violence in Northern Ireland. In the United States in particular, the Republican movement had lost that battle. 'I believe this is the greatest opportunity there is to turn that around,' I said. The British had always preferred to portray the war in Northern Ireland as a religious conflict between Catholics and Protestants, with them as unwilling referees. Such a scenario ignored their own part in creating the partition of Ireland which caused all the trouble in 1921, and their backing for the blatantly sectarian fifty years of Orange misrule which excluded Catholics and which eventually led to the renewed outbreak of violence in 1969.

Ted said that for years Sinn Féin had been seeking to involve the international community, particularly the US, on the issue of Northern Ireland. But it had been an uphill climb for Sinn Féin. Internationally they were pariahs as long as the campaign of violence continued. In the US they would always retain a hardcore group of supporters but had little hope of attracting a wider constituency as long as the British were able to kick them around on the issue of terrorism and violence. There had been many slow and stale years while the issue languished exactly where the British wanted it, as an internal problem for them, and them only, to solve and manage. But in the undergrowth something was stirring. There was a palpable war weariness on all sides as the conflict entered its twenty-fifth year. The powerful surges for peace in South Africa and the Middle East had sent shock waves around the world. The South African situation, in particular, weighed heavily in Belfast where Mandela's turn from the gun and his successful transition to power had made a huge impact. Just as the Easter 1916 Rising in Dublin had a profound effect on other independence groups throughout the world, the Mandela example had a major impact on Sinn Féin. Gerry Adams had made no secret of his total admiration for the ANC leader.

I then outlined what I had come up with as a plan of action. I talked for forty-five minutes with no interruption. I drew diagrams on napkins. I expanded on the 'Outside the box theory'. I had no idea what he was thinking; maybe that I was some crazy American over to try his patience with a hare-brained scheme. I told him I would put a group of leading Irish Americans together to visit Northern Ireland where we would meet with all sides, including Sinn Féin, who at the time were blacklisted for most American visits. Before the trip I would signal the White House that we were going and that something would happen while we were there. What I was asking for was no less than an IRA ceasefire during our visit to send the message to the White House that Sinn Féin was interested in engaging with them. Such a sign could trigger a whole new era in American involvement in the Irish situation. When the group returned to the US we would use the IRA cessation to show that the movement was serious about peace and that the US could play a huge role in bringing about that opening for peace. I stressed that my group would have no official status from the White House when we came over, but that we would be well connected. When we returned, we would use the trip as leverage to bring the US into the game in the immediate sense, either through the appointment of a peace envoy or to gain a visa for Gerry Adams to visit America.

When I had finished, Ted didn't laugh out loud, which was helpful. In fact, he listened without betraying any reaction. He gave no indication as to whether my request sounded outrageous or reasonable to his ears. He talked about the importance of the American link to his movement and the various efforts that had been made over the years to engage the US. I was aware of most of those, from my own sources, from reports in my newspaper and elsewhere. However, Sinn Féin was in a deep bind in the United States, the Noraid faithful who supported the organisation through thick and thin had little or no real political clout in Washington and were widely considered terrorist supporters by every government involved in the issue. But the work of people like Ciaran Staunton in trying to open up the process, and the success of the MacBride Principles had pointed a way forward for Sinn Féin. If they were able to build a coalition of grassroot forces and work to an agreed agenda, and through that gain access to the White House and to powerful Irish American senators such as Senator Edward Kennedy, then the outlook would be transformed for them. It was the ultimate nightmare of the British government – that the US would get seriously involved in peace efforts in Ireland.

I asked Ted about what was happening with other relationships they were developing. Albert Reynolds, the new Irish Prime Minister, had made clear his commitment to solving the issue of Northern Ireland when assuming office, though many commentators had dismissed his pledges as just lip service. Back in 1988, Gerry Adams had been involved in negotiations with SDLP leader John Hume which led to an interesting scenario of the two major nationalist parties in Northern Ireland agreeing a joint way forward. However, nothing had been heard publicly about those talks in several years. I got the impression from Ted that there was the beginnings of an opening in Ireland and that events were perhaps starting to come together. I was operating in the dark, however, as to the extent of those developments. There was, indeed, a very large effort underway of which I was unaware. Secret negotiations between the IRA and the British government, which were occurring at the time of my meeting with Ted, would become a sensational story later in 1993. These contacts were established in 1990 and were initiated by the British. The head of MI6, Michael Oatley, code name 'Mountain Climber', had initiated them when he contacted Martin McGuinness of Sinn Féin and told him that the British government was interested in opening dialogue. As evidence of British goodwill, an advance copy of a crucial speech which the Northern Secretary of State, Peter Brooke, was going to deliver was sent to Sinn Féin. That speech, which Brooke delivered on 9 November 1990, stated that Britain had no 'strategic or economic interest' in Ireland and would accept the unification of Ireland 'by consent'. It was the first step back by the British from their long held article of faith that Northern Ireland was forever British. The speech caused a major stir. The contacts continued, with the British sending Sinn Féin internal assessments of where the British government saw the conflict, and advance copies of further important speeches.

The contacts went ahead even when the IRA tried to blow up the British Cabinet on 7 February 1991. A rocket launcher was set up in a nondescript van parked just a few hundred yards from the Prime Minister's residence in Whitehall, London. The rocket landed in the garden of 10 Downing Street, right at the time when Major's cabinet was meeting. It was the most audacious of all IRA attacks, matched only by the bomb at the Tory Party conference in Brighton in 1987 which almost killed Margaret Thatcher. The talks were reaching a crescendo right at the time I was meeting with Ted. On 12 January of that year, the British officials stressed the seriousness of their approach to the IRA in a memo. The memo also stated that 'an easing off' of violence would start the ball rolling in a significant way. On 26 February, the IRA were informed by the British government that they had agreed to hold talks with Sinn Féin, which, if they went well, would be announced publicly. Suggested venues for the talks included Sweden, Scotland or the Isle of Man. The British stance in the secret talks made nonsense of their long held position of 'no talks with terrorists'. However, a more disturbing question about the secret talks would shortly raise its head following their breakdown. Did the British enter into them in good faith or in an inspired attempt to split the IRA? Most of the media in Ireland had long since dismissed any rumblings of progress as yet another false dawn in the twenty-five-year conflict, yet I was certain in my gut after my conversation with Ted that something was about to change.

As he left, I emphasised to Ted that the election of Clinton was an opportunity that should not be passed up by Sinn Féin. I was encouraged by the meeting, but, not for the last time, was left in the dark by his phlegmatic 'quiet man' approach. As to what his real views on the meeting, or of me were, I had no way of knowing. I just had to hope, with the scenario that was unfolding, that he had been sufficiently persuaded that America meant business this time. We agreed on methods of communication if all of this went ahead. All documents would be destroyed after reading them. A rough code was agreed upon: the Irish American effort was to be called 'the project', Gerry Adams was to be called 'Chairman', letters were to be hand delivered, sent with trusted airline passengers. Phone calls from the US could only be made to specific numbers. The IRA would be the 'local football team', a phrase that I think originated with author Tim Pat Coogan, an expert on the IRA. Tim was a dear friend, one of my first mentors in journalism, who had gone from the old *Irish Press* newspaper to become the foremost author and expert on the IRA and their role in Irish history. He was a great listening post over the next few years.

The peace process would be known as 'the Holy Ghost' and questions would be asked such as, 'Where is the Holy Ghost playing, forward or back?' 'Forward' meant it was good, 'back' was bad and 'on the sidelines' meant that there were great difficulties. Father Alec Reid, a key intermediary between the Dublin government and the IRA, was '*An sagart*', Irish for 'the priest'. 'An sagart is travelling' was a real sign that things were moving. Ambassador Jean Kennedy Smith in Dublin was '*An spéirbhean*', a mythical figure in Gaelic poetry which meant 'dream woman' and her brother, Senator Edward Kennedy, was merely known as 'the brother'. I walked away from the meeting with a sense of relief. I had not been laughed out of court; the American connection was up and running. Our friends in the White House and elsewhere would be glad to hear that there was contact and, as far as I could judge, progress.

Chapter 33

GATHERING PACE

I t was a cold and wet evening in mid-January 1992. I was on my
way to P J Clarke's, one of the best known watering holes in Manhattan, close by the Queensboro Bridge. A few days earlier, Bill Clinton had made clear his contempt for British Prime Minister John Major,
who had openly sided with his opponent George Bush in the election,
a most extraordinary act. Major's government had conducted a search
of their passport files to see if Clinton had tried to change nationalities
to avoid service in Vietnam when he was at Oxford. Clinton was
clearly stung: 'When I met John Major the other night he slapped me
on the shoulder and said, "You look nothing like your passport photographs," and I said, I really appreciate that, John, and that there is nothing personal in what you tried to do to me, and next week I'll send you
a note to that effect through Jimmy Breslin when I name him as our
envoy to Ireland.'

Breslin was, of course, the famous Irish American columnist who
had adopted a bitter anti-British line on the North. It was an interesting
quote, and, I thought, offered us a clear opening to exploit this divide.

Now I was on my way to meet with one of the most extraordinary
men I ever knew, to take advantage of this historical opportunity and
ask him to help with securing an IRA ceasefire and a huge breakthrough in the infant Irish peace process. His name was Chuck Feeney,
then sixty-six, son of an insurance clerk who grew up in humble surroundings in Elizabeth, New Jersey, an old smokestack town not far

past the Lincoln Tunnel as you exit Manhattan. By now, he was one of the richest men in the world, but his reputation was not based on his ability to accumulate wealth, rather in giving it away. He was, in fact, the greatest philanthropist of the twentieth century. Maureen Dowd of the *New York Times,* who attended an event hosted by my magazine, *Irish America,* where Feeney had been present and had made his only public speech, wrote later: 'I have never met a billionaire who is shy and retiring, who doesn't own a house, a car, a Rolex, who likes to take the subway and fly economy, who goes to the supermarket and worries about the price of carrots, who gives away most of his money, because, as he puts it, "You can only wear one pair of shoes at a time".' Later in the same article, Dowd noted that '*American Benefactor Magazine* stated that Feeney was on course to be "the greatest American giver of all times, surpassing the Mellons, Rockefellers and the Du Ponts".'

A deeply private man, his munificence had only come to light when his company was being sold and the details of his extraordinary generosity to charitable causes became known. The *New York Times* revealed him as one of the world's great philanthropists in a front page story in early 1997 and reckoned that he had given away $600 million anonymously, and was on his way to giving $3.3 billion more. In 2004, the *Wall Street Journal* said he still had another $4 billion to give to needy causes. *Time* magazine made him runner up for Man of the Year in 1997, noting in their citation that his story was a 'tale of such unsung goodness that some almost wished its secrecy had been preserved. The recipients did not know why the gifts came or how to ask for more. But still the money drizzled in, to universities and hospitals and service groups around the world, paid in cashiers checks and accompanied only by word that the giver wished to remain anonymous.'

Feeney had come from unpromising beginnings. Elizabeth is 'Soprano' Country and Feeney was raised in a hardscrabble environment which neighbourhood men rarely left, and where finishing high school was an accomplishment. He did considerably better, winning a scholarship to Cornell where he became known as the Sandwich Board Man as he worked his way through the Ivy League school and graduated in 1956. Soon afterwards, he joined the army in the Far East, eventually settling in Hawaii where he noticed that Japanese tourists liked to shop in large groups together when they came to the island. The concept of Duty Free Shops was born. Now, in addition to DFS, he owned businesses in all five continents, from oil wells to nursing homes, from Wall Street investment firms to hotels in his beloved Ireland. The companies existed for one reason only, however, to keep the spigot open and continue the flow of funds for his worthy projects.

I had been quoted in the *New York Times* story and in a subsequent *Newsweek* report about him. I was privileged to know him and call him friend and now I was about to ask him to join me on a quest to bring peace to the ancestral land he loved so much. I had met him through my magazine, receiving a call one day from him asking to meet because he wanted to discuss the Irish American Partnership, an organisation he had helped found. A mutual friend, John Healy, who also worked for Feeney, facilitated the meeting. I was used to such calls. After we started the magazine, Irish Americans of every stripe and background called up looking for help or publicity for one project or another. I assumed Feeney would be in the same category. I first met him at Tommy Makem's Bar on 57th Street and a few days later in a gritty coffee shop at 59 East 59th Street, between Madison and Fifth Avenue. It was a nondescript place, poorly lit, and hardly somewhere you would expect one of the richest men in the world to hang out. Yet it was his local when he was in New York. He was traumatised when it closed down years later. He had his favourite waitress who treated him with something close to contempt, yet with good humour. He loved it, and I'm sure they had no idea who he was.

That first time, he was sitting at a table in the back when I entered, his ever-present raincoat slung over a chair. A small man, with intense blue eyes, he had a half-grin on his face whenever we met, as if we had a private joke going between us. He usually had several newspapers with him and would cut out articles for you to read. He hated to be taken seriously, which is why, I think, we got along famously. He had an Irish wit, a self-deprecating air, and he loved when you skewered some holy cow or famous institution. He had a wonderful sense of the ridiculous. People with important titles meant nothing to him; respect had to be earned, not conferred. He judged everything on his own personal instincts, what he called his 'smell test'. His closest friends were those he had gone to high school with. No doubt he could have had acolytes slobbering all over him, given half a chance. He did not encourage it. He kept his feet on the ground, determinedly so, and it was soon evident to me that the working class Irish Catholic kid from Jersey was never going to forget where he came from. In fact, I think that was what kept him sane and normal. He looked at fame and failure and treated them both as the impostors they were.

In our first conversation we talked about Irish America, whether it even existed, and whether the Irish had all become so WASP [White Anglo-Saxon Protestant] that there was no longer a difference. I told him 'no'. He said 'yes', and I was glad in subsequent years to prove him wrong. I think he was glad, too. After our first meeting we met most times he was in town and became fast friends. His life spanned a huge arc around the world, constantly travelling to his far-flung empire, from Australia to Britain and Ireland and back again. He always travelled coach, and *Forbes* magazine noted that he seemed happiest at 36,000 feet. *Forbes* said Feeney was 'a hyperactive man who values his family and does not dress to impress'. The magazine also quoted someone who worked for him as saying that he once observed him with a safety pin holding up his pants. But he had a loving family, and his kids, one son and three daughters, were as normal as you could find. He insisted that they knew they would inherit very little from him. And I think they were much the better for knowing that. He lived in a small apartment. Indeed, in New York he had a studio with a Murphy bed which folded into the wall when you finished with it; his watch probably cost $5 and his reading glasses not much more. He was frugal but very generous, which wasn't a contradiction.

He refused to spend much money on himself, but loved to entertain friends, and while many profiles portrayed him as shy, he was far from that among close friends. He could be eccentric. Once, on a weekend in Connecticut where he used to have a house, we went for a walk that took us almost three miles along a long, winding road which crossed train tracks before ending up in the local village. There we promptly went to the library where he rummaged through the leftover magazines that people dropped off in a container, before taking some of them home. It was his way of keeping things in perspective. He was an incredible traveller. On one of our trips to Northern Ireland, Feeney flew direct to New York from Australia, attended an extensive briefing on the trip, then we all flew directly on to Ireland. He arrived in Belfast the next day fresher than any of us. On plane flights he simply curled up and fell fast asleep right after takeoff, or he read everything in sight, clipping articles from magazines and newspapers for future perusal. I was used to receiving bundles of such articles from wherever he was in the world, with some key phrases or sentences underlined. Oftentimes it would be articles on Ireland from the *South China News* or some newspaper in Indonesia, Bali or Australia.

I had known him for years and yet never knew how incredible his story was until *Forbes* magazine first broke his cover in 1990 by revealing the amount of his wealth. The extent to which he had been a mystery to me was evident then when I read that. I always knew he was wealthy and that he was a philanthropist, but he never ever discussed it. Now I found out that he was one of the world's richest men, and, more amazingly, was hell bent on giving all his money away.

Feeney despised the mentality of a Donald Trump who, fittingly, trumpeted everything he did, whether it was dating the latest super-model, building the biggest building or giving, for him, small sums to charity. He employed several public relations people to make sure that every such move he made was reported. Feeney deplored those who cashed in so publicly on the fact that they loved to make money and believed they had some divine right to insight and adulation as a result. He was famously quoted as saying that 'there are no pockets in a shroud'. His contempt for many of his fellow CEOs who gave away little of their money and spent most of their time trying to make it onto one rich list or another was total. From his point of view, the only list worth publishing was of those most committed to giving away, rather than accumulating, funds.

He had an abiding affection for Ireland and everything Irish, but never seemed particularly political. I knew, however, that he had a deep concern about the Troubles in Ireland and I felt he would do anything to try to help. I also knew that he would not be intimidated by the problem, which scared away so many Irish Americans. He would not believe the 'experts' who said it was insoluble, and he certainly would be prepared to listen to those whose voices were rarely heard or had been frozen out of negotiations to that point. He was, above all, a risk taker, and I was gambling that the chance to help make history in Ireland would appeal to him. We talked over dinner and he had his usual couple of glasses of white wine. He listened patiently. As usual, his mind was in overdrive and he was probably working three or four steps ahead of me as I talked. He had a habit of drumming his fingers when people began to bore him. Now his fingers were silent, however, and I kept my remarks as short as possible. I told him I believed there was a unique and historic opportunity to play a huge part in bringing peace to Ireland but that it involved significant personal risk, and for him, a constant fear of being exposed in the media. We would be unofficial emissaries from the White House, easy targets and denied on all sides if it went wrong. There was also some physical danger, as our mission would certainly become known before too long and we could be targets for Loyalist paramilitaries as a result. It was a long shot, I told him, but if it worked, it would bring the US into the conflict as honest brokers and could change the whole face of one of the longest running conflicts in the world.

I had never put such a proposition to anyone before. Yes, we were friends, but our friendship was based on a shared heritage and similar political outlook. This was something different, a major step into the unknown for a man who, if he wanted, could easily become one of the most famous in the world. I felt he was quite likely to tell me that he just didn't feel he had the expertise to deal with this issue and that he would be afraid of public exposure of any kind. I would have had to accept that. He would also have been aware that at some point there would be a need for considerable financial input from him if the process was advancing. I knew that one of his charities already spent significant sums in the North, but this would be of an entirely different nature.

When I finished, there was not even a brief pause. Without apparently giving it a moment's thought, he fixed his clear blue eyes on me and said that he definitely wanted to be involved. It was that quick and simple, and very typical of a man who had lived all his live by the creed of listening to his own voice first. He told me he had been particularly affected by a gruesome incident on 8 November 1987 in Enniskillen, in Fermanagh, where some of his ancestors came from. The IRA had detonated a bomb at a Remembrance Day parade which killed eleven civilians and left sixty people injured, many seriously. There were horrific scenes as family members desperately searched for those injured. In one case it resulted in Gordon Wilson, a local businessman, springing to international attention. Wilson's daughter, Marie, a young student nurse, had been mortally injured in the blast. She never had a chance. The IRA bomb, exploding at the base of the cenotaph, had hurled her a dozen feet in the air and she landed amid the rubble and ruin of what moments before had been a festive occasion and had suddenly become a great carnage. Her father was buried in the rubble beside her. Wilson later told the BBC, 'She held my hand tightly, and gripped me as hard as she could. She said, "Daddy, I love you very much." Those were her exact words to me, and those were the last words I ever heard her say.' To the astonishment of listeners, Wilson went on to add, 'But I bear no ill will. I bear no grudge. Dirty sort of talk is not going to bring her back to life. She was a great wee lassie. She loved her profession. She was a pet. She's dead. She's in heaven and we shall meet again. I will pray for these men tonight and every night.'

As historian Jonathan Bardon commented, 'No words in more than twenty-five years of violence in Northern Ireland had such a powerful, emotional impact'. They certainly impacted Chuck Feeney. Watching the carnage that day from America, Feeney cried, and swore that if the occasion arose he would do his very best to try to accomplish something to end the violence.

'If we can stop even one Enniskillen we should put everything we have into it,' he said to me. 'You have my complete support. I will go there anytime you want.'

I walked away from P J Clarke's energised and excited despite the gloom as a damp fog descended and the only light visible was from street lamps which threw off a ghostly halo. I could have cared less, however. I had signed up the most important figure in the crusade. A major American figure was prepared to put his reputation and money on the line. It was a very good start.

Chapter 34

COMPLETING THE A-TEAM

My next target for the peace project was leading business-man Bill Flynn who ran the Mutual of America Insurance Company in New York. Flynn was in his sixties, tall and always impeccably well groomed; the consummate insider in New York, who had a handle on every major politician, businessman and deal going down. He was an unlikely-looking revolutionary to enlist for the mission I was going to propose to him, but I knew that, inside, a rebel heart was beating. Despite his business success, Flynn had a deep philosophical bent. He was a philosophy major and had briefly contemplated the priesthood. Issues of war and peace occupied his mind as much as insurance. His company had sponsored numerous peace forums, including the 'Anatomy of Hate' conference in Oslo a few years before. Elie Wiesel was prominent on his board and Flynn learned much about making peace from the Holocaust survivor and Nobel prizewinner.

His interest in Ireland had started in earnest a few years before. Flynn had attended an FBI training course for business executives in defensive driving at an Air Force base in upstate New York. A friend of his from Syracuse, Jack Mannion, Chairman and CEO of United Mutual Life Insurance Company, was on the same course. Over beer and sandwiches, the issue of Northern Ireland came up. Flynn's mother had come to the US from County Mayo and his father from County Down, so he was deeply interested in the Irish issue. Mannion tackled him on his views and stated that he himself understood armed resistance to the British in the North by the IRA, something that astonished Flynn. They argued some, and Mannion promised to send two men who led the militant pro-IRA group, Irish Northern Aid, in the US to meet him. A few weeks later, back in his office, he opened the door and two hardline supporters of the IRA walked in. Flynn sat down with the two men. 'I could not agree with using violence, I told them,' said Flynn. 'Although I told them I was deeply supportive of a United Ireland.' They said, "Well what the hell do you support? What are you doing about it?"'The former marine suddenly felt like a draft dodger. He responded, 'You're right. I hear the bell.'

Within two weeks, Flynn was on his way to Northern Ireland to try and find a way to get involved. Soon afterwards he was organising lunches for visiting dignitaries from Northern Ireland as he sought to gain traction on the issue. One of the lunches he hosted was for Sir Patrick Mayhew, then Secretary of State for Northern Ireland. Flynn received enormous criticism from some in the community for this gesture. I was at the lunch and enormously impressed with his courage in taking the initiative. I decided I should try to enlist him. Like Feeney, Flynn hardly hesitated when I asked if he would become involved. He came right to the point, as he usually did.

'It's time. My God, imagine if we could help achieve a state of peace over there,' he said. 'The odds will be against us, though.'

Flynn also brought on board an invaluable ally, Bill Barry, head of his own security firm, one of the closest friends of the Kennedys, who had been with Bobby when he was assassinated in Los Angeles in 1968. Flynn reckoned that we would all be in danger once we stepped on Irish soil and he wanted Barry along as protection. It was a wise move. True to their leftist credentials, Sinn Féin wanted a leading Labour figure involved. Joe Jameson, head of the Irish American Labour Coalition, was the perfect man. Low key, unassuming and a great listener, Jameson, too, was committed to trying to achieve American intervention in Northern Ireland. I did not want to head up the delegation or be its public face. I believed that person should come from the US, and not speak with an Irish accent, as I did. There was one obvious choice, Congressman Bruce Morrison from Connecticut, who had distinguished himself years earlier by ramming though Congress an immigration bill that provided relief for tens of thousands of Irish undocumented. He had become a hero in the Irish American community as a result. He was an unlikely hero, a Lutheran with no real Irish background. But he was incredibly sharp on the issue from the time he was elected, when it became clear that there was a large Irish constituency in his district outside New Haven. Even more importantly, he was a *bona fide* friend of Bill and Hillary Clinton, having attended Yale with Hillary and worked in free legal aid with her.

Over the years I marvelled at how well Morrison grasped the issue. Most Americans will get tripped up somewhere in the often obscure vernacular that is Northern Irish politics. Not Morrison. He always had an impeccable grasp, and in a short time knew more than most of the Irish themselves about what was going on and who the players were. There was one final link in the chain. Sinn Féin were concerned that a top notch current politician needed to get involved. Boston Mayor Ray Flynn was the obvious person. He had a growing national profile, was deeply interested in the Irish issue and was considered a very live candidate for cabinet status in any Democratic administration. I met with Ray Flynn and his aides in a room in Fitzpatrick's Hotel in Manhattan. I was very impressed with the questions Flynn was asking about the offer of an IRA ceasefire that I was trying to negotiate. Surrounded by his army of aides, Flynn certainly gave the impression of maximum competence on the issue, never once referring questions to them. Flynn agreed with some enthusiasm to go. I no longer felt alone in my perceptions that a peace effort might succeed.

As each successive person fell into line I became emboldened by their support. That famous American optimism was beginning to take over. The recent depression which had dragged me to my knees had vanished. I was spending long hours on the phone every day trying to calculate angles, press buttons, whatever it took to find an opening in Northern Ireland. In short, I had become obsessed. The die was now cast. My bunch of amateur diplomats, a hybrid mixture of business, media, labour and political backgrounds, was now dressed and ready to go, just awaiting word from the IRA. Years later, Hillary Clinton told me that a group such as this was of immense importance to American efforts to make a difference in conflict resolutions. When she became Secretary of State, she tried to recruit similar groups from among large ethnic bases such as Indian and Pakistani Americans and Arab and Israeli Americans and to set us up with meetings between them and us in order to show how an activist ethnic group could make a huge difference in helping shape American foreign policy.

There is no question in my mind that without the Connolly House Group, as we became known (so called because it was at their West Belfast offices of that name that we met with Sinn Féin), the IRA ceasefire which was the underpinning of the entire peace process might never have been achieved, or would certainly have been delayed for a long time. Out of that group came the entire outreach ascending all the way to the president of the United States. The history books are full of efforts by Irish American leaders and Irish leaders such as Eamon de Valera to reach the president of the United States and get him to intervene in Northern Ireland. Now we had one hand on the Holy Grail.

I still shake my head at how many organisations and individual politicians would subsequently claim a major role in resolving the Northern Ireland situation. The harsh reality was that most Irish American groups were petrified of the issue and played safe throughout the Troubles. Those who did become involved, such as Irish Northern Aid, were far too pro IRA to make any huge difference. Most politicians gave it lip service, but never did anything, with honourable exceptions such as Congressman Peter King, former Congressman Bruce Robinson and Congressman Ritchie Neal. The American Ireland Fund did a remarkable job after the process was underway, and in later years, under chairman Loretta Brennan Glucksman, they became very effective indeed in helping out.

Years later, when celebrating the success of the peace process became a cottage industry, I often found myself astounded at how much credit groups who never took the slightest risk heaped upon themselves. The reality was that, in my opinion, until the Connolly House Group made the overtures, Irish America was largely missing in action.

Chapter 35

READY TO GO

Now that the delegation was in place, I felt it was time again to contact Sinn Féin and the IRA. This was done through a courier who carried a letter to my contact in Belfast. I thought long and hard about the letter. I could not over-promise, equally I could not undersell the reality that senior political and business figures were coming from America and for the first time would engage with Sinn Féin and the IRA. It still seemed a long shot when the letter finally went out. Would there be a response from the other side? I waited over a week and the silence was deafening. Then, one day, a stranger arrived at my office and asked to see me. He came in and handed me a letter, then left without saying a word. The letter was written in very guarded Irish and English. My heart leapt as I read it.

An informal seven-day ceasefire would be in place when we got to Ireland, beginning on 4 May 1993. There would be no announcement and nothing in writing; we would have to take their word for it. I could not disclose any of this publicly. I read and reread the letter. Yes, it was as clear as such a statement could be. The IRA, apart from an annual three-day ceasefire at Christmas, had not called a cessation of any kind since the 1970s when they felt badly burned after the British took advantage of a long cessation to target key members. The letter was the green light. As the May date approached, I found myself swamped with a list of things to arrange and do. Finalising travel plans was just one of them. There was also much further discussion with the members of the group, telling them that we had a green light, but not being specific about it. I was driving myself intensely to make everything work on schedule. Finally, the itinerary was set. We would meet every major political party we could, North and South, and spend the best part of a day with Sinn Féin, thus breaking their international isolation.

Then, just the week beforehand, the phone lines to Mayor Flynn's offices went dead and I could not make contact despite repeated efforts. At first I was not too worried; he was a busy man with a hectic schedule, and he had given me his word. As the days passed, however, I became increasingly worried. I tried to reach his press secretary, Mike Quinlan, who was on vacation in Aruba. Utter Silence. The trip would unravel if Flynn was not going. He was a key figure, the best known face on the trip, and a big city mayor. I began pacing the floors in my apartment, afraid even to contemplate the outcome if he had double crossed me after all his sweet talk. For several days I was manic.

Mayor Flynn had pulled out. I eventually received the call from Quinlan. I knew he was embarrassed to make it and I always considered him a decent guy.

'He's not going,' he told me. 'Pressure of work.'

'Bullshit. Mike, you can't do this to me. This has been set up with the IRA and the White House.'

'I'm sorry, but he just can't make it.'

'Oh fuck. Don't say this to me.'

'I know it's devastating, but I can't tell you anything else.'

The reason given was that his schedule did not allow him to go. It was the kind of pro-forma response he must have given to hundreds of people who organised events that they wanted him to go to. I was utterly shattered. The IRA now had a ceasefire planned, but no one would ever know about it. The fine dreams of involving the White House and a new departure from America in helping sort out the Troubles seemed in ruins. My life was flashing in front of my eyes and the whole thing ran like a tragicomedy, about a fool on a fool's errand. Worse, I now had to tell Ted and the other Sinn Féin leaders that the deal was off.

I went into my office on a Saturday morning and dialled a prearranged number. There was no time for couriers or anything else; this was too urgent, the trip was just days away. The number answered and I was switched to another number. Ted picked up the phone. Over the months I had come to admire his laconic style, but even he could not conceal his shock when I told him.

'Jesus, that is a disaster,' he told me. 'I'm in the shit.'

'I know and I'm sorry,' I said. 'I want to get on a plane and see you guys to explain everything.'

I knew what he was thinking: their movement had been set up and the news would come out that they had been planning an undeclared ceasefire. I couldn't discuss that with him on the phone. I had to see him and his fellow leaders face to face. I walked in Central Park later that evening, my mind racing. I had not slept for three days or so when the first inkling of trouble from the Ray Flynn camp had become evident. I was quickly learning why people avoided the issue of Northern Ireland like the plague. I had adopted a simple approach which, instead of landing me inside the charmed circle where peace could be made, had instead sent me boomeranging off into the outer hemisphere. Put not your faith in politicians was a lesson I should never have needed to learn. Flynn, of course, had taken the idea that I had presented to him, broken the agreement to keep it secret and ran it by several groups, including the Irish government, and perhaps the British, for all I knew. They had immediately counselled caution against getting mixed up with a bunch of amateurs on a fool's mission. That was the main reason he had pulled out.

Chapter 36

A DANGEROUS JOURNEY

A day later I got a call from Ted. It was brief and to the point: 'You have to come over. This is very serious.'

I put down the phone and considered my options. I could step away from the whole sorry mess now. I wasn't in too deep, and more and more the notion of trying to help end Europe's oldest war seemed far-fetched. I was having major doubts about my abilities to galvanise a movement from America. On the other hand, I didn't feel I could quit. The IRA had shown faith in me and I needed to live up to it. I had alerted Senator Kennedy, and through him National Security Council Deputy Director Nancy Soderberg who was keeping the President informed, that the deal was afoot in Ireland. I would look like a complete idiot in their eyes. I tossed and turned for a night before sending a message back. I'd be there a few days later. I really felt I had little option, and, besides, a little of that American can-do spirit had returned.

However, on the flight over, the old doubts gripped me in a merciless vice. Who did I think I was, they repeated over and over. I stared out at the black night. What was I getting myself into? The trip never seemed so long. Finally the plane swooped into Dublin Airport. It was raining, of course, the rivulets streaking off the windows as we dropped from the sky. My mood was as dark as the weather outside. I travelled to Belfast by train. It always fascinated me when the train approached the border. There was no demarcation line, no mountain range or other natural boundary. Instead you went from one man's fields in the South to another man's in the North and you were in a different country.

I was in a state of paranoia. Supposing my telephone conversations were bugged? What if there was someone on this train who was following me? I shifted uncomfortably and looked around. Maybe the man I had seen devouring the cholesterol-raising breakfast of bacon, eggs and sausages? He returned my gaze quizzically. No, I didn't think so. Maybe the young woman with the backpack who looked like a student? She got off before the border, however. There was really no point in speculating.

On arrival, I took a taxi to Dukes hotel, not far from Queen's University, where the rendezvous had been arranged. It was a comfortable but very basic sort of place. The Troubles had meant that when it came to tourism Northern Ireland was far behind. I was sitting in a corner of the lobby, with a copy of *The Irish Times* open in front of me. That was the sign by which the person who was picking me up would recognise me. I stared out at the torrents of rain being whisked along the drains to the gutters. I could still cut and run. I thought about it for a moment. No, I had to stay. Where *was* this guy? Suddenly a young man entered the foyer and looked around. He was of medium height, dressed in a denim jacket and jeans. He was clearly looking for someone. His eyes fell on me and he came over quickly.

'Hello,' he said, reaching for my hand. 'I'm your driver.'

That was it. We went outside to where his car was parked and I sat in the back, rather than beside him, as would be normal. It must have seemed a strange thing to do, but I was unconsciously thinking of taking a cab in New York. He drove off without a word. We headed towards the city centre and then in the direction of West Belfast, the redoubt of the Falls Road where Sinn Féin and the IRA reigned supreme. Cheek by jowl with the Falls is the Shankill Road, headquarters of the most violent Loyalist gangs. The places are so close together that you can only tell by the colour of the graffiti on the kerbstones where you are: red white and blue for Loyalist, green for Republican. Some of the worst murders of the Troubles occurred in these mean streets.

The driver suddenly took a sharp left turn into a hospital, drove up a dead end, reversed out and went back the way we had come. Obviously he was seeking to throw off any pursuer, or worse, completely baffle me. I was petrified now. What if he was a British agent sent to intercept me? What if he was a member of a Loyalist hit squad who knew what my mission was? I had every right to be worried. There had been several cases of collusion between Loyalist killer squads and the local army and police. Supposing I was being set up after my phone calls had been intercepted? Or had someone told others of the plan? I looked down at my hands and realised that the knuckles were white from gripping the briefcase I was carrying. The bright lights of New York never seemed so far away and I wondered briefly if I would ever see them again.

He was really driving now. Quick left and right turns, a double back and then, finally, and to my immense relief, I saw that we were close to the Falls Road. We drove up past serried files of black taxis which are the local mode of transport. We took a left and then several other turns, amid a maze of streets. Through the pounding rain I kept my eyes firmly on the kerbstones and on the graffiti. I was in IRA territory all right. I felt a huge surge of relief. Halfway up the street he stopped and told me to get out and knock on a door opposite. It was a quiet, nondescript street, indistinguishable from hundreds of other working class areas. As he roared off, I was left clutching my briefcase, a slightly ridiculous figure, I'm sure, dressed in a smart suit and tie in a neighbourhood where someone dressed like that would stick out like a sore thumb. I complimented myself on my foresight as I made my way up the short path and knocked on the door.

There was no answer. I knocked again and suddenly an upstairs window flew open. It was Ted. I don't think I have ever been so pleased to see anyone in my life. He came downstairs and let me in and then escorted me into the nearby living room. I just had time to notice the closed circuit TV system monitoring everything on the street, and the iron gate that blocked access to the upstairs area. There were about six people in the room. I recognised Gerry Adams immediately. I hadn't seen him in some years and incongruously I found myself noticing how tall he was and how large his feet were. The man had presence, of that there was no question. At least two of the others were familiar to me, by reputation only, as senior figures in the IRA. The other two I did not know. It was a sparsely furnished room with some religious and republican icons on the wall. The ever reliable Virgin Mary stared vacantly at me; there was a cross made by inmates from Long Kesh where the hunger strikers had died, and a wedding picture. The couple looked impossibly young.

The men were friendly and motioned me to sit down. It had all the hallmarks of an interrogation: me sitting alone on the settee, clutching a briefcase, the seven spread out in chairs around me. I suddenly wanted to take a leak very badly. Adams opened the meeting by saying how much he appreciated me coming over. He left me in no doubt, however, how serious the situation now was. Another speaker told me that the IRA had moved heaven and earth to get the unannounced ceasefire and now it had blown up in their faces. He stated that Ted had put himself on the line and had suffered as a result. Why had this happened? I had already made a decision to be as straight as I could. There was no point, with people such as these, in being anything else. I explained the entire Ray Flynn scenario to them and what had happened to the delegation. I set out as clearly as possible just how difficult a task it was to set up a group to come over and the problems I had encountered. I went through each of the people I had recruited and what their strengths and talents were. They listened impassively. I had no idea what they were thinking. I talked for a good hour. Outside, the rain was pounding the pavements and the room had grown semi-dark.

When I had finished there were some very pointed questions, especially from the men from the IRA. Why did I think the White House was interested? What if I failed again? Did I intend to add anyone to the mix next time? I answered as straight as I could. At least two hours had elapsed before a woman came in bearing sandwiches. I suddenly realised I was famished. The conversation turned to small talk, but I still felt very uneasy. Did they believe what I had told them? I sensed they needed time to talk something over, so I made excuses and went to use the bathroom.

When I came back, Adams spoke. He told me they accepted my explanation, and that I had been honest with them about it. He explained again how careful the organisation had to be that they were not being duped or set up in some way. I told him I understood. They asked if it would be possible to reconstitute the group. I said I thought it would and that I would aim for a September date.

That was it. They had been clinical and focused, and had come to the point very quickly. There was even time for some light humour as I recounted my trip with the driver. We parted on good terms and a different driver took me back to the hotel, this time directly, which took only a few minutes. Overhead, I noticed a British Army helicopter poised motionless in the sky over the nationalist area, the sound of its blades drowned out in the traffic. I wondered who they were looking for or listening to. I was happy, but utterly drained. I took the next available train back to Dublin and slept in my sister Triona's home for what seemed like twelve hours.

The following day on the plane back to New York I suddenly felt weak. I barely made it to the bathroom to douse my face with water for fear I would collapse. This was all taking its toll, but at least the operation was back on.

Meanwhile, back in Belfast, the IRA ad hoc ceasefire went ahead on 4 May; it had been too late for them to call it off. It lasted thirty-six hours before a bomb was thrown at a British Army patrol in Belfast.

Chapter 37

INTO THE CAULDRON

I t was August before I could reconstitute the group and plan the trip to Ireland. Through secret communications, I had a letter pledging another IRA ceasefire for one week, starting at midnight on 3 September. I could not share the contents of the note with any of the group until we were in Ireland; then I had promised to destroy it. We travelled to Ireland on 6 September 1993. Our party was small – Bruce Morrison, Chuck Feeney, Bill Flynn and myself. The ceasefire was already in effect. We travelled separately so that no suspicions would be raised. We met in the Westbury Hotel in Dublin. As we sipped coffee I took the document from the IRA out of my briefcase. There was a deathly silence as each read it in turn, with its message of a ceasefire on our behalf. Suddenly we all realised that this was the real thing. I then destroyed the document, as agreed.

We had arranged a meeting with Prime Minister Albert Reynolds in his office. A blunt, plain-speaking man, Reynolds threw all of his advisors out of his office and held a two-hour seminar with us on what was happening with the peace process. His relations with British Prime Minster John Major were very good and he felt that this could form the basis of a new outreach to end the Troubles. Though only in government a few months, Reynolds had promised to make peace in Ireland his top priority and was trying to deliver on that pledge now. He did not know of the ceasefire, and obviously we did not enlighten him. We knew there had been no IRA activity since Friday, 3 September. The ceasefire was in effect for over forty-eight hours when we arrived. We listened to each news bulletin with bated breath, but the ceasefire was holding.

After the Reynolds meeting we met with the US Ambassador to Ireland, Jean Kennedy Smith, in her office. She was new to the job and her nervousness showed. Later she would become a key figure in the American involvement in the peace process, but on that day she was just reading herself into her brief and said very little as we outlined the case for American involvement. Her brother, Teddy, had flexed his Irish muscle and delivered the job for her, and there were many who felt that she would not be up to it. Certainly, when we talked to her she was still extremely tentative, but that was soon to change.

The media was now following us with great interest as it had become evident that this was much more than just another American delegation. We were clearly getting access at a high level all round and the make-up of the group: businessmen and a journalist – no politicians, at least no active ones – was very different to the usual one from America. But no one could quite figure out what we were hoping to achieve. At the end of the first day, I activated the chain of communication with the White House and called Trina Vargo to tell her what had gone on. Amazingly, the White House knew the actual details of the short-term IRA. ceasefire even though the British and Irish governments did not. They had known well in advance of the mission and they were keeping a very close eye on us. Of course, we were on a hiding to nothing. If anything went wrong they had total deniability and I believe there was quite a discussion in the White House about whether we were just a bunch of know-nothing amateurs stumbling around, or serious players. This became a pattern for us. We knew the White House was a looming but invisible presence, somewhere out there in the ether.

The ceasefire was aimed solely at the White House to let them know that the Republican movement was serious about making a major outreach. It was unannounced to everyone but them.

Nancy Soderberg was the key official with whom our group was liaising in the White House. As Deputy National Security Advisor, she was a close confidante of Clinton and on the wall in her office was a framed photograph from the President in which he had written: 'To Nancy, first you tell me what to say, then if I miss a beat you actually write it out word for word. Those who say I think for myself should never see this picture. Thanks.'

Soderberg had worked for Ted Kennedy, Walter Mondale and Michael Dukakis, and then as foreign policy director in the Clinton campaign. She had access to the very top, but she was distrustful of me because I had written a number of articles that were critical of Democratic Party foreign policy on Northern Ireland. Still, I was aware that, from the President on down, they were intrigued with the notion of an IRA ceasefire that was now being dangled in front of them.

Because I was working through Kennedy's office, I knew that anything I told them could be verified by them and there was no opportunity for massaging the truth on any side. Gaining the full trust of the White House was going to be a difficult road. What we were proposing meant that they would be going against their strongest and longest ally in the world. We would have to be certain of how to proceed.

On the second day of our visit, we drove to Belfast. I had become convinced that our driver, who had been recruited in Belfast, was listening in on our conversations. I was paranoid enough to warn people to communicate only with notes and to keep all conversation inconsequential. In Northern Ireland, as I quickly learned, everyone was watching. That was further brought home to me when I picked up the phone at Dukes Hotel to make a call. There was already someone on the line, saying 'the Americans' had arrived. I quickly put down the receiver. The Northern Ireland media had also started to sniff around the story of the group of Irish Americans who had landed on their doorstep. By the time of our first meeting they had begun following us around. Before we came we had been put under considerable pressure not to meet various people. 'We were warned not to speak to several groups, as if somehow by listening to them we would be contaminated by their agenda,' Congressman Bruce Morrison reported. In the end, we succeeded in talking to everyone. We were attempting to break new ground by meeting both the unionist parties and Sinn Féin. It would be the first time that the unionists would agree to such meetings, as anyone who stated that they were meeting Sinn Féin was automatically blacklisted. The fact that the unionists had agreed to meet us, knowing we were meeting Sinn Féin, was a major breakthrough.

We met with the Ulster Unionist Party leadership. It was the first time I'd encountered David Trimble, who was then still seen as a hardliner and a threat to leader James Molyneaux. Strangely, Trimble clicked his heels when he shook hands with us, a bizarre gesture that I was unsure how to interpret. In subsequent meetings I found him impossible to decipher.

The Sinn Féin meeting, was, inevitably, the highlight. We met in a large and gloomy auditorium on the Falls Road. The media was there in large numbers. Sinn Féin had brought together several groups of nationalists whose families had suffered death or injury throughout the Troubles. They were arranged in little groups around the room, waiting to speak to us. We realised then just how important it was that we were there. We were the first Americans most had ever met and it was clear from their stories that they had great faith that if America became involved things would get better. Their confidence was touching, and I only hoped we could deliver. I was stopped in my tracks by one woman who had lost a son in the Troubles, shot down, she said, by the British Army in a case of mistaken identity. She did not seem to bear any bitterness, but I could tell by the hard lines on her face and her careworn posture that she had suffered greatly. She told me the story of her son and I listened, feeling completely inadequate. When she was finished she grabbed my hand, and said, 'Thank you for not treating us like animals.'

The comment brought tears to my eyes. I was beginning to see just how demonised this community had become. The very act of talking to someone from outside who believed they were important enough to listen to was clearly an immense sense of relief to them. The meeting underscored my core belief on these issues: that you have to go first hand to see what is happening in a given conflict. Some media had done an excellent job of depicting this community as IRA-loving, terrorist-harbouring natives. The reality was that they, like everyone else, were caught up in the spiral of a deadly conflict where hurt, injury and death fed upon itself and helped create the next cycle.

We saw the opposite side of the coin the following morning when we met with representatives of the Loyalist paramilitaries on the Protestant side. Among them was Gusty Spence, a revered Loyalist leader, and David Irvine. Once again, we found incredibly articulate and emotional men and women who desperately needed to be heard.

When they talked about the horrendous unemployment, drug problems and desperate need for American investment, the two communities were like a mirror of each other, albeit two communities seemingly locked in a death embrace. It was easy for the 'respectable' politicians to avoid such people. They had no voice or influence, really. It was also very easy to categorise them as sub human, the perpetrators of Europe's longest running war. The middle and upper classes and their political leaders were thus able to foist all the responsibility onto those who were left on the front lines, facing each other across neighbourhoods where a few dozen strides in the wrong direction brought you to a dangerous place.

From this meeting an entire outreach from Irish America to Loyalism commenced, spurred on by Bill Flynn and carried forward by his successor as CEO at Mutual of America, Tom Moran. Moran was a dogged and persistent believer in the same vision that Bill Flynn had of Northern Ireland. He created space for the Loyalists in America, made them welcome and took enormous time and effort to ensure they felt appreciated on the US side of the Atlantic. He personified the best of the Irish American involvement, unselfish, willing to take risks and always committed to the peace process.

Our second meeting with Gerry Adams and the top Sinn Féin leadership at their heavily fortified office went well. It was an intense few hours where we emphasised that we felt the White House could move in our direction now that the IRA were able to deliver. We told them that we would make the granting of a visa for Gerry Adams to come to the United States our objective. If we succeeded, we would overturn over 200 years of British hegemony over American policy on Ireland. It was a tall order, but we were sure going to try. We walked away believing that there was an amazing possibility for a peace breakthrough in Ireland.

The story of the IRA ceasefire for the American delegation broke on 11 September, the day we were leaving. I was astonished that it had stayed secret that long. Even Albert Reynolds was amazed at the news; the first he heard of it was in *The Irish Times*.

Chapter 38

PRELUDE TO A VISA

B ack in New York, the pressure soon mounted to deliver on our promises. I was receiving phone calls every week to check on progress. Clearly, the IRA felt that they had delivered and now it was our turn. I don't think they ever really understood the huge odds we were up against. It was time for action. On a Wednesday afternoon, I went to Bill Flynn's club, the University Club on Fifth Avenue, close by St Patrick's Cathedral. Flynn, as always, was the soul of hospitality, ushering me in and listening carefully as I explained the visa issue. Amid the stacks of library books, the soaring ceilings, the hushed courtiers and the muted sound of Fifth Avenue traffic, we came up with a plan. Adams had been turned down for a visa a dozen times or so, the latest when New York Mayor David Dinkins requested it. How would we be able to overcome that? We talked strategy. Flynn was chairman of a foreign affairs think-thank group, called the National Committee on American Foreign Policy. He wondered if we might use that forum as a vehicle to invite Adams.

I decided we should go and talk it over with Ciaran Staunton, my original Sinn Féin contact, who was someone Flynn now needed to meet. We were soon heading down Fifth Avenue in Flynn's limousine. Ciaran worked at Muldoons, a popular Irish watering spot on 43rd Street and Third. Flynn, in his expensive suit and tie, looked slightly out of place with the mid-afternoon blue collar drinkers. Ciaran was busy and could only spare a few minutes. It was important to all of us that our talk was conducted in strict privacy and we decided that the safest place was somewhere innocuous, like Ray's Pizza, a block or so away. We must have made a strange threesome as we walked to the pizza parlour: Ciaran in his white shirt and dark pants bar outfit, Flynn in his expensive suit, and I was wearing a large sweater I had donned because of the chill in the autumn air. Once inside, we made ourselves comfortable. Flynn was now hot on the idea of inviting Adams to attend the conference that we were cooking up. We decided that the way to do it was to invite all the party leaders from Northern Ireland. After all, if we did it within that framework it would remove one of the biggest objections – that Adams would be free to give only the Sinn Féin point of view. We talked about who we would need to get onside.

The key figure was Senator Edward Kennedy. He owned the Irish issue in Congress and nothing succeeded unless he was in favour of it. As I was already dealing with Kennedy's office, I was assigned the task. I knew Kennedy would listen first and foremost to John Hume, the main nationalist leader in Northern Ireland, who went on to win the Nobel Peace Prize. Convincing Hume would be just as important, and it placed him in an invidious position. After years of being the Irish nationalist kingpin in America, Hume was being asked to share the spotlight with the president of Sinn Féin, whose own star glowed brightly because of all the media attention he drew. After a protracted conversation, we made our decision: we would create a conference specifically for this purpose, hosted by Flynn's organisation. The chances were at least better than zero that we could persuade the White House that it was all bona fide. I loved Flynn's attitude.

'We'll either go down in flames or make this work,' he said. 'We're not going to fade into the wallpaper on this one.'

We walked away from the pizza parlour content that with our secret meeting we had set the visa battle in motion. We might not have been so sanguine had we known exactly where we had just dined. It later transpired that Ray's Pizza was the centre of a huge coke smuggling ring. Some weeks after we left, the FBI swept in and arrested twenty-nine people from three organised crime families from Italy. They were part of the Naples Camorra, and Ray's owner, Aniello Ambrosia, was using the restaurant to arrange drug shipments and hide narcotics in the basement. The FBI had been conducting a major surveillance operation of the place. So, our 'secure' location, where we had conspired to get a notorious 'terrorist' figure into the United States, was the most bugged building in Manhattan at the time! I often wonder what the FBI had made of the conversation of the three Irish Americans wandering into the middle of their sting.

The following week I blasted the news of the conference across the front page of the *Irish Voice* and it was quickly picked up by wire services and newspapers all over Europe and the United States. The visa battle had begun. Years later, many people stepped in to claim credit for the visa, including a slew of politicians. Although talk of a visa and efforts to secure one had gone on for many years, none of them ever had a chance. Bill Flynn helped spring the deadlock, along with Ciaran and me. There was simply no one else directly involved.

Chapter 39

THE VISA BATTLE

Now that the visa issue was out in the open, the *New York Times* and other major newspapers were writing editorials on the question. The *Times* support was invaluable. The British media, was, as might be expected, apoplectic at the idea of Adams coming to America when he was banned from travelling to London. The British embassy had a willing servant to carry their water, House Speaker Tom Foley, who, despite his ethnic background, was a prized friend of the British and was pushing hard to have the White House deny the visa. He told Ambassador Jean Kennedy Smith that he thought it was a dreadful idea. How deeply he felt about it was obvious from a comment from *Washington Post* columnist Mary McGrory to Conor O'Clery as reported in his book *Daring Diplomacy:* 'It was hard to figure out the Speaker. He had the whole business of the House to worry about, but the only thing I ever saw him get passionate about was Ireland.' He had also made it clear in many conversations that he absolutely opposed a visa for Adams.

At a house party that Foley attended, he shocked guests by shouting at someone who tried to defend the visa idea. Kennedy Smith was not the only one taking heat. In one of the more bizarre incidents, British actor Hugh Grant rudely interrupted a speech that George Stephanopoulos was making at a private dinner in Washington and began shouting about the White House encouraging terrorists. Grant had come from a reception at the British embassy, where, no doubt, Adams was the chief topic of conversation. Meanwhile, within the White House itself, a battle royal was shaping up. On one side were Secretary of State Warren Christopher, Attorney General Janet Reno, the CIA and the FBI, all opposing the visa. On the other side were the National Security Council staffers, Deputy National Security Advisor Nancy Soderberg, and her boss, Tony Lake, who were actively considering the issue. The key was President Clinton himself, and he gave a tantalising insight into his thinking in a year-end interview with Conor O'Clery in *The Irish Times* when he stated that the Adams visa issue was 'under review', an enormous step forward from a point blank refusal. O'Clery was an invaluable reporter, in my opinion one of the best ever to come out of Ireland. When on the scent of a story, he was like a bloodhound, and the visa one had all the ingredients of a major scoop. We were also lucky that RTÉ, Ireland's national television station, had a great reporter in Mark Little in place at the time in Washington.

There were other straws in the wind. That autumn, Yasser Arafat had come to the White House and shaken hands with Israeli Prime Minister Yitzhak Rabin; many were asking if an historic breakthrough could happen in the Middle East, why not in Ireland? In the Dublin embassy, Jean Kennedy Smith had to face down a revolt in her own ranks. Four senior embassy officials signed a letter dissenting against her recommendation that Adams be granted a visa. It poisoned the atmosphere in the embassy and led to a lengthy State Department inquiry. Jean was an important supporter, but we had an even better friend. Senator Ted Kennedy had come on board. His sister had played a large role in convincing him to support it, but it was the backing of John Hume that made the difference. Hume and Kennedy met at Tip O'Neill's funeral in Boston and Kennedy asked him straight out if he supported the visa idea. Hume answered 'yes'. The stage was thus set for a major row as the days ticked down to the visa decision. The conference was arranged for the end of January.

The White House was now pressing hard to get a strong statement from Adams on violence before the decision on the visa was made. As I was the conduit, it involved exhausting hours on the phone between Washington and Belfast, trying to find a formula of words. Both sides were talking past each other. Washington could not understand why Adams could not just come out and denounce violence. Adams could not understand why they wanted him to do that when he knew it would destroy his credibility with the IRA. There was a complete language stalemate. The White House wanted clear and concise language in deploring violence. Adams knew that such language would render his role useless if he complied.

He confided to me on several occasions that he was worried that he was being set up, that he would make a statement and the visa would be denied and he would be left useless. It was a legitimate fear. The White House demands kept changing, clearly a sign that the internal dispute over the visa was in full flight. Bit by bit I tried to tease out a form of words acceptable to both sides. As Adams remarked, thousands of lives could ride on a successful outcome to the negotiation. I felt a major responsibility in this area. Sinn Féin and the White House both spoke their own version of bureaucratese. Though an accomplished creative writer himself, Adams often fell into the Sinn Féin language trap of over-elaborate and careful qualification of everything so that the core message was unclear, particularly to an American audience. Often, the White House would call, exasperated because they had no idea whatever what the phrases really meant and which ones indicated progress. My job on those occasions was to bring about a clarification that made sense to both sides.

There had been two almost fatal incidents in this regard. In the first, the White House had been about to issue a damaging statement, based on British pressure to get Adams to renounce violence. In effect, the White House statement would say that Adams could have a visa if he renounced violence. It all seemed so simple on the surface; after all, what sane person would not renounce violence? But what the British omitted to tell the White House was that if Adams were to be pushed into such an explicit renunciation, he could bid farewell to his position of influence with the IRA and within Sinn Féin, and the Irish peace process would be deader than a dodo. He was clearly the only man alive who could significantly influence the IRA to give up their campaign voluntarily, and he would not do it by denying them. In the highly nuanced world of Irish republican politics, Adams had stated that he wanted to see the gun out of Irish politics, which was as far as he could go. Yet the imminent White House statement called for him to use the British term of renouncing violence – a bridge too far. The statement got as far as the White House press office before we intercepted it and managed to head it off. I was within a few minutes of calling Adams and telling him the bad news, before news reached me to say that the White House had withdrawn the statement.

Then, two days before the visa decision was made, Adams was called to the US consulate in Belfast for an interview. He found the questioning hostile and was told when leaving the building that he would not get the visa. I had wanted him to go to the US Embassy in Dublin for the interview, as Ambassador Jean Kennedy Smith was clearly far better disposed to the visa request. Indeed, a key element in securing the visa had been put in place by having Adams apply at the Dublin embassy in the first place. We felt that a positive recommendation from Ambassador Smith would have a huge impact back at the State Department. Moreover, we knew that the Belfast consulate where, technically, he should have applied, would route his request through London, where the anglophile Ambassador Raymond Seitz would quickly issue a negative report back to Washington. However, at the time Adams was too fatigued, and had not made any security arrangements to travel to Dublin, thereby making Belfast the venue for the vital interview. What Adams did not know was that he was by then in the middle of a major power game being played out between the National Security Council and the Irish lobby who favoured the visa, and the British government, State Department and Justice Department who did not. Naturally, the State Department personnel who conducted the interview had put the most negative spin possible on it. With the world media awaiting a statement on his meeting with the consular officials, Adams, unaware that the State Department attitude did not reflect the total US government view, scripted a strongly worded statement thanking his supporters in the US and expressing strong regret that the government would not grant the visa.

I had arranged to talk to him before any statement was issued and finally reached him with great difficulty as the media was clamouring for his press release. My heart sank as he read it to me.

'If we release this, Gerry, we lose the battle,' I told him. 'That is not the true situation. It's a complex issue, but the State Department are not running this policy, much as they would like to. You have to issue a neutral statement.'

Adams then told me he had been stopped and searched by the Northern police force, the Royal Ulster Constabulary (RUC), outside the American consulate. He was obviously immensely irritated by the RUC action and, not for the first time, he had questions about the American strategy and whether we were reading it right. Both those incidents had made me aware of how crucial the element of trust was between the Clinton administration and Adams. There was a mutual sense that they could do business, but translating that into reality was proving difficult. And so much was riding on the relationship, including a vital element of the peace process in Ireland. A slew of rumours circulated that the visa had been lost, fed, I'm sure, by the British who were now increasingly nervous. The *New York Times* clearly believed the rumours, publishing an editorial on 28 January that assumed it had been denied, and stating, 'A broad spectrum of Irish-Americans now see an opportunity for engaging Mr. Adams in serious discussion of joining a promising peace initiative. Whether or not to allow him into the country was a close call, but Mr. Clinton would better have honored the principle of openness by admitting him.'

I knew different: that the game was still on. The deadline for the visa was almost upon us and still there was no decision from the White House. It was a nerve-racking period, where every time the phone rang my mouth went cotton dry as I picked up the receiver. After every false alarm I became just a little more anxious than before. Why was it all taking so long?

Chapter 40

THE SAN DIEGO INCIDENT

T he White House finally made contact at 7pm on the Saturday before the visa decision had to be made. The call came via Senator Edward Kennedy's office just as I had stepped into the shower. Dripping wet and grabbing a towel in one hand, I grasped the receiver, thinking it was likely another query from a friend or participant as to what was going on. The caller was Trina Vargo, Foreign Affairs aide to Senator Kennedy and one of the people I worked closest with in the entire process. She was relaying a disturbing message. The White House wanted immediate direct contact with me. They had been leaning in favour of granting Gerry Adams the visa, but something had come up. There was something in Vargo's voice that got me distinctly worried. She seemed downright agitated. One awful thought was foremost in my mind. Had there been an IRA atrocity? No, said Vargo, nothing that she knew about. But I had better discuss the matter with them right away. They would call me. I was in a fever of anticipation.

Whatever it was must have been serious enough to throw the entire question into the melting pot again. We had been quietly confident that the issue was heading in our direction again since the tremendous *New York Times* editorial the day before which had urged the President to admit Adams. But now the anxious feeling in the pit of my stomach returned. There was an enormous amount at stake, over three years of painstaking work, involving hundreds of people and the future of a fragile daisy chain of communication that had been established, linking the guerilla leaders of IRA/Sinn Féin in Belfast all the way up to the White House. As the conduit between Sinn Féin and the White House and the person who set up most of those lines of communication, it was shaping up to be one of the best, or alternately, one of the worst days of my life. Not alone was President Clinton on the verge of break-ing a twenty-five-year international ban on Gerry Adams, he would also be interjecting the United States directly into the Irish question for the first time in history. The ramifications of a positive decision over the objections of the British Government and his own State Depart-ment would be enormous. The potential for the ending of the longest guerilla war in Europe was on the line, as was, if the British media was to be believed, the state of the 'special relationship' between the Brit-ish and US governments, which had lasted since they made up after the Revolutionary War.

Throughout the previous two weeks we had been told that a deci-sion was imminent. Adams was booked for a conference at the Wal-dorf Astoria, New York, on Monday, 2 February. Yet, late on the Saturday evening before the conference, there was still no decision from the White House. A few moments after Vargo's call, the tinny sound of my phone interrupted my thoughts again. It was Nancy Soderberg, ringing from the White House.

'We brought the Adams issue to the President today and he feels good about it,' she said. A pause. 'However, there is one snag.'

I held my breath. 'What now?'

'You need to talk to him about the San Diego incident.'

San Diego? My mind went blank. What had the Sinn Féin leader got to do with San Diego?

'I'm sorry, Nancy,' I told her. 'I haven't heard anything about the San Diego incident.'

She seemed embarrassed telling me. As a former staffer for Senator Kennedy and the White House expert on Irish issues, she knew what she was about to relay to me sounded farfetched.

'It appears that the IRA may have planted some devices in British-owned stores in San Diego. We have a wire story saying that two suspect devices were found by police in British-owned stores and that a phone call claiming responsibility by the IRA was made and that they want Adams to get a visa or there will be more trouble. The FBI are very worried and the President wants a firm denial by Adams of any IRA involvement before he signs off on this visa.'

I could hardly believe my ears.

'You've got to be kidding me,' I sputtered. 'You know that the IRA has never operated in the US. It would be completely suicidal for them to do so, particularly at this time. This is clearly a dirty tricks operation to stop the visa. You guys can't fall for this,' I added desperately.

Nancy ventured no opinion on that. 'We need a statement from Adams disavowing it,' she said. 'As soon as possible.'

'He's going to think I'm nuts if I call him with this,' I told her. 'I also have to be able to tell him he has the visa. I can't expose him to ridicule on this if he fails to get the visa as well.'

'It's with the President.' she said. 'He wants to do it, but we need this first, and it has to be public.'

She rang off. I was stunned. Anyone dealing with the Provisionals knows that there is always the possibility that an atrocity by the IRA could wreck delicate political negotiations. The Shankill Road bomb that had killed ten innocent Protestants just a few weeks before was but the latest example. But bombs in San Diego? I had hardly time to think it through before the phone rang again. It was Senator Edward Kennedy whose support for the Adams visa had helped turned the whole issue around and who had been a major influence in shaping the White House debate on it. The senator had been an unseen hand in the debate over the visa for several weeks, as had the White House. At all times I was very aware that they both had to have deniability about what was going on. Dealing with 'international terrorists,' even through intermediaries such as me, was not going to add to their stature if it became public before the pieces were put in place.

'Niall, I can't believe this nonsense in San Diego,' he said, clear anger in his voice. 'How will Adams react to it?'

I told him what I thought. Adams had become quite tetchy at times in my dealings with him over the previous few weeks as the visa battle peaked. I understood how he felt. We had drafted a statement together for the White House on where he stood on violence. I had asked him to give me his most recent and most positive statement on the issue, then I had worked it with him, so that it reflected some of the concerns the White House were voicing, as far as it could. During our back and forth, Adams had remarked that the whole game on the visa to America issue could be a set up by the British, with the Americans in tow, in order to get him to go further out on a limb with his own people by dangling the carrot of an American visa before him. It was a plausible scenario, but I strongly didn't believe that was the case. That scenario, of course, would also have implied that I was an unwitting pawn in this game. It was an unpleasant feeling. Throughout the week leading up to the visa decision, I had been constantly on the phone to him, trying to get a satisfactory form of words on different issues for the White House as their decision-making on the visa evolved.

I told Senator Kennedy that I wouldn't be surprised if Adams dismissed the whole issue and refused to go any further. Kennedy was reassuring.

'This has to be dealt with,' he said. 'Tell him I personally told you to say that he can trust us on this. There's no stopping the momentum on giving him the visa now.'

I put down the phone and called Gerry Adams. It was the middle of the night, his time, and here I was, having to tell him what I was convinced was a cock and bull story about IRA bombs in San Diego and asking him to disavow it publicly. Adams would have been justified in thinking that he had just taken up residence in Kafka's *Castle* when it came to dealing with these Americans. His phone rang for what seemed an interminable period before a tired, but surprisingly good-humoured Adams picked up the phone. Our conversation was, of course, taped by the British, as all his calls are, but I was surprised to see large chunks of it brazenly repeated almost verbatim in the pages of the London *Sunday Times* the following week, even though the paper characterised it as a direct call between the White House and Adams, which it was not. He did not seem all that surprised by the bogus bomb story. I told him I thought the visa was a sure thing if we could satisfy the White House on this San Diego issue. I told him I was completely bowled over by the San Diego development and that it had 'come from left field' as far as I was concerned.

'This is what Mary Robinson went through,' he said.

He explained that the Irish President had determined that she would meet Adams on a visit to West Belfast in August of the previous year. The British did everything, short of physically stopping her, to scupper the meeting. They gave out her private home number, threatened to withdraw security around her for her visit, and orchestrated a media campaign of vilification against her. Despite it all, she bravely went ahead and shook Adams's hand in a brief meeting. It was a symbolic but highly significant step in ending the ostracisation of Sinn Féin.

After recalling the Robinson incident, we quickly moved on to the San Diego issue and the necessity to issue a public statement. If this was all that stood between him and the visa he said he would do it. He felt the incident was so clearly the work of an *agent provocateur* that it would be widely seen as another effort by the British to blacken him with his own people. But would his denial guarantee him a visa? We discussed the request for twenty minutes and I told him that Senator Kennedy believed it would. More than ever, I needed Adams to believe me now that the chips were down. Finally he broke the tension with a joke.

'Ask the White House if this means I have to issue a statement denying responsibility every time an Irishman upsets an Englishman in a pub over there,' he said.

I knew then we had the visa in the bag. He drafted a brief statement condemning the incident. I took it down, hung up and called the White House to read it to Nancy Soderberg. She said she needed to consult her colleagues, and after what seemed an interminable ten minutes, she called back to approve it. She seemed satisfied, but wanted to ensure it was released publicly. Would Adams have the visa then?

'It looks good,' she told me.

Still no definite yes. Now another problem arose. Releasing the statement was to prove harder than I thought. On my first two tries I called the wire services in New York cold and met with quizzical replies from hardened journalists, wondering why an Irishman was calling them up at this hour replying to a story they weren't even aware existed. One even asked gently if I hadn't been imbibing a little, perhaps. I called every journalist I knew, even though it was close on midnight. In desperation I reached Conor O'Clery of *The Irish Times* who had superb contacts in the US, Britain and Ireland. Conor was at a house party, and it was too late for his own newspaper, but he gave me the number for the Associated Press editors in London. Eventually, after lengthy debate, the Associated Press agreed to handle it through their London office. Sinn Féin personnel were roused from their beds and the complete statement was faxed through to them from my newspaper office in order that they could release it directly. Standing over the fax machine at my office at 1am, faxing a message from their own party president back to the Sinn Féin press office about a hoax bomb in San Diego, in order for them to release it in London, was only one of the many ironic moments of a very strange night. But the job seemed done.

In an interesting sidebar, the arrival of a fax on Sinn Féin headed notepaper at the National Security Council at the White House apparently caused a huge ripple. 'For the first time it became real that we were engaging with these people,' a security council staffer later told me. That night, President Clinton had attended a dinner in Washington. He was seated between Warren Christopher and Speaker of the House Tom Foley, two avowed enemies of granting the visa, a scenario that would have made us shudder if we had known. On leaving the function, Clinton was handed the Adams' denial by Sandy Berger, the second in command at the National Security Council. With the statement in hand he issued the order allowing Gerry Adams into the United States on a forty-eight-hour visa. It was 31 January 1994.

The news was to be released at a press briefing the following morning. It was an historic decision that would have huge ramifications for the embryonic peace process in Ireland. By then, I was almost too tired to care. The hectic weeks leading up to the visa decision began to finally impact on me and I was bone weary. Without the adrenalin rush, there was instead a deep sense of anti-climax and I neglected to call some of those who had been closest in the battle with me. Some were rightfully annoyed the next day when they heard it first on the radio. I did call the other members of the Connolly House Group. Of all of them, Flynn hardly seemed surprised.

'I never doubted this would happen,' he said.

I wish I had shared his confidence.

Chapter 41

THE MEDIA GO WILD

T he next morning, after a full night's sleep, the immensity of the victory hit me. Every news bulletin in America was leading with the story that the head of the Sinn Féin/IRA guerilla movement was coming to America after being banned for twenty-five years. The British were going crazy. The *Daily Telegraph* called it 'the Worst Rift Since Suez' while the *Daily Express* described Clinton's decision as 'a coarse insult from a country we thought was our friend'. The tabloid *Sun* hissed, 'Yanks, keep your noses out of Ulster.' The *Sunday Times* attacked Nancy Soderberg. The British ambassador in Washington stated, 'When I listen to Gerry Adams, I think, as we all do, it's reminiscent of Dr. Goebbels.'

Chat show host Larry King announced that Adams would be appearing on his programme. Every television network in the US was clamouring to have him on. The *New York Times* led with it on their front page. Sinn Féin said they could not remember anything like it since the death of Bobby Sands on hunger strike in 1981. The media madness that would surround the visit itself was already shaping up. The British were apoplectic. Their media was to turn highly venomous over the next seventy-two hours, but initially they were reacting out of a sense of shock. Suddenly two hundred years of the 'special relationship' had been breached by a US president and an upstart Irish lobby they felt certain they long had the measure of. So certain were their diplomats in Washington of their position that they rated the chances of an

Adams visa at 'about 10%' just a week before the decision. A senior British diplomat had bet a colleague on the Irish side, with whom he had an excellent relationship, an expensive dinner on the outcome. He was so upset when the decision came down that he would not take calls.

I was unable to reach Adams on the day of the visa announcement as he had left for Dublin where he was appearing on Irish radio and television, another recent breakthrough for Sinn Féin who had long been banned from the airwaves in the Irish Republic under the provisions of Section 31 of the Broadcasting Act. He was due on the Aer Lingus flight into New York the following day, and within hours I was in negotiations with the White House on exactly what he could and could not accomplish during his stay. Nancy Soderberg was extremely keen that there be no Irish Northern Aid direct fundraising associated with the visit. Noraid had long been fingered by the US government as a conduit for IRA arms. I willingly gave her that assurance and told her that the public meeting would be managed by Americans for a New Irish Agenda, (ANIA) the group which grew out of Irish Americans for Clinton/Gore and was composed of leading Irish American politicians and community leaders.

The White House were specifically worried that Adams would say or do something that would embarrass them. They were only beginning to feel the full wrath of the British media reaction to the Adams visit. Worse, the British Embassy in Washington, after a relatively restrained original reaction, was launching a diplomatic counter offensive against the decision. Their point man was Speaker of the House Tom Foley, who despite his Irish origins was a committed Anglophile and who had personally lobbied Clinton against granting the visa. Ending the complete demonisation of Adams and the job of assuring key people that he was indeed intent on the path to peace would prove to be a difficult task. I felt that many of the White House people and the media I spoke with expected him to show up in America with horns on his head. Clearly, years of guerilla warfare and some of the more notorious atrocities had left their impact, as had the British spin that Sinn Féin/ IRA were a terrorist criminal gang with no political intent. But the British did their own cause no good by their overreaction. It was to become a familiar pattern.

Whenever the White House would make a positive decision for Adams, the British overreaction would make a bad situation for them much worse. Instead of downplaying the Adams visa, they instead helped make it a huge international incident involving the very fundamental nature of their dealings with the United States, the 'special relationship' as they liked to refer to it. Years later, I took enormous satisfaction from the fact that John Major and senior diplomats, among others, admitted that the visa decision had in fact been the right one.

However, in the post Cold War era the special relationship was no longer as paramount as it once was. In President Clinton's case there was also the fact that the British Conservative party had sent two of their top operatives to the US to help George Bush get re-elected. And, just before the election, British Foreign Secretary Douglas Hurd had sent a pointed message of support to President Bush, all of which hardly endeared them to the new young president from Arkansas. Into the widening gap between the President and the British government, the Irish lobby had now driven a coach and four, by swinging the visa for Gerry Adams. But none of us involved in winning that decision had any real sense of how huge the ramifications for the US/British relationship really were.

Chapter 42

ADAMS ARRIVES

I did not go to the airport to greet Gerry Adams. I spoke to him the night before he left Dublin. He sounded exhausted already and I warned him of the mayhem that would ensue once he arrived, but he was already well aware of it. I told him how proud Irish Americans were that his voice would finally be heard in the United States and that a key element in his speeches would be to thank President Clinton for the opportunity. He requested that I look over his speech for the National Committee on American Foreign Policy, the group which had invited him, and which he would deliver on Tuesday. I agreed.

I also had to cover things on the home front. The arrival of Adams had thrown my *Irish Voice* into a headlong battle to stretch our deadlines in order to cover the visit. Normally we would go to press on Tuesday afternoon for Wednesday morning newsstand delivery. Now we had to stretch everything to the limit. We had one ace in the hole – the column that Gerry Adams regularly contributed to the newspaper. Now, having a firsthand account of his visit would be of great benefit to us. My morning was spent deciding some crucial elements of the visit in tandem with Ciaran Staunton, the Sinn Féin representative. For the public meeting, the Americans for a New Irish Agenda had already made the decision to hire the largest hall available in New York – at the Sheraton Hotel – capable of holding up to 5,000 people. The question of who would introduce Adams was critical. Former Congressman Bruce Morrison was the obvious choice. He was not identified in any

258

way with Noraid, was a personal friend of President Clinton and a member of the 'Gang of Four'. There would also be a role for Paul O'Dwyer, the legendary 84-year old patriarch of the Irish in New York who had worked harder and waited longer than anyone in New York for this day.

Adams finally flew in to JFK airport on Aer Lingus flight 105 on Sunday, 1 February, 1994. He was met by a bevy of cameras from every major network and by Congressman Peter King of Long Island, a long time supporter. Already the desire to be part of the momentous event was causing friction. The Sinn Féin personnel and the National Committee on American Foreign Policy group, who were sponsoring his conference appearance, had a sometimes acerbic argument over who would officially meet Adams. In the end, he was brought to the interview area and surrounded by officials of both groups and some key supporters. Bruce Morrison was one of a number of people who went into the baggage customs area to greet Adams on his arrival.

Seeing him on TV at the podium at JFK Airport, I had to do a double take. It seemed an extraordinary breakthrough moment, which so many had worked long and hard to accomplish, and even though I had been on the inside, I still had difficulty believing what I was seeing. Adams, however, seemed his usually unperturbed self. Later that night there was a private reception, hosted by Bill Flynn, for Adams and for John Hume, the other Irish nationalist leader, who was attending the conference. The sight of the two men together, an extremely rare occurrence, heightened the sense of history around the conference. Adams was relaxed, though already exhibiting the signs of the deep fatigue he was feeling.

After the reception we went up to his room so I could give my opinion on his speech. My heart sank when I read it. It was a Sinn Féin boilerplate speech, suffused with much of the cant and historical polemics that would be completely lost on an American audience. Clearly,

Adams's advisors had decided his New York speech would be a restatement of basic principles, but it read like someone dictating the telephone book. There was also no way to work around it. I sat down on the bed, preparing to do my best with it, while Adams went to take a shower. After a few moments he emerged, puzzled, from the bathroom.

'What's wrong with this shower, eh? I can't get it to work.'

Like most Irish people in America for the first time, the Sinn Féin leader had been baffled by the switch mechanism which changed the water flow from the taps to the shower. That done, I went back to my text. Adams came out of the shower and immediately tackled the drinks cabinet, which included some food snacks. After he had wrestled with the handles for a few minutes I went over to help him, content in my superior knowledge that I would soon sort it out. Alas, it baffled me too and the key usually available to unlock it was nowhere to be found. I abandoned the speech and for the next twenty minutes the two of us tried to wrestle the door of the cabinet into submission. Adams was ravenous and even tried the 'Open Sesame' routine from *Ali Baba*, to no avail.

'Don't tell anyone you're a complete klutz, Gerry. It might destroy the image!' I told him.

Amazingly, we hardly got back to the speech. We were both too exhausted and he was starving

Chapter 43

A ROCK STAR RECEPTION

The media had been briefed by the British that Adams had agreed to renounce violence in return for the visa to America. Though it was a classic piece of disinformation, it dogged Adams for the forty-eight hours he was in America as the supine press gladly pushed the line. No such assurance was ever given or asked for. The media throngs were extraordinary; from early in the morning they surrounded the Waldorf Astoria hotel, covering every move. Each of the conference speakers had been issued a fake identity to protect their privacy. This worked fine until John Hume turned up at Reception and couldn't remember who he was supposed to be. After a long debate he finally got the key to his room.

Early that morning, Slobo Galisowizc, aka Gerry Adams, slipped out of the hotel for a round of meetings. The White House were clearly unnerved by the fallout from their decision. I received hourly calls checking that Adams was not going to say or do anything outside the parameters we had agreed. Again, the extent of the demonisation of the man struck me. I felt he was one of the most astute political figures ever to set foot in the US and he was surely not going to blow his reception by saying something to embarrass his hosts. On the morning before the conference, Adams had his first meeting with Trina Vargo, who was dispatched to the conference by Senator Kennedy. The meeting was more crucial for Adams than he could possibly have known at the time. Ted Kennedy had a key role in delivering the visa and his take on Adams would weigh heavily on Capitol Hill. The meeting took place in Vargo's room in the Waldorf and we reached there after having to throw several reporters off the trail. The discussion was dominated by the question of an IRA ceasefire. Adams had made it clear that if he could get a sufficiently extensive range of proposals together he would take a proposition to the IRA. But no, he was not at that point.

I have always admired Adams's negotiating manner. He is immensely patient. I have often sat in meetings with him where speakers went on far too long on some trivial point, and watched him exude an almost Buddha-like patience on those occasions. Similarly in his management of the peace process. He appeared to go for weeks and months without shifting off his stated position. Then a new word or phrase would be introduced into his statements, and would be worked assiduously for another period of time, before yet another miniscule shift would occur. In the end, the significance of the overall shift would be apparent to everyone, but it would have happened so gradually that, unless you were watching closely, it would never have occurred that it was going on. He, of course, had to be a skilled negotiator. In attempting to manage a process which brought an armed revolutionary movement into a political accommodation, he was trying what previous Irish leaders had done and failed.

In the most immediate example, the ruinous Irish civil war of 1921 and the death of Michael Collins had resulted from the failure to bring the IRA into politics. In his meeting with Vargo, Adams reiterated most or all of the points that he had stated previously on where his movement stood on the issues. However, he did make it absolutely clear that President Clinton's issuance of the visa was a huge boost for his movement and would be a major factor in the internal debate. Following his meeting with Vargo, I spoke with her.

'He's really got to deliver,' she told me. 'We have the President and the senior senator on the Irish issue on the hook here. I really hope he understands this. There are a lot of people who want us to fail.'

I told her he did, of course, but that he had his own internal pressures. I then broke the bad news on the conference speech, which didn't help her confidence.

'Look, we have to work with him on this kind of thing,' I told her. 'It's not that easy just to drop into the middle of such a huge media circus.'

Adams had proceeded from our meeting to the conference, where, as I feared, his speech went over like a lead balloon with most of the audience. 'More suitable for a Republican commemoration service in Tyrone,' said one cynical observer. The star, in fact, was John Hume, who spoke passionately and without any notes. He outlined his vision of an 'agreed Ireland' as against a United Ireland or a continuing British-controlled Northern Ireland. It was a speech I had mostly heard before from Hume but it was a very moving exposé of the type of generosity that was needed in Northern Ireland. Earlier, sitting behind Adams, it was easy to feel for Hume, who was all but ignored in the media crush to film and photograph Adams. After spending many years building his American contacts all the way to the White House, Hume was inevitably playing second fiddle on this day. The other speaker at the conference, moderate Alliance party leader Dr John Alderdice, also acquitted himself very well.

The most moving and perhaps revealing moment of Adams's visit occurred the following evening when he spoke to a 5,000 plus audience at the Sheraton Hotel, with many more locked out. Even without advance notice, throngs showed up from as far away as Chicago, Boston and Philadelphia to hear the man who, in the long tradition of Sinn Féin leaders, had been kept out of the US for so many years. Many, particularly the older people, were in tears around me when he stood up to speak. My thoughts went back to the same kind of crowds who had stood for hours when Eamon de Valera, as head of Sinn Féin in 1919, had visited America for the first time as leader of the Provisional Irish Government after the War of Independence. Then, the poor Irish, from the house maids to the labourers, turned out in their tens of thousands to greet their new Irish hero, only to see their dreams shattered a few years later when partition and the Irish civil war ensued.

Their descendants stood in line this night, all those years later, and a new generation of young Irish who had emigrated during the 1970s and 1980s joined them, creating the most extraordinary atmosphere I have ever witnessed at an Irish American event. Would they, too, be disappointed? It was also the first inkling of the extraordinary emotional impact Adams has on audiences of Irish Americans. Much of Irish American history starts with the mass emigration after the Famine. Partition, civil war and the Troubles were bloody signposts on a miserable trail. Now the latest leader of Sinn Féin, with his talk of peace and his recent victory over the British on the visa issue was finally delivering good news. There was a sense among ordinary Irish Americans that at last the pieces in the chess game were lining up together: the Irish government, John Hume, Gerry Adams and now President Clinton and Irish America. The people in the room that night sensed that an irresistible momentum was building up. Like all the other involved groups, many of them had become war weary after a quarter century of conflict, a reality that struck me the more Adams met large crowds on his American trips.

On a subsequent Adams visit, an old man in Glastonbury, Connecticut, stated it best when he said, 'It's great to have something to celebrate after all the tragedy. We all feel renewed by this peace process.' There is no question in my mind that without the Connolly House Group, the IRA ceasefire, which was the underpinning of the entire peace process, might never have been achieved, or would certainly have been delayed for a long time. Out of that group came the entire outreach reaching up to the president of the United States.

Gerry Adams's appearance on 'Larry King Live' was the media centerpiece of his visit. In a scenario even he could not have invented in his wildest dreams, the British authorities jammed the live satellite link into Britain in order to dub his voice, as he was not allowed to speak over the airwaves in Britain. This caused enormous bemusement on the American side where free speech remains the most cherished amendment to the Constitution, and ultimately led to the British dropping their absurd broadcasting ban.

Before he left, I met Adams at the offices of Bill Flynn who had been his gracious host throughout. He was plainly exhausted and had hardly slept since his madcap trip began. Now, with his security and Sinn Féin advisors hovering outside the door, we had a rushed meeting shortly before he went back to Ireland. We agreed that the American agenda had come a long way since our original meeting. He asked that I continue the current arrangement of serving as the go-between with the White House, and I readily agreed. I put it to him that there were inevitable expectations at the White House as a result of the dramatic breakthrough that had been accomplished, but was careful to leave it at that. He would sort that through in his own good time, I felt. Adams was clearly happy about how the historic visit had gone.

'It's come a long way', he said to me as we parted.

'Further than maybe we both believed,' I responded, as I thought back to the stuttering and uncertain beginning to the Irish American involvement in the peace process. It was a long and hard road that had defeated many other leaders before Adams. I have often been asked about how the Sinn Féin leader managed to deliver the IRA and how we made a part of that possible. I always reply with one word: 'patience'. It was a quality I learnt when dealing with Sinn Féin on a regular basis. The trick was to make others – all the way up to the American President – understand that 'more haste, less speed' was the operative principle when trying to force Sinn Féin to go faster.

Chapter 44

TOUGH WORDS AT
THE WHITE HOUSE

The White House decided to hold a major event on Saint Patrick's night 1994. It was officially called a 'Celebration of Ireland' but was informally named a 'Hooley at the White House'. It started out as a state dinner for Taoiseach Albert Reynolds, but so many wanted to be involved that one White House source told the *Irish Voice,* 'There are 44 million Irish Americans and it looks like 43 million want to come'.

It was the beginning of the White House outreach to Ireland and it is a tradition that has continued ever since, through the Bush years and into the Obama term. On this one night a year, the Irish now get the run of the American seat of power. It is a remarkable occasion and other ethnic groups would give their eye teeth for it.

The numbers were capped at 350, thus starting an elephant's ballet of manoeuvres for the coveted invitations. The list that was finally chosen drew heavily from our *Irish America* magazine Top 100 list. For the first time I experienced what it was like to be the most popular guy in town as perfect strangers corralled me, explained their deep affection for me and asked if, by the way, I might have a White House ticket.

There was a deeper purpose to the event than simply a 'hooley'. Clinton wanted to make a statement to Sinn Féin and others that he had bought in, was fully committed after the Adams visa and was now waiting for a return on his investment.

On the night, President Clinton did not mess around when I met him on the receiving line.'What are the IRA up to?' he asked, referring to the fact that they had just hit Heathrow Airport three times with home-made mortars which deliberately did not explode but left panic and consternation in their wake.

I tried to explain, quickly, that paradoxically I felt it was a sign that they were serious about a cessation, arguing that it made them look stronger and clearly in control of their actions and that the ceasefire would come from a position of strength, not weakness. In truth, I thought the Heathrow bombs were a disaster, believing for some time that the IRA were too often utterly tone deaf to political realities as others tried to bring them in from the cold.

Later at the party, where stars like Paul Newman, Joanne Woodward, Richard Harris and Michael Keaton mixed with the old and new guard of Irish America, any celebratory feelings I was enjoying were quickly quenched. National Security Advisor Tony Lake and his deputy Nancy Soderberg ushered me into a quiet corner. For the first time, I realised the pressure they were facing. Lake was furious about the Heathrow bombs, saying that it made the British right all along: that the Republican movement could not be trusted. Soderberg left me in no doubt that she shared Lake's feelings. I responded that it was an internal game at the moment within the Republican movement and that despite Heathrow I was convinced it was heading in the right direction. I had only the word of Ted Howell and Gerry Adams for that, but I believed both men implicitly.

In Clinton's speech he slammed the IRA mortar attacks at Heathrow in very strong language. I swore he looked directly at me as he spoke. I just hoped I was right in putting my faith in Sinn Féin.

Chapter 45

WAITING FOR THE CEASEFIRE

In August 1994 the Connolly House Group returned to Ireland. I had received a communication that the IRA was about to move and declare a ceasefire. The note was typically cryptic, only advising me when to take my vacation and announcing that new arrangements would soon be in place. It was the only document I saved from my years of dealing with them.

We went to Belfast the weekend before the announcement. The city was abuzz with speculation as to what was about to happen. Everywhere we went, camera crews followed us, believing we knew something, which we did, but were sworn to secrecy. Earlier in the week, we had met Taoiseach Albert Reynolds and Deputy Leader Dick Spring. They had asked us to carry a message to the IRA that only a complete ceasefire would work. There had been lots of speculation about a ceasefire that would last for a few weeks or maybe a month. Reynolds left us in no doubt what the government wanted and needed – a complete cessation. We went North not knowing what to expect. The delegation was divided over what the IRA would do. We knew we were on the verge of an historic announcement but we didn't know what that announcement would say.

The minute we met Adams and the other leaders I knew it was a complete ceasefire. I had never seen Adams look so confident and rested. It seemed he had crossed the Rubicon on the issue of the IRA campaign and was now fully committed to the new path. They told us we could expect a major announcement on 31 August. 'Wait for the Angelus Bell' said one of them, giving us the time frame of 12 noon.

A few days later, I was exercising in the workout room of a Dublin hotel when the radio presenter broke into a music programme to announce that an IRA statement was imminent. It moved me to tears when I heard it. All the pressure, the personal strain, the years of grappling with such a complex issue, seemed to boil to the surface. The longest running guerilla war in Europe was finally over. It was 31 August 1994.

Within an hour, Ted Kennedy's booming voice was on the line, congratulating me. 'Good Morning America' wanted an interview and so did the 'Today Show'; the media enquiries were flooding in. It was a beautiful, bright and clear day in Dublin. Suddenly, a new frontier had opened up for every Irish person and Irish American alive.

On the 'Today Show', America's top-rated programme, I was taken on by Sir Patrick Mayhew, who at the time was the Northern Secretary. I had thought that the British would grab the ceasefire with both hands, accept the bona fides of Adams and McGuinness, and immediately set to work on creating the political framework to sustain it. Now it seemed that I had been incredibly naïve in my expectations. Instead of being joyful, Mayhew appeared irritable and ill at ease and we clashed repeatedly. He kept stressing the word 'permanent' which the IRA had not used in their statement. It was an early indicator that the British were not going to accept the peace chalice with the alacrity that I had hoped.

The British foot-dragging was to have serious consequences. Try as I might, I could not fault how Adams and McGuinness were handling the process. They had done what no other Irish Republican leadership in history had done – bring the armed revolutionary movement onto a political path. Of course, there were problems, and many dissidents remained, both inside and outside the ranks, but it was a time to help them achieve their final goal, not stand in the way, especially with spurious objections on whether the truce was 'permanent' or not.

The Americans would play a critical role in ensuring that the peace train stayed on track during the fraught months and years ahead. We had pushed strongly for President Clinton to visit Northern Ireland to cement the peace. It was an uphill task, with many in his administration listening to the British naysayers who wanted to keep America out at all costs. I found that I now had the ear of the White House. The IRA ceasefire had been a great feather in the cap for the President and he was very willing to listen to advice from the core group that had put the plan for American intervention together. However, the mood music from Northern Ireland was worrying. As far as the Sinn Féin leadership was concerned, certain commitments had been made and were not being kept. There was still political naivety there, a belief that what politicians promised they should be held to. In fairness, there was frustration on the other side too, especially on the part of the Irish government, with the slow pace of developments within Sinn Féin, where very step forward was hedged with caveats and need for assurances.

Another crisis almost derailed the process before it got underway. Gerry Adams was allowed back into America in September 1994 once the ceasefire had been achieved. A delegation of Unionists had been to the White House and met with Vice President Al Gore the week before Adams was due. The British government, still smarting from the visa defeat, managed to convince the White House that Adams should not be allowed to visit the building or meet with Gore. For Adams, this created an enormous problem. It would appear that Unionists were being treated more favourably than Republicans in America. The parity of esteem issue was always a major one for them. At stake was the end of the direct White House ban on contact with Adams – a key sticking point for the Sinn Féin leader and his supporters.

Adams was still not in direct contact with the White House and I was the intermediary. A flurry of phone calls ensued, trying to find a way in which Adams could be seen to be treated the same way as everyone else without meeting the Vice President. It came to a head on Saturday morning, 2 October when Tony Lake called me at home and we commenced a kabuki dance all day long trying to find a way to resolve what was turning into a nasty standoff. Eventually Ciaran Staunton, who was travelling with Adams, came up with the idea of a phone call from the Vice President to Adams, which I took to Lake and managed to persuade him to accept, after hours of wrangling. Obviously the British had pinned their hopes on Lake refusing any such deal and I have rarely had to negotiate harder to win a point. But won it was. For the first time ever, the White House would now be in direct contact with a Sinn Féin leader. Even Eamon de Valera had never achieved that.

Then there was a problem trying to locate Adams in an era before cell phones were widespread. As time ticked by and the window for confirming the phone call with the Vice President began to close, it became even more urgent. I found myself in the surreal circumstance of dialling the situation room in the White House at the instigation of Lake and telling them where I thought they could find Adams as quickly as possible. Because the White House could not speak directly to him, he had to call me. Thus it was that Adams was finally tracked down at the airport in Philadelphia, when Staunton was approached by a security officer and told to call me.

At 8.35 the following morning, Sunday, 3 October, the White House rang Gerry Adams who took the call from Vice President Gore at Bobby Kennedy's residence in Hickory Hills, Virginia where Adams was staying with Bobby's widow, Ethel, Bobby's niece, Courtney Kennedy and her husband, former Guildford Four member Paul Hill. A crisis had been averted and some history made.

There was soon more history in the making – the first Clinton visit to Northern Ireland, which took place in October and November 1995. Foolishly, I had left it to the morning of the flight to fly to Washington to go with the travelling party. I awoke to a sudden and unexpected snow storm in New York and spent some of the worst hours of my life cursing my stupidity and waiting to take off for Washington when the weather cleared. I made the flight from Dulles Airport by the skin of my teeth. We flew on Air Force Two, which we were told had been Lyndon Johnson's Air Force One. On board also were a slew of Irish American leaders from every major Clinton stronghold, and Commerce Secretary Ron Brown, who would later be tragically killed on an economic mission in the old Yugoslavia.

It was an amazing experience to accompany Clinton over the next few days; the world from inside the White House bubble was a very different place. Everyone moved to your beat. Nobody moved until Clinton did. All information was carefully screened and the sense of how difficult it is for a president to live a normal life became very clear to me. All anyone wanted to do was give good news to the President on what was happening in the North. But I had received a disturbing and very different signal. Bruce Morrison and I broke away from the presidential party to meet with Republican leaders at a secret location in a working class neighbourhood in west Belfast.

As we entered the house, Bruce and I were still basking in the warm glow of seeing the incredible reception that Clinton had received. Our good humour was soon challenged. The news was grim. The British were not living up to their side of the deal and the IRA was under increasing strain. We were asked to make a special plea to Clinton to intervene and to warn him of the impending crisis. The portents were ominous. We argued back and forth, trying to explain how incredible it was to have an American president visit Northern Ireland, and what it meant for the future. But it was clear that another insider game was underway within the Republican movement and the people I was speaking to were very worried indeed that they were losing out. Later I would pass the message on to Clinton himself during a conversation at the American Embassy in Dublin. I told him the ceasefire was on thin ice, that the British foot-dragging had imperilled internal unity in Sinn Féin, and that some believed they were merely being strung along. He immediately understood its importance .

We left the Republican meeting feeling shaken. Suddenly the joy of the visit dimmed. We both knew what was at stake now and were unsure of the future. Apart from everything else, had we brought the American President into a no-win situation, where the peace process would break down and his noble work would go for naught? We could only imagine what the naysayers would say. We made our way to the town centre where Bill and Hillary Clinton were set to light the Christmas tree. We stood in the softly falling rain in Belfast, surrounded by about 100,000 Catholics and Protestants who were chanting Clinton's name. *New York Times* columnist Maureen Dowd called it the best two days of his presidency. Clinton agreed and later wrote as much in his memoir. Unfortunately, we knew that the ship was listing badly.

Chapter 46

IRA BREAKDOWN

Just a few months later, in early February 1996, the IRA ceasefire collapsed. I will always remember it as one of the worst days of my life. A bomb at Canary Wharf in London killed two people and caused hundreds of millions of dollars worth of damage. All seemed lost. The British delaying by their insistence on decommissioning and the use of the world 'permanent' had caused a fissure in the IRA ranks. An opinion poll by the *Sunday Independent* showed that most people in the Irish Republic blamed the British for the breakdown. The conspiracy theories began, of course, postulating that it was all a plan by the British to set up and divide the IRA and how the IRA were never truly on board.

I received an anguished call from Taoiseach John Bruton urging me to get on the phone to Republicans and demand that the ceasefire be restored. Bruton had come to power in a bizarre series of events that saw Albert Reynolds – who had done an amazing job in working with Sinn Féin in securing the ceasefire – fall from office. John Bruton was far more suspicious of the IRA and their motives than his predecessor had been, and his government did not have the same tight connections with Republicans. Now he was appealing to me to get involved.

What he did not understand was that Sinn Féin or the IRA never responded to public demands. The way to work with them was to close the door quietly and engage in extremely direct talks about where the situation was headed. Underlying the reality of Northern Ireland was a full acknowledgement by the IRA that they could never win the war by military attrition. They were smart enough to know that they, like everyone else, were in a fatal bind that had resulted in the situation spiralling out of control. But public rancour as expressed by Bruton, and demands made on them, were never going to work.

I also received a call from a senior official at the White House, telling me that they were baffled by the latest turn of events. What was the real story? What could I find out? I picked up the phone and dialled the number for Gerry Adams. I had always found him brutally honest in his assessments. He did not disappoint me this time either. I asked a fundamental question – could the ceasefire be restored? His answer was brief: yes, it could – with an awful lot of work and good faith on all sides. I put down the phone, very much relieved. I knew now that it was possible to get it back. Adams would never have made such a statement unless be believed it. I called the White House and relayed the conversation. I could hear the sigh of relief on the other end.

It was not going to be an easy task to restore peace, but a key element was the election of Bertie Ahern as Taoiseach in the 1997 election. I had met with Ahern and his advisor, Martin Mansergh, soon after Ahern came to power. It was clear to me that he had a direct input to the process, was talking to the Republicans, and that he was determined as his first priority to restore the IRA ceasefire. What he was saying was mirrored by what I was hearing from Republican leaders. Conditions were coming back into place for the ceasefire to be restored. On 19 July 1997 it happened. There were no bells and whistles this time, no worldwide clamour, merely a sense that a huge obstacle had been overcome and that it was time for everyone to buckle down and make it all work.

Buckle down they did. Led by US Senator George Mitchell, the peace talks continued, often excruciatingly slowly. Mitchell was perfect for the job. Before he went over to Northern Ireland I met with him at his midtown law office. He sat perfectly still and listened as I talked for a good forty-five minutes about what I thought the future could be in Northern Ireland. Then he asked a dozen or so penetrating questions. That skill of patience and forbearance was what he brought to the peace process, as well as an American can-do attitude that allowed him to instill even in the most cynical of Northern Irish observers a sense that the impossible was possible.

And it was. On a grey Good Friday morning in April 1988 the historic Good Friday Agreement was signed. I was in touch with Republican negotiators several times the night before. For a while it seemed that all was lost, then won, then lost again. Sometime in the early morning hours, with a tentative deal on the table, George Mitchell made the decisive move, demanding that all the parties sign up to what was on offer. They agreed, though a badly splintered Ulster Unionist Party was a portent of battles to come.

I knew that President Clinton had made some decisive calls to party leaders, including Adams, as the seconds ticked down that fateful night. At 4.45, Washington time, on Good Friday morning, Adams woke Bill Clinton up to tell him the deal was on. I received a call shortly after from an excited White House staff member to say that the final roadblocks had been pushed aside. As I looked at the weary, though exultant faces on television, 3000 miles away, I sensed an incredible moment of hope. I felt that nothing could stop peace in Ireland now, and, despite many stumbles and setbacks since then, that now seems the case. It was one of the proudest moments of my life.

Although I was most certainly not in it for personal gain, the peace process did bring me fame and recognition. RTÉ and US Public Television did a one-hour documentary on my work, entitled 'An Irish Voice'. Conor O'Clery's book, *Daring Diplomacy*, outlined my role in the peace process in great detail. The *Guardian* newspaper cited me as the person at the centre of the web of how America got involved. It was heady stuff.

Chapter 47

9/11 AND THE AFTERMATH

O ver the next few years, far away from the peace process which continued to stumble along with occasional American intervention to keep it ticking over, I continued my life in America. Around 8.45am on 11 September 2001, I was in my Manhattan apartment preparing to go to work. Alana had just been dropped off at the playschool by her nanny, Margaret, and Debbie and I were getting ready to leave. It had been a special day for me, the first time I had voted in an American election. I had always been too lazy to register for local New York races, but had finally done so. Little did I know that I picked the one election where the result would not count because balloting would shortly be suspended. As I made my way back to my apartment on 93rd and Second Street after voting I remember thinking what a glorious autumn day it was.

Suddenly the phone rang. It was a friend, Stephen Travers, telling us that a plane had flown into the World Trade Centre. We switched on the TV and soon the horrific drama unfolded.

Coincidentally I had just finished reading a book by my friend Jim Dwyer called *Two Seconds Under the World: Terror Comes to America* on the 1993 World Trade Centre bombing, also carried out by Muslim extremists. I remembered that bombing well. I had been stuck in traffic on the West Side Highway for hours on my way to a Wall Street meeting with Denis Kelleher and Noel Pearson, the Irish filmmaker. I had an eerie feeling that history was about to repeat itself.

The phone rang again and it was Irish radio calling for news on what was happening. The 'Joe Duffy Show' was obviously seeing the same horrific scenes as I was. He was the first on air to broadcast the news. I told them what I knew, and that it was almost certainly a terrorist attack. The words seemed strange and unreal to me, as if I was weaving some work of fiction into everyday life. Terrorist attack in broad daylight in Manhattan? Who could have imagined it?

Unfortunately, it was all too real. An hour or so later, having collected my daughter from pre-school, I climbed onto the roof of our apartment building and joined several dozen others gazing at the massive cloud of smoke that hung over downtown Manhattan in the distance. Some were praying as they watched, several on their knees. We did not know what that cloud of smoke held, there was a wild rumour about radiation and that a nuclear device had been activated. I hugged my daughter close. We watched as the smoke cloud lazily slipped across the horizon, heading in the direction of Queens. Though we were three miles distant, the acrid smell of burning was carried on the wind. Outside, the streets were deserted and no traffic hum or noise could be heard. It was eerily quiet.

I walked to my office, concerned that people who were already in work might not be able to get home, as all transport was shut down. Sure enough, we had several people with nowhere to go. I took them back to my apartment and we watched, mostly in stunned silence, as the events unfolded.

I called Conor O'Clery of *The Irish Times* who lived within a stone's throw of the World Trade Centre. He had witnessed people desperately clinging on to life and eventually jumping to their deaths from the windows, and firetrucks flattened into pancakes when the buildings fell. Jim Dwyer was frantically searching for his daughter who attended school in the area. Fortunately, she was safe.

The next few days were like a nightmare as the city struggled to cope. Four days after the attack, a friendly cop in a senior position brought me down to Ground Zero and showed me around. On the way, we passed army tanks on the streets – the stuff of movie myth happening in front of our eyes. The World Trade Centre site looked like a scene from a nuclear winter. White ash covered the area for miles and it cast a strange and luminous glow on everyone around it. On top of the massive pile of debris, ant-like workers were frantically searching for bodies. But seeing that pile you felt that no one could have survived. The entire complex had been flattened, from 110 storeys to less than 30 feet in height. Apart from a few miraculous escapes, everything and everyone in the buildings was pulverised on the spot: humans, office furniture, concrete.

I had been on the roof of the World Trade Centre once after an Irish event there. It was a massive expanse of space, covered with communication dishes and other devices, but the view was stunning. Now it was no more. As I walked along the side streets this day I saw an Irish pub with a tricolour covered in fine white ash. All around, rescue workers and cops were moving gingerly through the rubble, picking up someone's shoes here, someone's briefcase there. It was a scene from hell. Already every pole and free space was plastered with posters by families desperately looking for lost ones who would never return. It was indescribably sad.

Late that night, Conor O'Clery and I walked to a nearby fire station that had lost four firefighters in the tragedy. Thousands had filled the street outside and were holding candles. The sense of grief and devastation was something I had never felt before.

I knew some of those who had been killed. *Irish America* had held an event at the WTC that summer, to celebrate our Wall Street 50, a listing of the top Irish on Wall Street that we do every year, and two of our Wall Street 50 had died in their offices a few months later. I also knew some cops and firefighters who were missing.

I began writing a book about the Irish at the WTC soon after. They were such an incredible part of the story, from the cops and firefighters who rushed in to save lives as others rushed out, to incredible men like Ron Clifford from Cork who was in the WTC that day and barely escaped with his life. He only found out later that his sister and his niece were in one of the planes that slammed into the building he was in.

The book, called *Fire in the Morning,* tried to capture their stories. I came across such bravery and belief in the course of writing it that it deeply affected me, such was their great forbearance and strength in impossibly trying circumstances. I hope I did them justice. It was wonderful to see the book sell very well in Ireland, where the ties between Ireland and America never seemed so strong as in the immediate aftermath, with the Irish government declaring a national day of mourning and thousands signing books of condolence at the American Embassy.

Chapter 48

BATTLING FOR THE
UNDOCUMENTED IRISH

I f Northern Ireland was the hardy perennial in Irish American life, illegal immigration had become a close second. Because of the changes in the 1965 Immigration Act, Irish people were essentially barred from coming to America legally. But there was a centuries-old tradition of them coming, especially in hard times. Every thirty years or so in the twentieth century a wave came, fleeing from the civil war in the 1920s, the economic wasteland in the 1950s or harsh economic times in the 1980s.

The huge influx in the 1980s became a major issue in the Irish American community. New Irish neighbourhoods sprang up, old Irish organisations were revitalised, sports teams thrived, but underlying it all was the fact that almost everyone who came did so illegally. Some felt that anyone who knowingly entered the US illegally deserved what they got, but the reality for those immigrants was that often the only alternative back in Ireland was a soul-destroying life on the dole.

In the 1980s I attended the inaugural meeting of the Irish Immigration Reform Movement, headed by two young Corkmen, Sean Minihane and Pat Hurley. With the help of the *Irish Voice*, they created a powerful lobby that was eventually successful in winning the Morrison and Donnelly visa program for undocumented Irish. It allowed 45,000 or so Irish to claim the visas and come and work legally in America, though some of the visas were never taken up.

In the early years of this century, the numbers started creeping up again. Even with the Celtic Tiger there were many in Ireland who could not find work and followed the well worn path to America. And, of course, the changed economic circumstances in Ireland recently have seen a new surge of young people leaving for the US.

The issue became a major one in Irish politics, with politicians being lobbied daily by anxious families trying to help their loved ones trapped in America. There was no organisation in America coming to their aid, but following a meeting with the then Irish Ambassador Noel Fahey, I decided to start one. Thus was born the Irish Lobby for Immigration Reform, created in December 2005 with the express idea of legalising the 50,000 or so undocumented Irish. Ciaran Staunton joined me on stage on the first night of the group when we held a public meeting in Manhattan.

It was a different landscape from the 1980s; the American mood had darkened towards immigrants, especially after 9/11, and there was a sense that the right wing of the Republican Party was controlling the agenda. We held some very successful organisational meetings in various cities but little seemed to be changing on the national landscape. I thought it might be time to take the battle direct to Washington. Americans as a whole are not terribly exercised about much, unlike in the Vietnam War days when very public battle was joined. There is a political vacuum where small groups can punch way above their weight by appearing ever present in the corridors of power.

I decided that a series of Irish rallies on Capitol Hill might be just the opportunity to force some recognition of the issue. With Ciaran Staunton and Kelly Fincham, the two other officers in ILIR, we decided on a bold strategy of bussing thousands of Irish direct to Washington DC. If it went wrong we would have egg on our face, but we needed to do something to make our mark. I contacted Senator Kennedy and Senator Hillary Clinton directly and asked if they would appear at our rally. They both agreed immediately. For Kennedy there was a sense of an opportunity to right a wrong for which he had been partly responsible. As author of the 1965 Immigration Act, he had unwittingly locked out the Irish and I knew he wanted to make amends.

On the appointed day, 7 March 2006, busloads and plane loads of Irish descended on Washington. They came from New York, Boston, Florida, Chicago, California and even Texas. We had each of them wear a 'Legalize the Irish' tee shirt, which proved our smartest move. As the throngs of young, enthusiastic Irish flooded Capitol Hill, wearing the distinctive tee shirt, the staffers came out to see what all the commotion was. Washington is the only legislature where the public can literally walk in the door of a congressman or senator's office and make their case. That first day we visited all 100 senators' offices and close to 500 congressional offices.

In the afternoon we held a rally addressed by Senator Kennedy and Senator Clinton, as well as many other luminaries. The day was a profound success and showed how, even without massive numbers, we could make a massive impact. From then on, we were considered major players in the debate – because, I think, of those tee shirts.

We repeated the mass rallies on two other occasions, with similar success. One of the highlights was the day I was asked to testify before the Senate Subcommittee on Immigration, with Senator Arlen Specter from Pennsylvania presiding and Ted Kennedy as the ranking Democrat. I was there with three others who were experts on immigration issues. When it came to Senator Kennedy's turn to speak, he spent considerable time outlining all I had done on the issue and on Northern Ireland.

He stated: 'This gentleman here played an absolutely indispensable role. You all acknowledge the great role that our friend and former colleague George Mitchell played, but Niall was an enormously important figure in the earliest days in developing the ceasefire and the support for the figures.'

It was a wonderful moment for me and I was very gratified. I wish I could say the same for the other experts, who were none too pleased that the lion of the senate essentially ignored them.

All our work was aimed at passage of the Kennedy/McCain Immigration Reform Bill in 2007, and it was shattering blow when, despite major support from the White House and leading Democrats and Republicans, the Bill failed. It was incredibly difficult to go back to the community and share with them the bleak result. However, it is an issue I believe will return to the top of the agenda under President Obama. When it does, I intend to be there on behalf of the undocumented Irish as an illegal immigrant myself once upon a time. I will never forget that.

Chapter 49

IRISH CENTRAL LAUNCHES

On 15 March 2009, I launched IrishCentral.com, a major undertaking to seek out the global Irish and give them a home on the internet. Taoiseach Brian Cowen performed the launch at the American Irish Historical Society on Fifth Avenue in New York where I am a board member. Cowen had impressed me since he became Taoiseach as very sharp, very focused, with a deep instinctive knowledge of Irish America. It was his misfortune to take over at a time when the Irish economy had fallen on very lean times.

It was my fourth launch of a media publication and I knew it would be the toughest. Times had turned very sour at the end of George Bush's reign and Barack Obama had inherited a disastrous financial situation. Despite that, my loyal friends had come together to support the new site and to help launch it. Among them were Donald Keough, former President of Coca Cola; Denis Kelleher, CEO of Wall Street Access; Doctor Kevin Cahill, a noted New York physician and Director General of the American Irish Historical Society, and Chuck Feeney, my comrade in arms on Northern Ireland. Two of my brothers, Fergus and Michael, came over from Ireland for the launch, and as the night progressed I found myself wistful yet excited about what lay ahead. I looked at my little daughter Alana, nine years old and full of life, and hoped that someday she would remember this night and the extraordinary adventure that lay ahead of all of us.

Also there was noted actress Vanessa Redgrave, mother of Natasha

Richardson who was married to Liam Neeson, a key figure on the board of the society. In one of those astounding 'stranger than fiction' realities, Vanessa would be back there a week later at the wake of her beloved daughter which was held at the society. The day after our launch, Natasha died in a freak ski slope accident in Canada, a story that would occupy us very much in the early days of our site.

A few months later, in September 2009, I attended the first ever Diaspora forum held by the Irish government in Dublin's elegant Farmleigh House in the Phoenix Park. One hundred and eighty business leaders had flown in from all over the globe. It was the first real recognition by an Irish government of the potential of the Diaspora, potential which had been clearly on display during the peace process.

Some years ago I wrote an op-ed piece for *The Irish Times* which mentioned the word Diaspora and had received a few letters asking what a Diaspora was. The fact that 70 million people worldwide had Irish roots deeply differentiated Ireland from other countries. We had a footprint all over the world and it was exciting to see the government, led by Taoiseach Cowen, finally grasp its importance at Farmleigh.

Mary Robinson, both in her inauguration speech and in her address to the Houses of the Oireachtas in 1995, entitled 'Cherishing the Diaspora' is recognised as the person who created awareness of the term – certainly in Ireland – and what it stood for, and famously installed the 'light in the window' of the presidential residence, Áras an Uachtaráin. By doing so she brought the idea of the exiled Irish home in a way that Irish people in Ireland had never fully appreciated.

Since the 1840s half of the population of people born in Ireland has left the country. It is an astonishing figure, yet until Robinson no one in power had ever really reached out to them. The outreach she began has continued under her successor, President Mary McAleese.

I felt that our website launch in March had helped kick off this new recognition of the potential of the Diaspora, as had two conferences on the subject we held in conjunction with University College Dublin. Now the new website would attempt to link up the Irish on a global basis. Like any new media venture, especially in these times, the odds of success were long, but that's how I liked it.

A few months later, we did our 'Legal 100' event at Irish Ambassador Michael Collins's residence in Washington. The Chief Justice of the US Supreme Court, John Roberts, and his wife, Jane, attended and I had a nice chat with him about the tradition of thatching in Ireland where he and his wife have a time-share cottage.

It was the kind of access to the most powerful jurist in America that makes you realise the potential of the Diaspora. Through our networks of the 'Business 100', 'Education 50', 'Wall Street 50', 'Legal 100' we have created a roadmap on how these Irish Americans of influence can be found.

Ireland is an incredible brand, with 70 million around the world who have strong feelings about their heritage. I believe that at last the Irish government are beginning to understand that clout and its potential. I have been living it these past thirty years since my first newspaper in California.

The reality is that much of my life has been a journey into the unknown, beginning with leaving Ireland that June day long ago. This time I had a great crew, a great wife, Debbie, and daughter Alana and a fair wind behind us. Success or failure lay ahead, but for that night it hardly seemed important as much as sharing with those who had made my life such a wonderful adventure. I had known presidents and paupers along the way but in the end it came back to those nearest and dearest, family and friends, like all of life does. A line from Yeats ran through my head … 'And say my glory was I had such friends.' Indeed it was, and remains so.

Go n-éirí linn. (That we may succeed.)